British Library Occasional Papers 12

Women's Studies

British Library Occasional Papers 12

Women's Studies

Papers presented at a colloquium
at The British Library
4 April 1989

Edited by Albertine Gaur and
Penelope Tuson

The British Library 1990

© 1990 The Contributors

First published 1990 by
The British Library
Great Russell Street
London WC1B 3DG

British Library Cataloguing in Publication Data
Women's studies: papers presented at a colloquium at the
   British Library, 4 April 1989. — (British Library
   occasional papers; 12).
   1. Great Britain. Women's studies. Information sources
   I. Gaur, Albertine   II. Tuson, Penelope   III. British
   Library   IV. Series
   305.407

ISBN 0–7123–0184–4

Designed by Alan Bartram
Typeset in Lasercomp Bembo
by August Filmsetting, Haydock, St Helens
Printed in England on permanent paper ⊛ by Henry Ling (Printers) Ltd,
Dorchester, Dorset

Contents

Editors' preface		vii
List of participants		ix
The state of women's studies at British universities	Mary Evans	1
Discussion		6

British Library Resources 1
Printed books and newspapers

The English Language Branch and women's studies	Barbara James and Ilse Sternberg	7
A female novelist in the nineteenth century	Elizabeth James	16
Nineteenth-century black American women's writing	Carole Holden	23
Newspapers as source material for women's studies, 1830s–1930s	Eamon Dyas	33
French resources for women's studies	Morna Daniels	46
Holdings on women's studies in Italy	Christine Burden	52
Resources for a study of the women's movement in Germany until 1945	Rosamond Eden	55
Women's studies in West and East Germany	Brigid Haines	61
Dutch resources	Janet Gilbert	67
Scandinavian publications since the mid-1970s	Tom Geddes	75
Norwegian women writers	Barbara Hawes	85
Women in the Soviet Union from 1917 to the present: sources for research	Janet Zmroczek	88
Discussion		97

British Library Resources 2
Archival and manuscript

Suffragettes and saris: resources for women's studies in the India Office Library and Records	Penelope Tuson	98
The life of Asian women as depicted in oriental manuscript illustrations	Albertine Gaur	109
Katherine Mansfield's letters in the Department of Manuscripts	Sally Brown	116
Rich and poor widows: eighteenth century women in the Althorp Papers	Frances Harris	124
Oral history: governesses and teachers, 1890–1989	Annie Gilbert	129
Discussion		133

Collection Development: The British Library and other United Kingdom Research Libraries

Collection development and women's studies	*B C Bloomfield*	134
Small is beautiful – but is it feasible? Small special women's collections in the UK	*Pat Darter*	140
The Fawcett Library	*David Doughan*	148
Women missionaries as represented in the Missionary Collections in the School of Oriental and African Studies Library	*Rosemary Seton*	156
Feminist publishing	*Ursula Owen*	165
Discussion		175

The user perspective

How can the British Library help feminist research?	*Rosalind Delmar*	176
Discussion, recommendations and suggestions.		182
Summing up	*Albertine Gaur*	184
Appendix: *Changing views of women*: a British Library exhibition		187

Editors' Preface
Albertine Gaur and Penelope Tuson

The Colloquium on Resources for Women's Studies held on 4 April 1989 was the twelfth in a series organised by the British Library to bring together librarians, information scientists, writers and publishers, to share their knowledge, experience and ideas.

Previous colloquia have concentrated on a single area of study. Women's Studies provided a wider brief by involving all categories of the Library's holdings. This also seemed a particularly opportune time to consider the rôle of the Library after the move to the new site at St Pancras.

We are very grateful to everyone who attended the Colloquium and who helped to make it such a lively and stimulating event. We wanted to achieve two results: to advertise more widely the Library's resources, and to stimulate positive criticism and constructive discussion about the Library's rôle in the provision of resources for women's studies. At a very early stage in the organisation it became clear that there was far more material than we could possibly discuss in the short time available; it was also evident that there were far more potential participants than we could accommodate in the limited space of the Novello Room. We hope that this publication will provide an introduction to the wide range of resources in the British Library and that it will stimulate more bibliographic and other work in that area.

Particular thanks to Steve Ashton for taking on the rôle of rapporteur so efficiently and also to the chairpersons of each session who helped to keep us to the almost impossible timetable we had drawn up.

List of participants

Hayfa Alankary	School of Oriental and African Studies
Sally Alexander	History Workshop Journal
Ziggi Alexander	Writer
Steve Ashton	Education Service, British Library
Melanie Aspey	News International
Alison Bailey	Public Services, British Library
Patricia Barr	Writer
Jacqueline Beevers	Public Services, British Library
Barry Bloomfield	Collection Development, British Library
Jean Boyd	Writer
Deborah Bragan-Turner	University Library, Nottingham
Christine Burden	Research and Development, British Library
Anita Burdett	Institute of Commonwealth Studies
Barbara Burton	School of Oriental and African Studies Library
Jackie Canning	British Library Bibliographic Services
Jane Carr	Marketing and Publishing Office, British Library
Dee Carter	Avon County
Sylvia Collicott	Polytechnic of North London
Ruth Coman	British Library, St Pancras Planning
Morna Daniels	Collection Development (West European), British Library
Pat Darter	Equal Opportunities Commission
Ruth Davies	Anglia Higher Education College
Anna Davin	History Workshop Journal
Rosalind Delmar	Writer, translator and lecturer/member of Virago's Advisory Group
Paola Di Cori	British Museum
David Doughan	Fawcett Library
Eamon Dyas	Newspaper Library, British Library
Rosamond Eden	Collection Development (West European), British Library
Mary Evans	University of Kent
Tony Farrington	India Office Library and Records, British Library
Mirjam Foot	Collection Development (West European), British Library
Wendy Frankland	British Library Document Supply Centre, Boston Spa
Albertine Gaur	Oriental Collections, British Library
Tom Geddes	Collection Development (West European), British Library
Annie Gilbert	Preservation Service, British Library
Janet Gilbert	Collection Development (West European), British Library
Sarah Graham-Brown	Writer
Sally Graves	British Library Bibliographic Services
Brigid Haines	British Library, St Pancras Planning
Catherine Hall	Feminist Review
Frances Harris	Special Collections (Manuscripts), British Library
Judith Harrison	Public Services, British Library
Barbara Hawes	Collection Development (West European), British Library
Richard Hayward	Schoolmistresses and Governesses Benevolent Association

Edward Higgs	Public Record Office
Susan Hills	Planning and Administration, British Library
Carole Holden	Collection Development (Overseas English), British Library
Barbara James	Collection Development (English Language Branch), British Library
Elizabeth James	Collection Development (English Language Branch), British Library
Eve Johansson	Newspaper Library, British Library
Patricia Kattenhorn	India Office Library and Records, British Library
May Katzen	University of Leceister
Mary Kennedy	Centre for Extra-Mural Studies, Birkbeck College
Diane Leonard	Institute of Education, University of London
Julia Leslie	Centre for Cross-Cultural Research on Women, Oxford
Margaret Makepeace	India Office Library and Records, British Library
Keith McClelland	University of Reading
Dawn Olney	British Library, St Pancras Planning
Avril Powell	School of Oriental and African Studies
Jane Priestland	Freelance researcher
Jane Rendall	University of York
Maureen Ritchie	University of Kent
Lyndal Roper	Royal Holloway and Bedford New College, University of London
Catherine Ross	Waltham Forest Education Authority
Rosemary Seton	School of Oriental and African Studies Library
Dorothy Sheridan	University of Sussex
Liz Stanley	University of Manchester
Ilse Sternberg	Collection Development (English Language Branch), British Library
Anne Summers	Wellcome Unit for the History of Medicine, Oxford University
Chris Thomas	Collection Development (Slavonic and East European), British Library
Lesley Turano	Collection Development (West European), British Library
Penelope Tuson	British Library Consultancy Services
Rozina Visram	Writer
Ken Watson	Sheffield City Polytechnic
Jeffrey Weeks	Council for National Academic Awards
Halina Whiteside	British Library, Public Services
Annabel Wigner	Plumstead Manor School
Frances Wood	Oriental Collections, British Library
Christine Zmroczek	Women's Studies International Forum
Janet Zmroczek	Collection Development (Slavonic and East European), British Library

Mary Evans

The state of women's studies at British universities

Women's studies at British Universities flourish. This unequivocal assertion has, however, to be qualified hastily by the remark that whilst women's studies flourish they do so against a background of financial constraint and uncertainty in British higher education. The post-Robbins era of expansion and expansiveness has given way to a period of retrenchment. Nevertheless, the last twenty years have seen systematic and probably irreversible changes in British universities: the numbers of women students have substantially increased, the single honours degree has given way to the more common pattern of combined or joint honours and subjects, and their human embodiment in the form of teachers in higher education, have become more willing to consider the enriching possibilities of multi and inter-disciplinary work. None of these changes is absolute; we must note, for example, that women still remain under-represented (both as students and as staff) in the faculties of natural science, technology and pure and applied mathematics. Equally, whilst women have become more notable consumers of higher education they are still not to be found in positions of institutional or academic influence, let alone power. There is, as yet, no woman Vice Chancellor and much general discussion about higher education, its needs and problems, tends to assume a male student as the 'normal' person.

But for all that, women's studies has, in a relatively short time, established itself as an important and vital subject area. Ten years ago no postgraduate degrees in the area existed and the number of undergraduate courses was very limited. Today there are at least six postgraduate MA degrees in women's studies, numerous undergraduate courses, and the possibility, in the not too distant future, that students will be able to take women's studies as a component part of an undergraduate degree. Whilst these remarks apply to universities, a similar degree of activity and vitality exists at polytechnics and colleges of higher education. A mailing list of all those associated with women's studies in higher education in general would now be extensive. A list in 1979 was not short, today it would probably constitute one of the longest (and I tend to think the more interesting) specialist lists of British Academics.

So what do all these people (largely – although not exclusively – female people) do? In one sense the answer is obvious: they teach in university departments and have specialist interests in women's studies. But in another sense the answer is more complicated, for we need to know which disciplines most of these individuals are drawn from, the relationship of their interests in women's studies to their particular discipline and the institutional context in which an academic interest in women's studies ceases to be an academic twinkle in the eye and is translated into the weightier and more visible form of teaching, book lists, degree structures and so on. The answers to some of these questions are relatively straight-forward; the majority of people who teach women's studies are drawn from either the social sciences or the humanities and it is generally (although not exclusively) the case that women's studies courses and degrees have been established with greater ease in those universities which already have established faculty and inter-discipline structures which promote and encourage multi-disciplinary work. It was therefore no coincidence that the first two MA degrees in women's studies to be established in the UK were located at the University of Kent at Canterbury and at the University of York. Both these 'new' universities had commitments to the importance of inter-disciplinary work and internal organisations that made possible the necessary co-operation and exchange between specialist subjects that is involved in multi-disciplinarity. Again, the third MA in women's studies to be organised was at another new university, in this case the University of Warwick.

For various institutional reasons, therefore, the early years of courses and degrees in women's studies have been easier in 'new' universities. But the reasons for this more encouraging climate are not exclusively institutional. Obviously, it is an enormous help for anyone beginning, or thinking of beginning a new and innovative venture in a university to be in an institution where the boundaries of academic subjects are not set in a straight-jacket of habit and venerable practice. Yet a greater receptivity to new associations and liasons between subjects would get nowhere were it not for individuals to implement and give institutional coherence to general ideas about interesting new developments. 'Interesting new developments' are part of the very fabric and language of academic life; they are what we hope for, hope to be, and hope to encourage. Without people, however, no new development is going to emerge into the academic daylight. Here, then, we come to the more complex issue of where, and why, women's studies courses and degrees have been established. Two points have to be made: the courses and degrees have been established, without exception, where women academics have taken the initiative in proposing and organising the development of women's studies. Women academics appointed in the post-Robbins expansion were part of a generation which created contemporary feminism; by no means all women appointed were feminists and many women already appointed were feminists long before Germaine Greer had a university job. But those women who were appointed in the late 1960s and early 1970s took into the academy an openness and an eagerness (created in part by the academy itself) to the idea of new possibilities and new issues and questions in traditional subjects.

In summary of the above it can safely be said that women created women's studies. The second point that has to be made is that women's studies courses and degrees created, very often by the mere suggestion of their existence, a new sense of gender divisions in both the social and intellectual world in general and the academy in particular. The hostility which greeted some early proposals for teaching women's studies opened many eyes; I think that it would be fair to say that many people – feminists and others – were taken aback by the vehemence expressed against the mere idea that sexual divisions should be considered by academics and that the concept of the male as the definitive human being was not one that should go unchallenged. Endless examples exist of the way in which feminism challenged existing attitudes. For example, in the early 1970s one of the livelier areas of debate amongst feminists concerned that of housework. Somewhat esoteric aspects of the debate focussed on the issue of whether or not housework could be considered as productive labour. This inevitably led to endless jokes amongst feminists about the new burden of having to think about housework as well as do it. Amongst others, however, it led less to mirth than to consternation and incredulity that something so apparently 'natural' and certainly taken-for-granted should now become a subject of academic discussion. Yet with hindsight the debate was one of the more important of the early 1970s; it made visible women's unpaid work in the home, it demonstrated the 'double shift' that employed women work and it provided an utterly convincing explanation of the failure of many women in employment to seek promotion or further training. The irony is now that for demographic reasons employers are being asked by the Secretary of State for Employment to consider the domestic responsibilities of their female employees. A new battle clearly exists about re-defining domestic (and child-care) responsibilities as part of men's lives as much as women's but for the time being what we can observe as having been established (as a matter of public record and not unspoken common knowledge) is the work that is necessary to maintain and care for a home and dependents.

Over fifteen years of academic feminism have thus provided for the public world a string of arguments, books, articles, research projects, films and daily practices which challenge the idea of the gender neutrality of the human being, the social actor and the social subject. The impact of much of the work has been considerable; in the areas of health care, employment and education institutional ideologies and practises that failed to consider the best interests of women have been scrutinised and demonstrated as inadequate. I would argue therefore that women's studies in the academy has made an impact outside the world of universities. Moreover, it is also the case that to a very limited extent universities have recognised women's studies: a post exists in the subject at the University of York, the MA in Women's Studies at the University of Kent has been validated by the Economic and Social Research Council and recent innovations and developments in the area (much as the establishment of further graduate degrees and undergraduate courses at the Universities of Swansea and Liverpool respectively) have been positively welcomed by the relevant institutions. All this is a long way from some of the more aggressive reactions of historical record. In so far as any member of any social science or humanities department is guaranteed employment in the present context of university funding, there is no reason to suppose that those teaching women's studies (or the teaching of women's studies itself) are more vulnerable than anyone else.

So to a certain extent, women's studies teaching at British universities has been institutionalised. There are MA degrees at Kent, York and Warwick and plans are being considered for further degrees at Lancaster, Swansea and Bristol. At the University of Bradford an MA in Applied Women's Studies is taught (with a concentration on social work practice), the University of Hull has a MA degree in Women and Literature and the Institute of Education at the University of London has a MA degree in Human Rights which allows students to specialise in women's studies. The undergraduate courses available are too numerous to list, but it can safely be said that the majority of universities now have courses either on such general topics as women in society, or gender and society, or more specialist, subject based courses on – for example – women and the law or women and the labour market. The subject has yet to reach maturity, but it is a long way out of its somewhat perilous infancy. The plant is thus well rooted. But what are its main characteristics, and how might it develop? In my concluding remarks I would like to make a few points about the present state and future development of women's studies. Three points stand out: first, the relationship of women's studies to traditional subjects, second, the institutional and intellectual future of the subject area and third, the issue of the extent to which the very impact and effectiveness of women's studies has made it doomed to disappearance.

The first point – that of the relationship of women's studies to traditional academic subjects – is also a question about the status of women's studies itself. From the first, many people (including myself) who have been working within the area of women's studies have resisted the idea that women's studies is a discipline, in the sense that we traditionally understand it. That is, an academic discipline has a specific method and a specific mode of inquiry. The area of interest of a discipline may be extensive but how it studies, rather than what it studies, is unique and definitive. This view – that women's studies is not a discipline – is not universally accepted. Those who reject the position argue that to analyse social and intellectual life in terms of gender, and gender divisions, is a method. The counter argument is that to analyse the world in terms of gender does not in itself constitute a discipline of women's studies *per se* but one that might be more appropriately described as sexual divisions. The problem with gender, as both feminists and anti-feminists agree, is that there are two. Attempting to enlarge the boundaries of women's studies so that relationships between the sexes become part of the subject area can be regarded with suspicion since this shift of emphasis tends to detract from the very considerable political and social impact of an intellectual space in the academy which is entirely about women. Almost every student that I have spoken to who has taken a women's studies course (and these students are virtually exclusively women) has endorsed the view that one of the greatest rewards of studying women's studies is the chance to study in a context that is largely for and about women. The costs to girls of co-education in secondary education have now been widely reported; the parallel case of the problems for women of the mixed-sex environment of higher education has yet to be discussed.

The advantages of the freedom given to women students (and teachers) of women's studies courses brings me to the consideration of the second point: the future of women's studies. The overall context of higher education in this country is not, at the moment, one of expansion. Equally, there do seem to be pressures on universities to teach subjects which are popular; the idea is that the 'market' should to a certain extent dictate academic choices and priorities. It will be interesting to see if this *laissez-faire* thinking applies to women's studies, which is consistently popular at both graduate and undergraduate level. Unfortunately, the evidence at the moment suggests that popularity is only allowed as a measure of academic viability if what is popular is also consistent with government policy. Women's studies, however academically respectable and even academicized it has become, still remains associated with feminism, and feminism (despite its long record of campaigns around now utterly taken-for-granted issues of civil rights) remains associated to many political minds with the break up of the family, society and social order. The telling evidence from the United States, so cogently suggested by Barbara Ehrenreich, that it is the free market philosophy of sexual and personal relations that destroys the family far more often than feminism has ever done, is not entertained by those who suspect feminism of socially destructive possibilities.

So my suspicion is that, at least for the present, women's studies will remain in the curious position of being immensely popular and intellectually highly productive but divorced from the mainstream of university politics and priorities. This enforced separation may paradoxically guarantee the long term survival of women's studies – and ensure, and here I would like to raise my third and final question, the long term survival of the subject area. Because of the success of people working in women's studies in demonstrating the importance of gender in any analysis of social life it is possible that others, in traditional disciplines, will absorb the issue of gender into their own work, thus annexing the very material of women's studies. To a certain extent this has already occurred; few university courses on the family, or the nineteenth century now omit the discussion of gender. But these courses remain in the mainstream, in traditional disciplines, and the persistent, enforced strength of women's studies is that it remains outside these established and traditional boundaries and so continues to permit work that is not designed to enrich or inform what already exists. To put it another way; there is nothing for women's studies to integrate itself into: there is no long history to confront and to re-order, no great theoretical tradition to amend and re-think. The dead weight of history can sit as heavily on academic subjects as it can on social life. The continuing vitality of women's studies suggests that so far the subject has managed to avoid the hardening of its intellectual arteries. Whilst the context of women's studies remains problematic – and the present under-funding of the liberal arts and social sciences subjects in universities I regard as a matter of major concern – the subject area itself is healthy and flourishing.

Discussion

In the subsequent discussion a number of points were raised:

The provision for women's studies at the Open University (The Faculty of Technology offers a scond-level course on the 'Changing Experience of Women' which consists of a study of Britain in the last 150 years); the need to emphasise that feminist research is not confined to women's studies in higher education or indeed within the formal education system (a wide range of alternatives and supplements exist); the extent to which women's studies might lose their distinct identity through integration across the curriculum; the need to recognise that half of the students in higher education are in the polytechnic sector (Sheffield Polytechnic and Cambridgeshire College of Art and Technology offer MA courses in women's studies; for undergraduates, a half degree is available at the Polytechnic of Central London).

The following participants took part in the discussion: Eamon Dyas (BL Newspaper Library); Liz Stanley (Manchester University); Penelope Tuson (BL, Consultancy Services); Jeffrey Weeks (Council for Natioinal Academic Awards).

Fig 1 Women's rights in seventeenth-century England: *The woman as good as the man, or, the equality of both sexes*, translated from the French by A L, London, 1677 (*see* pp.7–15). [8415.b.17]

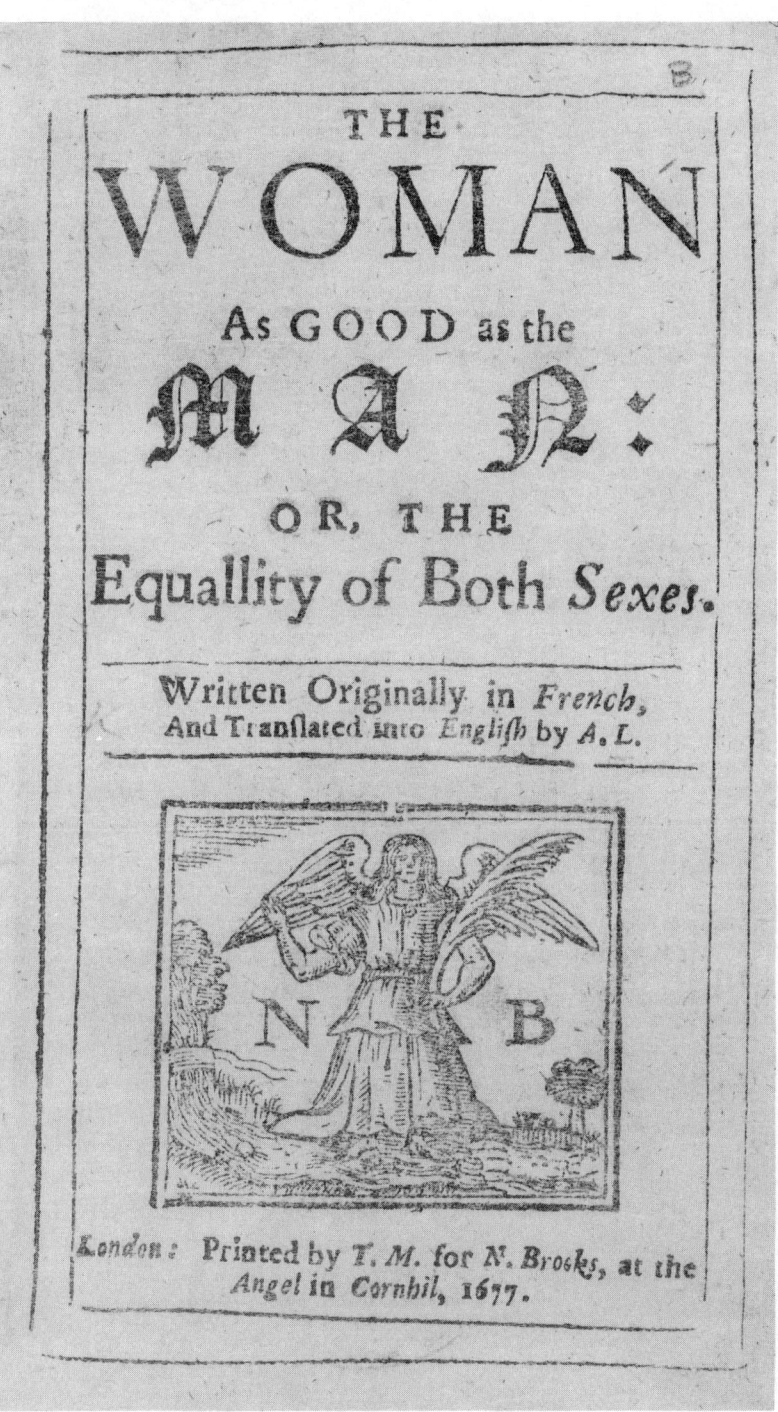

Fig 2 Black women poets: an autographed copy of Gwendolen Brooks's *Riot*, Detroit, 1969 (*see* pp.23–32). [x.909/37816]

Fig 3 Women and work in the Soviet Union: a poster encouraging women to work for collectivisation by becoming tractor drivers in *Seht her, Genossen!: Plakate aus der Soviet Union*, Dortmund, 1982 (*see* pp.88–96). [x.429/15087]

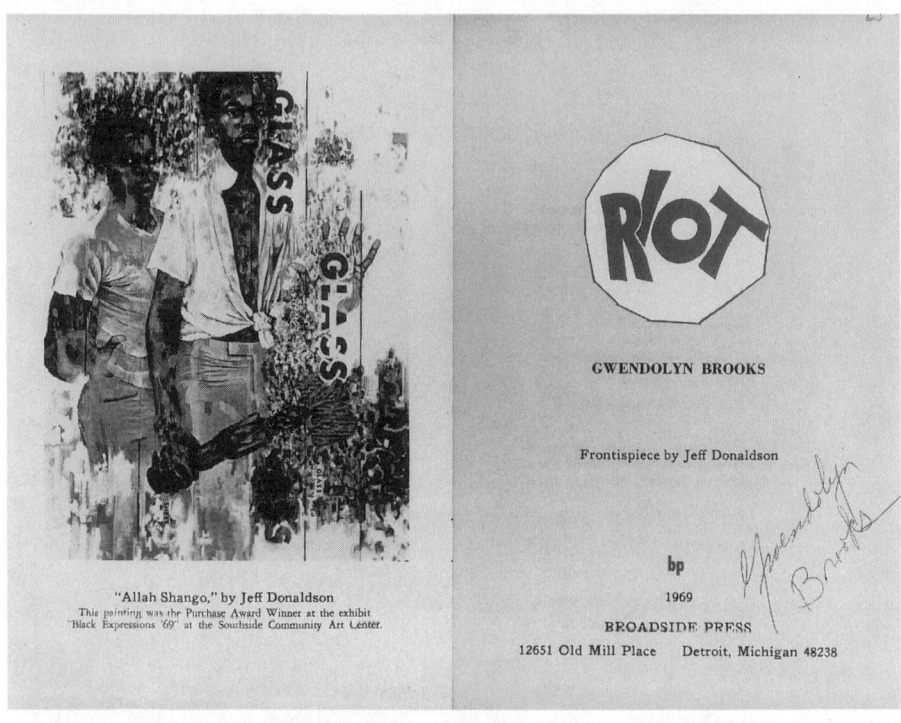

Fig 4 Women and politics in Germany: an illustration from Käthe Kern's *Frauen entscheidet euch!*, Berlin, 1931 (*see* pp.56–60). [YA.1987a.9265]

Reg. No. 1317.

STRI-DHARMA

OFFICIAL ORGAN OF THE WOMEN'S INDIAN ASSOCIATION

Vol. 5 No. 6]   April, 1922   [As. 5 Post free

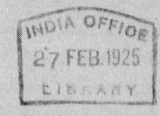

    Our symbol represents the ideal influence of woman, which it is the object of our Association to make an actuality in every detail of daily life in every part of India. The work has begun in the Madras Presidency (the place of the woman's feet), but its life-force springs from religion (her heart is in the region of Benares), and its intellect must be as clear and cool as the Himalayan regions into which rises her head.

    Serene and self-reliant must stand each member, with hands outstretched to sisters and brothers, both in the East and West, to give them from her active right hand Beauty and Prosperity represented by the lotus, the flower that bears within itself male and female qualities equally, and from the lamp in her left hand to extend the steady flame of inspiration which will light the fire of the united life of man and woman, the fire of devotion to our Sacred Religion and of love for humanity, the fire of patriotism, the fire of zeal for reform.

    Thus she represents Religion, Knowledge, Organisation, Service, Beauty, Prosperity, Inspiration and Co-operation, all offered freely to Mother India by each of her daughters.

Dedication

To the women of India to-day, and to the memory of the Indian Women of all past ages who have set an example of Courage, Wisdom and Devotion to Truth.

CONTENTS

Notes and Comments	...	சொந்த விஷயமாய் ஸ்த்ரீகளின் உரிமை	...	88
Social Service 83		வேண்டுகோள்	...	89
The Earl of Lytton's Reply to a Deputation of		சமாசார திரட்டுகள்	...	90
British Women Suffragists ... 84		శ్రీ ధర్మదీపిక-సము	...	92
		అక్షరాల ఆర్యంగ నామ్రములు	...	94
The "Lords of Creation" 85		వివిధ విషయములు	...	94
Women the World Over 86		Branch Reports		

The Editor will be glad to receive articles suitable for publication in English, Tamil, Telugu, or any Indian language. All Communications to be addressed to the Editor, Mrs. D. Jinarajadasa, Women's Indian Association, Adyar, Madras.

SUBSCRIPTION FOR 12 NUMBERS, POST FREE.

INDIA, Rs. 4   W. I. A. MEMBERS, Rs. 2   FOREIGN, 7 SHILLINGS.

Fig 6 Bulletin of the Indian women's movement, 1942 (*see* pp.99–108).

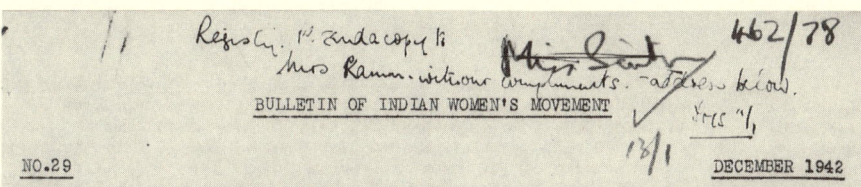

BULLETIN OF INDIAN WOMEN'S MOVEMENT

NO.29   DECEMBER 1942

(In connection with the Liaison Work of the
ALL INDIA WOMEN'S CONFERENCE)

This Bulletin is issued in connection with the Liaison Group of British Women's Societies (British Commonwealth League; Six Point Group; Women's Freedom League; Women's International League) that works in co-operation with the All India Women's Conference, and it is designed to give news which does not appear elsewhere in this country.

This Bulletin is sent post free every quarter* to yearly subscribers of 2/6 or more. Surplus funds, which constitute our only source of income are devoted to the work of the Liaison Group, whose objects are to strengthen the links between women of both countries, and to create a better understanding of the Indian Women's Movement. PLEASE NOTE THE NAME AND ADDRESS OF OUR NEW HON. TREASURER:

> MISS MAUD DICKINSON,
> 12 SOUTHEND ROAD,
> BECKENHAM, KENT.

ALL INDIA WOMEN'S CONFERENCE NEWS

The first All India Conference was held in January 1927. To these Conferences, in the five years prior to the outbreak of war, the Liaison Group has sent a Special British Delegate. Since 1927 the A.I.W.C. has had an unbroken record of annual meetings. A few weeks ago we cabled to the Hon. Secretary of the Conference for particulars of this year's Conference. Mrs. Mehta cabled back - "NO CONFERENCE, STANDING COMMITTEE MEETING ONLY CHRISTMAS WEEK." An airgraph letter from Begum Hamid Ali, just received by Mrs. Lankester and Miss Harrison - throws further light on this cable. In reply to the request made to her for news - Begum Haid Ali says ... "NO WONDER YOU DO NOT GET LETTERS. ALL YOUR FRIENDS ARE SAFELY HOUSED IN A PLACE WHERE THEY CAN NEITHER SEE, NOR HEAR, NOR WRITE - EXCEPT TO RELATIVES."

This sad news serves to show the reason the Conference cannot meet is because its effective leadership is under arrest. We understand that the following are amongst the number: The Hon.Mrs. V.L. Pandit (India's first woman Cabinet Minister, and President of the A.I.W.C.); Shrimati Kamaladevi - the President elect; Mrs. Sarojini Naidu; the Raj Kumari Amrit Kaur; Mrs. Brijlal Nehru. A scrutiny of Indian papers shows that women have taken a large part in the nation-wide protests that took place as a result of the arrests in August last. As meetings and processions of this character are disallowed - arrests have followed. At the moment we have no further details - either as regards the number of women arrested, nor what sentences they have received. But it is clear that a great many of India's outstanding women are either in prison or "detained", and their work in connection with the All India Women's Conference halted.

The above information should give us pause. The situation calls for intensive effort on the part of British women to end the present tragic impasse between our two countries. We should press too, for more detailed news about our Indian colleagues.

* * * * *

On behalf of the Liaison Group - Mrs. Corbett Ashby (Chairman) sent the following cable to Mrs. Mehta:
> "REGRET NO CONFERENCE. LIAISON GROUP SENDS GREETINGS STANDING
> COMMITTEE AND EAGERLY AWAITS NEWS."

Other cables were also sent by members of the Liaison Group.

---

*We regret that three, instead of four Bulletins have been issued during the year. But we feel sure that our subscribers will understand the reason has been our lack of news.

Fig 7 Women fetching water from the village well: album of mica paintings from southern India; c1850 (*see* pp.109–115). [Or.6540f.13]

Fig 8 Japanese courtesan reading a book: one of 167 girls depicted in *Ehon seirō bijan awase*, a picture book comparing the beauties of the 'Green Houses'. Edo, 1770 (*see* pp.109–115). [Or.75.g.34]

Fig 9 Taj al-Muluk bestowing slave girls on Sayf al-Muluk, watched by Sa'id: *Quissad-i Sayf al-Muluk va Badi al Jamal*, copied by Muhammad Warith, Thatta, 1755 (see pp.109–115). [Or.8758f.54(a)]

Fig 10 Radha is brought to Krishna by her girlfriend, another milk maid, who acts as go-between; the friend leaves and Radha and Krishna consummate their love: *Radha Krishna Keliskatha*, seventeenth-century palm-leaf manuscript from Orissa (*see* pp.109–115). [Or.11612, ff.17(a/b), 18(a)]

Fig 11 A Hindu wedding: a scene from Valmiki's *Ramayana* showing three couples being married. Sanskrit text, AD 1713 (*see* pp.109–115). [Add.15295, f.219(a)]

Fig 12 Social mores in eighteenth-century England: *The wonder of wonders: or a true and perfect narrative of a woman near Guildford in Surrey, who was delivered lately of seventeen rabbets, and the legs of a tabby cat... In a letter from a gentleman at Guildford to his friend, a physician at Ipswich, Suffolk...*, Ipswich, J Bognall, 1726 (*see* pp.124–128). [1178.h4.1–15]

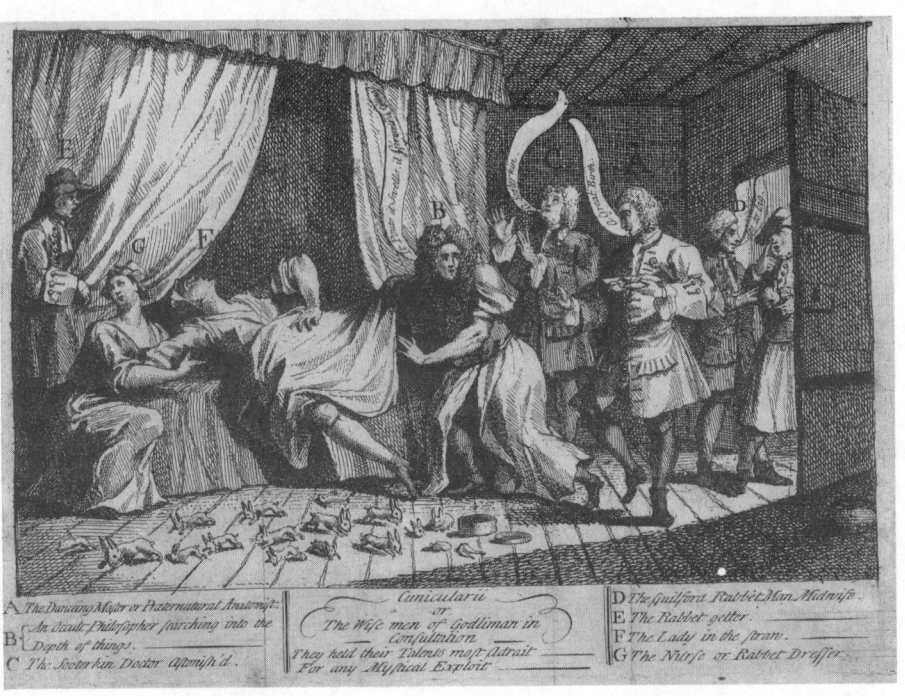

OPPOSITE

Fig 13 A group of British and American missionaries to China photographed in 1899 (*see* pp.156–164). [SOAS: Archive of the Women's Missionary Association, Presbyterian Church of England]

Fig 14 A group of missionaries of the London Missionary Society photographed after a committee meeting in Tientsin, *c*1900 (*see* pp.154–164). [SOAS: Archive of the Council for World Mission, China Photographs]

Fig 15 Intellectual pursuits open to women in the seventeenth century: portrait of Sor Juana Inés de la Cruz (1648–1695), perhaps one of Mexico's greatest poets, by Miguel Cabrera, as reproduced in Ezequiel A Chávez's *Ensayo de psicologia de Sor Juana Inés de la Cruz*, Barcelona, 1931 (*see* p.187). [4868.g.8]

Barbara James and Ilse Sternberg

The English Language Branch and women's studies

At a moment when the social position of women is daily becoming a question of greater and more general interest, it seems not inopportune to look back at her past history, and ascertain what has been the effect of the female character on human progress at particular periods, and under different degrees of civilisation.
Fullom *The history of woman*, 1855[1]

The increase in demand for women's studies over the past twenty years is not an isolated event arising from a new and previously unheard-of feminism. The past 500 years alone have seen periodic insistence on a redressing of a perceived imbalance or inaccuracy in popularly held ideology concerning woman's rôle in society. A 'friend to the sisterhood' in the three volume *Essay on old maids*, 1786, stating her intention to 'redress all the wrongs of the autumnal maiden, to place her, if possible, in a state of honour, content, and comfort' begins with a few remarks on 'the extreme cruelty and injustice of the sarcastic contempt so frequently lavished on old maids in general, and of the tendency which such treatment has to afflict, exasperate, and debase the character.'[2]

A vehement example, written originally in French, was published in Restoration London in 1677. It proclaimed that 'both sexes are equal; that is to say, that women are as noble, as perfect and as capable as men. This cannot be established, but by refuting two sorts of adversaries; the vulgar, and almost all the learned'.[3] The author sought to explain any difference between men and women in the matters of scientific or philosophical knowledge, manners, or even physical strength as simply a result of the education they receive. (*Plus ça change...*)

An even earlier work, its first edition printed in 1540, argues along the same lines, using a philosophical debate between two men to demonstrate that 'woman is not a creature imperfect, but as it seemeth is more perfit than manne'.[4] The dispute covers inventions by woman, intellectual accomplishments and the fact that even 'in armes women have ben found of no littell reputacion'[5]. It appears that in all these ages the proposition was made that it was lack of education rather than natural inferiority which placed women in their lesser position.

Despite the fact that women's studies programmes have been underway for some 20 years in North American and for over a decade in British academic institutions, no single definition of the subject has been agreed upon. All descriptions have the study of women at the core, but the field encompasses a wide range of views. This is largely due to the different political perspectives held by the scholars involved. A main point of contention continues to be the issue of autonomy versus integration. It is a debate common to other relatively new areas such as black studies, and even less controversial ones such as oriental studies. Radical feminist scholars tend to believe that it is only through a separately organised women's studies programme that there can be the desired review leading to a total restructuring of knowledge. Proponents of this standpoint hope to alter the focus of knowledge from its current androcentricity and to create a new scholarship based on a range of women's experience, thus leading to a redistribution of power, academic, economic and otherwise.

Integrationists, hoping to achieve reassessment of traditional fields of research from within those fields themselves, fear both the elitism and the ghettoisation possible in an autonomous programme. Within integrationist thought is a view which opposes the separatism of the other assessment. This school holds that it is desirable to aim towards a complete integration of women's studies into the traditional disciplines, which would thereby be essentially changed and more fully representational of reality. Ultimately the need for women's studies as a separate entity would be eliminated, and a higher general standard would result.

Scholars from both perspectives are involved in the development of a new feminist methodological approach to research, which has been influential in many disciplines, including psychology, history and sociology. This analysis rejects positivism and attempts to integrate women's experience into the research itself. The search for a new evaluation can include looking at a subject from a broader viewpoint than that of the single specialist discipline. Women's studies scholars tend to be as ultra-specialised as any other; an inter- or transdisciplinary approach will require significant changes in methodology. Women's studies, because of its origins in the women's movement, itself a result of the general unrest of the 1960s and 1970s, has a greater potential than many other fields for taking into account issues such as racism, class, sexuality and disability. The problem for any collection hoping to meet the needs of an area of study that in continually developing and reanalysing its terms, is to provide access to its holding from a wide range of indices.

The British Library's approach, if any, has tended to be integrationist. Often, areas of special interest, of a controversial nature or, in this case, only recently defined, tend to depend for their development on the concern of individuals within the institution. Here it would have had to have been the sympathetic consideration of a man. It was not until about 1920 that women were first allowed, theoretically, as staff at a curatorial level in the British Museum Library. However, it was only in 1931 that Marjorie Hoyle became the first woman to work at that grade in the Department of Manuscripts and not until 1934 that Norah Kenyon and Annie Gibson were employed by the Department of Printed Books. Even then women were not taken on in significant numbers until the continued shortage of male candidates forced a change of recruiting pattern. However, they were allowed to work only as long as they remained single, a situation which endured until the 1950s, in spite of the chronic shortage of staff from the mid-1930s onwards. Similar regulations applied at this time in other professions, such as nursing.

Nor, in the early days of the institution, would there have been a great deal of readership demand by women for feminist materials. As Barwick notes in his short history of the Reading Room published in 1933, initially 'it was not considered etiquette for ladies to study in the Library of the British Museum'.[6] Those who were grudgingly allowed to use the Library, had to appear in pairs, the first duo being admitted in 1762 and the second a year later. This practice continued into the nineteenth century although apparently not by regulation. In 1857 when the new Reading Room was opened, two tables were set aside for women. 'Ladies' who used the Reading Room when it became overcrowded in 1886 were attacked in the Press as an 'absolute nuisance' as they 'chattered, held little levees, read novels, painted pictures and rustled their skirts'. Their response was that men were just as bad and in addition often 'went to sleep and snored'[7]. The root of the problem was the reserved seats which the ladies, who were in any case few in numbers, began to ignore, taking the risk of sitting next to a man in order to be near the reference books they required. By 1906 'lady' readers were about one-fifth the daily average. This increased to one-third in 1913 with approximate parity being reached by 1933.

In theory, the Licensing Act of 1662 which provided for the submission to the King's Library of all books published in England or any other part of His Majesty's Dominions should have ensured that all titles published in Britain since that date came with the Old Royal Library to the British Museum Library. In fact, it was not until after 1852 when Panizzi began enforcing the deposit clause of the revised Act of 1842, that it became general practice for most UK publishers to deposit their works at the British Museum Library. With the deposit provision strengthened, a wide range of what would now be classified as women's studies materials were received. The reiteration of copyright in the 'British Dominions' which caused the Act of 1842 to be known as the Imperial Copyright Act, did not provide adequate sanctions to ensure deposit from the British overseas territories. With the assistance of the India and the Colonial Offices, British Museum officials finally succeeded during the 1880s in having local copyright acts passed in some such areas and for the next 50 years until about the period of the Second World War, titles were received by 'Colonial copyright' deposit. As well as the outpourings of the commercial presses, many items published by government printers in British Africa, Asia, North America, the Caribbean, Pacific Islands, and so on were sent to the BM Library.

The non-selective gathering and retention of much publishing from the British Empire and, in the case of government documents, also from those countries of Europe and Latin America with which the Library agreed to exchange official publications has resulted (to the benefit of contemporary research) in the preservation of material which if considered for purchase at the time might well have been thought to be of low academic value and, therefore, not worth the expenditure. It is the inevitably narrowed view of what is important in contemporary research which worries those of us who see the 'use' criterion for retention as restrictive of future scholarly independence.

The *omnium gatherum* approach of our 'forefathers' – one can hardly say 'foremothers' in this case – has given us, today, the benefit of a collection which contains a large proportion of the pivotal (that is not to say seminal) works such as the first edition of Mary Wollstonecraft's *A vindication of the rights of women* which was part of the foundation collections. Another copy with erasures, excisions and manuscript additions intended for a new edition was purchased in 1892. A copy of the second edition also published in 1792 was purchased for £18 in 1967 (this coincidentally is shelved next to the *Rules and regulations for the asylum of penitent females*). Also held are the six different editions published between 1869 and 1906 of J S Mill's *The subjection of women*. Three of theses were received by legal deposit, two donated and one purchased. Much official publishing contains relevant material. Dorothy Walker, on the staff of the Official Publications Library, compiled an exhibition for the recent bicentennial on 'Australian innovations in political democracy' which, using official documents to illustrate her points, reminded viewers that, although the first votes for women were granted in the Territory of Wyoming in 1869, Australia was in the forefront of the suffragette movement during the latter part of the nineteenth century. (Complete adult suffrage for the Commonwealth of Australia was granted in 1901 and in the last of the states, Victoria, in 1909, nearly two decades before similar rights were available in Britain.)

Alongside such books of proven research value one finds works by lesser figures, many now long forgotten, such as *Poems of progress* by Lizzie Doten, the poet and inspirational speaker said to be one of the best improvisers of nineteenth-century New England who became something of a recluse in her later life as she was unable to 'determine the point at which her personality ceased and the agency of spirit influence began'[8], *Edith Hale: a village story* by Ellen Putnam, a temperance writer, or the recently acquired *An island plant: a Nantucket story* by Mary Catherine Lee, a novelist of Springfield Massachusetts. Many of these nineteenth-century women writers are being rediscovered by women's publishers such as Virago, Hogarth, etc. Although a substantial number of these books are held, it is undoubtedly one of the areas which received little selection attention and the benefit of legal deposit or donation is most clearly demonstrated here.

With hindsight we see that the acquisition policy was not designed to create comprehensive collections in all areas. For example, the Library obtained, in at least one edition, the sociological and economic texts by Charlotte Perkins Gilman and in the case of *Women and economics*, some six, including one in Russian. Her highly acclaimed and groundbreaking short story *The yellow wallpaper*, however, was not acquired until it was received by copyright deposit when recently reprinted. Whether its omission was because it was considered too frivolous, too subversive, or simply unimportant remains unclear. More recently the controversial *Puberty blues* by the young Australian writer Kathy Lette was missed and will have to be searched in the second hand book market. Her recent *Girl's night out* published by Bloomsbury Press should be received by legal deposit.

Having reviewed the difficulties of defining women's studies and commented on the collectors and their selection parameters we will now look at approaches to the holdings, beyond the simple author search, both through conventional printed sources and through the newer automated listings. Measures include carefully constructed thesaural strategies and cybernetic serendipity.

When embarking on a search of a particular historical subject area (either to broaden a topic after the personal author approach has been exhausted or if personal authors are unknown) the starting point one might assume to be the *Subject index of modern works added to the Library of the British Museum in the years 1881–1900*. Compiled and edited by George Knottesford Fortescue when he was Superintendent of the Reading Room, the first three volumes, published in 1902, contain some 155,000 entries for works in western and eastern European languages. This index continued to be published covering five-yearly intervals, except for the decade 1961–70, until 1975 when it was discontinued in favour of another subject approach known as Precis (available on microfiche but now suspended). Fortescue in his introducction is full of apologies for the shortcomings of this work and he stresses its use as a supplement to the *General Catalogue*.

The earlier period of printing up to 1880 was indexed somewhat later, between 1933 and 1939 in three series, by the antiquarian bookseller R A Peddie. According to David Low, Peddie had come from St Bride's Library of Printing to join with Miss Fanny Hamel (who wrote as Frank Hamel) in 'the most uneasy, ill-assorted, and happiest of partnerships'[9] at the Coptic House of Gratton & Co, from where he compiled his index. Unlike the British Museum *Index* the work by Peddie was made up from many sources: the British Museum Library, the National Central Library, University College London, the Patent Office Library, his own collections and bibliographies and catalogues. He, like Fortescue, adopted a simple alphabetical approach using the most precise descriptors (*ie* 'Organ, Piano, Flute not Musical Instruments') considering that 'the more general a subject, the less need there has been for treating it at length'. Again he excludes the ordinary headings found in author catalogues, family histories, biographies, other personal works; and there was no attempt to re-evaluate the works in the light of 1930s academic fashion.

Thus Peddie, in his first series indexes 4 columns of titles under *Women*, $4\frac{1}{2}$ columns under *Witchcraft* and 2 columns under *Women's diseases* but only 11 titles under *Man* used in the sense of mankind. There are also 127 titles listed under *Obstetrics*, 23 under *Uterus*, 1 under *Ovary*, and 9 for *Testicle*, 2 for *Penis* and 4 for *Nymphomaniac* (six published between 1705 and 1836 in the three series). There are none under the male equivalent satyriasis but there is a French work listed under *Satyr* which describes them as brutes, monsters and demons. Not all of these works are found in the British Library, but other titles by the same author, or another with a similar name, can be found by searching Peddie authors in the *General Catalogue* (GK). From Peddie, J Burton *An essay towards a complete new system of midwifery*, 1751, proved to be, in the *General Catalogue*, John Burton, MD *of York*. Also in the GK there is J Burton *of Rochester?* whose *Lectures on female education and manners*, in 2 volumes, must have been very popular in the 1790s. The first edition published at Rochester, 1793, was followed by a second published in London, 1793, a third at Dublin in 1794 and the first American edition, New York, also in 1794.

Fortescue and his team at the British Museum perhaps reflected the growing interest in women's rights or maybe just the increased publishing output of the later nineteenth and early twentieth centuries. There are some 17 pages devoted to *Women* for the twenty year period 1881-1900 which had become 11 pages for the five years 1911-15 and which by 1971-75 had grown to 28 pages. Estimating between 50-60 items per page the progression of titles indexed per annum concerning women is something under 50 for the early period rising to 120 odd by the time of the First World War and 300 plus by the early 1970s.

It is interesting also to consider how the subject was indexed. In the first compilation the topic *Women* is divided into:

Part I: Social, economic, moral, political and religious works which include *history: women in various countries; criminal women; political works, female suffrage;* separately, *rights and emancipation of women; professions and work (legal, medical, public service, religious, factories); women and morality* and *women and socialism.*
Part II: medical works which are broken down into *general, periodical, electrical treatment and massage, homeopathic treatment, menstruation: change of life, monographs on various organs, diseases etc* and *hygiene, domestic medicine, etc.* By 1911-15 *medical works* was just one among the headings and was divided into *general works, monographs on various organs, etc* and *domestic medicine and hygiene.* New fields included under *professions, trades, etc.* were *agriculture* and *teaching* and there were separate headings for *women and war, women in books* and *women and sport. Criminal women* had become *women and crime*.

By the 1970s the headings had been further refined, the *general medical works* were now *general history of gynaecology* and *general works on gynaecology*. There was a new heading for the *psychology of women* but the number of works relating to *women and crime* still required separate mention despite the headings for psychology and law. The *bibliography of women* first indicated in the 1946-50 compilation led to Francis Lee Utley's *The crooked rib: an analytical index to the argument about women in English and Scots literature to the end of the year 1568*, Ohio State University, 1944. Utely's book looks at satires and defenses of women, which he defines as works that are exaggerated or controversial, and is rich in footnotes. Another early bibliography is Middleton Hussey and Roseanne Hudson's *The woman's collection: a bibliography of material in all matters pertaining to women's interests added to the Woman's College Library of North Carolina, 1937-1943, 1944-49* and a *1950 supplement*. A handwritten note in the first volume states: 'Close with the 1951 suppl. We shall not buy any more'.

Both BMSI and Peddie state in the introduction that there are conscious omissions in coverage and it is to universal bibliographies such as Robert Watt's *Biblioteca Britannica* or, more specifically, to the British Library *General Catalogue* that we now turn to further widen the search. In the British Library printed catalogue anonymous works, books with more than two authors, series, serials, and otherwise difficult to find titles, such as those which have authors designated by initials or epithets, are often listed using a key word approach. So under *Bawd* one finds *The insinuating bawd: and the repenting harlot. Written by a whore at Tunbridge, and dedicated to a bawd at Bath.* [1699]. See B,D. There is a second copy *To which is added, Love. An ode to a lady. By a Marry'd Gentleman. Spinster* reveals *The Truth about Man* by a Spinster, *Female* gives *To the unfortunate female*, London: Religious Tract Society [1810?] and *Knitting teacher* indicates *The knitting teacher's assistant*... New edition edited by E M.., author of "Ladies knitting", London, 1877; but *The standard guide to knitting*, 1879, is perhaps hidden from the unwary by its author a *Lady-manager*. Among the more unusual occupations for women is *The lady knife-thrower*, London, 1890, and *How to become a lady sanitary inspector* [1908]. It may surprise some to know that *The woman engineer*, the organ of the Women's Engineering Society has been published since 1919 or that the *First annual report*, of the Women's Gas Council covered the years 1935-36. More recently major bibliographies such as the Greenwood Press *Women in western European history*, 2 volumes (vol.1, 760 pages; vol.2, 1024 pages) provide a quick guide to material published in Europe, North America, Australia, etc in most of the languages of western Europe.

In addition to the word specific approach there are a number of general headings such as directories, ephermerides, collection of, etc, which deserve attention. One finds under *Directories III. [Professions, Trades, etc]* that there are listings for *Women workers, Women's wear* and Ephemerides gives, among others, the Massachusetts *Women's rights almanac* for 1858. Under the heading *Collection* are listed numerous holdings of songs, pamphlets, letters, valentines, treatises, etc, including *A collection of poems* by a Young Lady, (ie Jane Swinney) from 1792. Searches could also be made under other similar headings (eg miscellanea).

Number nine in the H&SS *Reader guide* series by Alison Gould is a key to named special collections in the former Department of Printed Books. This is a briefly annotated guide to those named collections which are shelved together in the Library. Items of interest here include the Maud Arncliffe-Sennett collection of 37 volumes of press clippings, pamphlets and other items relating to the women's suffrage movement between 1906 and 1936; and Marie Stope's collection of pamphlets and printed ephemera relating to birth control and health (c1861 to 1958).

More recently, and in the future a major source of information, the British Library computer services give access to a wide variety of bibliographic references. Key word and/or subject access is flexible and combinations of terms can produce very specific results. Data bases which cover a range of time periods and genre correspond to a broad spectrum of printed indexes. These automated files are presently searched by Library staff with the expertise to retrieve the maximum number of appropriate entries (a charged service). The Library is also developing an online catalogue (OPAC) which will give readers automated access to the catalogue records and when eventually linked to the automated book ordering system in St Pancras should not only increase the variety of methods for searching the collections but also speed the delivery to the researcher of required works.

Brief searches were carried out on three files. Two of these are union catalogues: the *Incunable Short Titles Catalogue* (ISTC), which aims to record all material printed before 1501 from moveable type and the *Eighteenth Century Short Title Catalogue* (ESTC), a file of works printed in any language in the British Isles or British colonies and items printed in English anywhere. The third file, the British Library Catalogue, is the general catalogue of H&SS which is being converted to a machine readable format. Only A-Hall was available when the search was undertaken. Accessible now as a preview to BLAISE subscribers the file should be complete in time for the move to St Pancras in 1993.

Since there are only 224 items in English recorded on ISTC, a search for the term wom#n results in only 8 entries (all indexed as women). Other terms, such as whore#, harlot#, female#, wife or wives do not appear at all. The file, however, contains some 17,000 Latin titles, and so searching for terms such as mulier: or muliebris will produce better results. Entries can also be found searching for French, German, Dutch, Italian and Spanish terms. As might be expected references to the Virgin Mary are profuse. In the ESTC file, wom#n results in 945 entries, spinster#, 147, femal: 652, dame: 425 and sapph: 56 (for those unfamiliar with searching techniques '#' replaces one letter and ':' allows for a number of alternative letters). The BLC, as yet a limited file, produced 6578 entries under wom#n, 63 for spinster#, 961 for femal: 202 for sapph: and 67 for whore:. Combining these terms with others would narrow the field.

Wider availability of some items is being facilitated by the microform publishing of titles from ESTC and from the BL nineteenth-century collections. The *Nineteenth century* does not list women's studies as an individual category in order that the titles retain their nineteenth-century context, but recent demand has resulted in the separate production of women writers. Already the list includes over four and a half thousand authors. Texts from the ESTC are also being produced and although again there is no series devoted to women, individual items are available in microform. The British Library has produced 19 microfiche reprints of texts dealing with *The emancipation of women*.

The brief of this paper is the English language collections in the Humanities and Social Sciences Division. To cover all the resources of the British Library in the space allocated is a tall order and inevitably, important aspects are given rapid treatment or totally omitted. In this case extensive resources not represented include the National Sound Archive, especially their collection of the spoken word, and the Document Supply Centre at Boston Spa, where staff recently compiled a select bibliography of their holdings of women's studies material for another conference. In discussing a subject approach to the collections our examples were naturally designed to elicit women's studies results. The same approach can be used with equally gratifying conclusions for most topics. Whatever approach is taken to recording and indexing a large general library there is no substitute for specialist analytical bibliography. How many researchers working on the development of education for black women in the United States will automatically reach for volume 2 of Fletcher's *History of Oberlin College*, to find that 'in 1850 Lucy Stanton, a colored girl, was even elected president of the Young Ladies' Association (later Ladies Literary Society),[10] or that Mary Jane Patterson was possibly the first African negro woman in the world to receive the AB degree in 1862[11]. We can but indicate likely avenues of approach.

In the development of this paper, a number of books were valuable. These include *Theories of women's studies* (edited by Gloria Bowles and Renate Duelli Klein, London: Routledge and Kegan Paul, 1983); *A women's thesaurus* (edited by Mary Ellen S

Capek, New York: Harper and Row, 1987); *Feminist scholarship* (Urbana: Universtiy of Illinois Press, 1985) and *Women's realities, women's choices* (Hunter College Women's Studies Collective, New York: Oxford University Press, 1983). *Women in LC's terms: a thesaurus of Library of Congress subject headings relating to women* by Ruth Dickstein, Victoria A Mills and Ellen J Wait, Pheonix: Dryx Press, 1988, provides valuable insight into a classification analysis of terms.

References

1. Fullom, Stephen Watson. *The history of woman, and her connexion with religion, civilization and domestic manners, from the earliest period.* 2 vols. London, 1855, Preface.
2. *A philosophical, history and moral essay on old maids by a Friend to the Sisterhood* [William Hayley]. 2nd edition (3 vols). London, 1786, p.xvi. Held in one Dublin and three London editions by the British Library.
3. L A. *The woman as good as the man; or the equality of both sexes.* Written originally in French [by F Poulain De la Barre] and translated by A C. London, 1677. Preface.
4. Elyot, Sir Thomas. *The defence of good women* London: T Berthelet, 1545. p.C5 verso.
5. *Ibid.* p.C7 verso.
6. Barwick, George Frederick. *The reading room of the British Museum* London: E Benn, 1929. p.65, quoting Bumpus, John Skelton. *Organists and composers of St Paul's Cathedral.* London: Printed for the Author, 1891 p.108.
7. *Ibid.* p.136.
8. *Nineteenth-century American literature by women.* Elaine Katz, Bookseller, Catalogue 32, item no.33.
9. Low, David, *With all faults.* Tehran: Amate Press, 1973, p.6.
10. Fletcher, Robert Samuel. *A history of Oberlin College, from its foundation through the Civil War.* Oberlin: Oberlin College, 1943, p.525.
11. *Ibid.* p.534.

Elizabeth James

A female novelist in the nineteenth century

There was a popular view, encouraged at the time by magazine articles, that nineteenth-century literature was distinguished by the unprecedented number of women writing for a largely female audience. Over the years some important work has been done in this area which will be familiar to many members of this Colloquium. The intention of this paper is simply to indicate afresh certain points about the rôle of women writers during the period, and to show how some of them are reflected in the career of one contemporary novelist.

The British Library is a convenient place in which to begin an investigation into the extent and circumstances of female authorship in the nineteenth century since it contains many useful sources of information about the book trade, as well as large numbers of the books themselves. The list of the holdings of literary works by women, currently in preparation by Dr Robin Alston, particularly emphasises this.[1] So far approximately 4,600 authors have been identified, and, if these figures are correct, it is already clear that a recent estimate of 4,000, extrapolated from census returns and *The Cambridge bibliography of English literature*, is in need of revision.[2] Although the precise numbers grow as more authors are recorded, pseudonyms unmasked, or anonymous books attributed, it will be interesting to see whether we also have to revise accepted perceptions of the proportion of women writers to men during the period. Until now the figure most often quoted is one in five: this was the average arrived at by R D Altick on the basis of entries in the CBEL,[3] it is within an acceptable range of the 17% of female applicants to the Royal Literary Fund,[4] and of the 18% of Civil List pensioners.[5]

Unlike their male counterparts, however, most of these women were limited, by their moderate level of basic education, to the writing of children's books or fiction. Such concentration of effort ensured that around 40% of all novels were written by women,[6] and is partly responsible for the impression that the literary market place was dominated by them. It is indeed tempting to see the Victorian novel as an area of female triumph. George Eliot, Frances Trollope and a host of familiar but less famous authors earned considerable sums for their work, while lower down the literary scale more and more women were still finding it possible to earn a living by writing. In truth, other than teaching, there were few respectable alternative means of employment for middle class women, and to say that some overcame the difficulties to achieve success is to evade the all-important questions about access to the profession. As Julia Swindells poses the problem in *Victorian writing and working women*:

How women were received by publishers, how women perceived themselves as literary professionals, and cumulatively, the difficulties of becoming and sustaining being a writer: these are the questions which are not simply answered quantitively according to labour power or profits.[7]

One obvious answer to the first part of the question is, of course, that many women side-stepped the issue by presenting their work anonymously. Charlotte Brontë explains her views:

> while we did not like to declare ourselves women, because ... we had a vague impression that authoresses are liable to be looked on with prejudice; we had noticed how critics sometimes use for their chastisement the weapon of personality, and for their reward, a flattery, which is not true praise.[8]

Could she have been thinking of the anonymous (male) reviewer of Julia Kavanagh's *English women of letters* in 1862?

> Two or three of these ten ladies evidently owe a good deal of their literary fame to their good looks. Mrs Inchbald, for example, and Mrs Opie would not have been authoresses if they had not first been pretty and charming women, and their intellects quickened by flirtation.[9]

On the other hand it should not be forgotten that a significant proportion of all novels, whether by men or women, were published anonymously or pseudonymously. The publication lists of Richard Bentley and Son reveal that this was true of 76% of novels published in 1830, for example. It is a reminder that novel writing was a dubious occupation for either sex during at least the first half of the century.

For obvious and practical reasons research has tended to concentrate on the best known authors and their relations with their publishers. A biographical approach via the personality of a leading writer is the surest means of holding an interest in what are, after all, essentially dry financial transactions, and in the second place, the archives relating to such authors and their publishers are more likely to have survived. Yet in order to answer the remaining parts of Swindells' question it is necessary to investigate the careers of the 'ordinary' writers – those whose works filled the shelves of the circulating libraries and railway bookstalls. This is not a straightforward undertaking (these women have earned no place in the literary histories and many of their publishers vanished without trace long ago) and often appears quite hopeless. The information has to be extracted from diverse published sources such as contemporary biographical dictionaries, reminiscences, library and publishers' catalogues, book trade journals, reports of charitable insitutions and societies connected with the profession of authorship, as well as a wide range of archives, of which those relating to printers, publishers or booksellers form only the most obvious group. The British Library is fortunate in having amongst its collections useful material in all of these categories, supplemented by microfilms of important items in other institutions, where these are available. It would be difficult, and perhaps tedious, in such a short space to list even the most obvious sources:

instead, the following study of a novelist, once popular but now quite forgotten, shows how some of them may be used to piece together a picture of even the most unpromising subject.

Emma Robinson was the author of about twenty books which achieved some success during the middle years of the nineteenth century, particularly in their cheap editions. Like many of her contemporaries however – and despite an entry in *The Cambridge bibliography of English literature* – she is now almost entirely unknown. Although she was chosen at random for this paper to represent the 'proletariat' of women who tried to earn their living by writing, her life and career proved to contain several interesting features when viewed from a women's studies perspective. How far these are to be taken as typical may be a matter for discussion.

Not a great deal is known about Emma Robinson herself, and much of the little information which is available comes from William Tinsely *Random recollections of an old publisher* (1900) or F Boase *Modern English biography* (1892-1921). She was born in 1814, the daughter of Joseph Robinson who is variously described as a bookseller or publisher in the *Post Office London Directory*. He was probably responsible for her education, for introducing her to the book trade through his own business, and to some extent for her subsequent literary career.

Her earliest recorded work is a play about Cardinal Richelieu, the manuscript of which was submitted under the signature of 'a cadet of Woolwich' to J R Planché in his capacity as 'reader' at Covent Garden in about 1840. Planché was unenthusiastic about the play's chance of success either on the stage or at the hands of the Licensor, but Emma Robinson was not easily deterred. She found another sponsor in Benjamin Webster, the famous actor and manager of the Haymarket Theatre, and in 1844 persuaded Henry Colburn to publish the text of the play, which she prefaced with a scathing essay about the system of licensing for the stage in general and the difficulties facing young dramatists in particular. (The play eventually received a licence in 1850, according to a note on the manuscript now amongst the Lord Chamberlain's Plays).

This was a controversial debut which aroused a considerable amount of speculation about the author's identity. Planché came near to guessing the truth, but Emma resisted all invitations to make herself, and her sex in particular, known to the public. 'I am not anxious' she wrote 'that anyone who hears I am a *lady* in *private* should win a reputation for courage by abusing me as a *gentleman* in *public*.[10] The 'Cadet of Woolwich' was not heard of again, but she continued to fuel curiosity by adhering to a principle of anonymity on one hand, while addressing the reader in a variety of prefatory notes on the other.[11]

The persona of the author is therefore very strong in many of Emma Robinson's novels. If contemporary gossip is to be believed there was good reason for this. In 1844 she also published her first novel, *Whitefriars*, dedicating it to her father from 'his friend, the author'. Soon it was being reported that the Joseph Robinson named in the dedication was himself the author, and that this was a clever device to link his name with the book. The British Library deposit copy bears a manuscript note to this effect, suggesting that the theory had received at least a degree of recognition. Tinsley's version, published many years later, is unequivocal.

Robinson was a seller of old books in or near Holborn, and during her father's absence at book auctions, Miss Robinson took his place and wrote; and handed the complete book to him, much to his surprise.

Strange to say, Robinson, for some years made a sort of mystery of the authorship, and almost, if not quite, led people to believe that he himself was the author.[12]

Emma Robinson's novels of the 1840s were historical stories of the type fashionable at the time. *Whitefriars* was reprinted three times in the first year of publication and has been her most enduring work, but all contributed to her reputation as a popular novelist. The majority of these early books were published by Henry Colburn, a former partner of Richard Bentley, and specialist in three volume novels for the circulating libraries.

These works, like many others from the Colburn and Bentley stables, were exactly the kind of material needed for the cheap reprint series coming on to the market. Routledge seized upon them for his Railway Library in the knowledge that Emma Robinson's name was still fresh, that there was a guaranteed sale for relatively new novels at the drastically reduced price of 2s, and confident that he would not have to pay much for the copyrights. *Whitefriars* appeared in 1851 in two volumes as numbers 28 and 29 in the series, followed by *Whitehall* (nos 53 and 54), *Caesar Borgia, Owen Tudor, The Maid of Orleans, The gold worshippers* and *Westminster Abbey*. The receipts for copyright payments on all these titles are preserved in the firm's archives. In each case the rights were leased for five years for sums ranging from £20 to £50, and the documents signed by Joseph Robinson.[13]

However, *The gold worshippers*, first published in 1851, marked the beginning of a succession of changes in Emma Robinson's career. At about that time Colburn's business was taken over and she was forced to find other publishers in firms such as C J Skeet, Bentley and John Maxwell. At the same time, she attempted to follow literary fashion by abandoning her well-tried pattern of historical fiction in favour of contemporary plots of a domestic nature, often incorporating a suprisingly forceful feminist message. Marriage became a favourite theme, particularly as a potential cause of deceit and misery. *Mauleverer's divorce*, subtitled 'a story of woman's wrongs', for example, was written in the aftermath of the introduction in Parliament of the Divorce and Matrimonial Clauses Bill. It is dedicated 'To the illustrious Minister of England ... [who] first of all English statesmen had commenced the generous justice of restoring the sexes to a legal equality ...'. Her last novel, *The matrimonial Vanity Fair* (1968) develops an earlier theme: that society's harsh treatment of single women was a direct cause of many unsuitable marriages. The novel opens with one of the chief characters contemplating marriage with an elderly, but wealthy widower: the alternative is to be 'turned out on nothing a-year, when I'm forty or so, by the heir of the entail. Rather too late, I should say for going a-governessing or anything of that sort...'[14]

These new themes may have been indicative of changes in her own personal circumstances – possibly of her father's death – for by the end of the 1850s she was signing documents herself, and openly corresponding with publishers in her own name. Henceforth the 'persona' of the novels is occasionally revealed in her true colours – no less forceful and independent than we had been led to expect.

Strength of personality and experience notwithstanding, her business affairs did not prosper. In 1858 she leased the rights in two more novels to Routledge on the same terms as before. Like many other comparable authors, she was seduced by his talent for wringing more sales out of copyrights which had appeared to be used up, and so failed to examine the facts sufficiently closely. When the original leases came up for renewal she happily agreed to an outright sale of her most valuable copyrights. Routledge thus purchased *Whitefriars, Whitehall, Caesar Borgia* and *Owen Tudor* for £70 in 1859, with the sole stipulation that they should not be transferred to any other firm. (It is salutory to remember that Sir Edward Bulwer Lytton, with – one might say – all the advantages of his sex and class, managed to extract £20,000 from Routledge for the inclusion of his novels in the Railway Library.) The extent of Emma Robinson's loss is apparent from the firm's Publication books. Seven thousand copies of *Whitehall* were printed between 1858 and 1871, also a similar number of *Caesar Borgia* between 1858 and 1877. During the same period 10,000 copies of the 2s edition of *Whitefriars* were printed at a unit cost which steadily declined from $10\frac{3}{4}d$ to $6\frac{1}{2}d$, while between 1884 and 1888 29,000 copies of a 6d edition were produced at a unit cost of $1\frac{1}{2}d$.[15] No further analysis is needed to show that, even allowing for discounts and overheads, Routledge made a considerable profit out of this single transaction.

Since Emma Robinson published no new works between 1858 and 1862, Routledge's £70 may have been her only literary income during this period. It is scarcely surprising that she turned to charitable sources for support. In 1861 she made her first approach to the Royal Literary Fund, a charity which had been set up in 1790 to assist struggling authors or their dependants. She was awarded a single payment of £60, after Routledge had confirmed the identity of 'the authoress of "Whitefriars"'.[16] In 1862 she was granted an annual Civil List pension of £75 in further recognition of her difficult circumstances. These pensions were intended to reward significant contributions in a variety of fields, but in practice – as critics of the system frequently stated – the money was allocated with a total disregard for merit.

As if to confirm these ominous signs of failure, the 1860s saw the end of her career as a published author. *Madeleine Graham* (1864) was sold for a mere £35 to John Maxwell, who subsequently transferred the copyright to Routledge. *Christmas at Old Court* (1864) and *Dorothy Firebrace* (1865) were published by the more famous Richard Bentley, but on precarious half-profit terms, before the latter was also transferred to Routledge in 1866. *Dorothy Firebrace* was in fact something of a desperate return to her original genre of historical fiction, but despite careful advertising the public appeared to have forgotten the earlier successes.[17] She had obtained an advance of £100 on the strength of her reputation in this field, but in August 1865 Bentley reported that he was the loser by £75, having 300 copies on hand.[18] Once again, Routledge's willingness to republish at a lower price seemed the only answer: a final memorandum in the firm's archives records that £60 was paid to Emma Robinson for all her rights 'past, present and future' in *The Maid of Orleans, Westminster Abbey* and *Dorothy Firebrace*.[19]

In 1869 she was forced to make a second application to the Royal Literary Fund in a letter which referred to her lack of success in the face of 'the great change that has taken place in the public taste in fiction'.[20] Ironically, this application was also sponsored by Routledge who continued to make a steady income from copyrights which he had purchased on such advantageous terms. It was twenty years before Emma Robinson appeared to realise the full significance of her loss, but by then it was too late. She made a third, breathless, appeal to the fund in 1887 in words which sum up the vulnerability of all authors.

A complication of misfortunes – a winter of severe disabling illness – the sudden, most unexpected and ruinous bankruptcy of my Trustee and confidential agent in the concerns of the little property I have ever been enabled to get together after above forty years of incessant literary labour, and who was in charge of the legal proceedings I have been obliged to institute against two London publishers for piracy (Messrs. Routledge & Sons and John Dicks) by which they have managed to cheat me... out of all I have in the emoluments of three editions published as late as last year without my knowledge or consent of the first and most celebrated of my numerous works... whereby the damage I hoped and still do not doubt to obtain from an English judge and jury are for a while postponed.[21]

Spirited to the last, she was granted £50 in respect of this appeal, and a further £40 in 1889, but died in the Middlesex County Lunatic Asylum on 19 Decembner 1980.

References

1. Alston, R C. *Checklist of women writers of fiction, verse and drama 1801-1900* (to be published by British Library Publications, and Greenwood Press).
2. Cross, Nigel. *The common writer: life in nineteenth-century Grub Street.* Cambridge, 1985. pp.3, 167.
3. Altick, R D 'The sociology of authorship'. In: *Bulletin of the New York Public Library.* vol.66, no.6 (June 1962), pp.389-404.
4. Cross, p.166.
5. This figure is based on details given in William Morris Colles *Literature and the Pension List.* London, 1889.
6. *A list of the principal publications issued from New Burlington Street* (London, 1893-1923) records the publications of Richard Bentley and Son, one of the foremost publishers of fiction during the nineteenth century. A calculation based on the novels published 1829-1834, 1855-1860, 1888 produces a figure of 46% – slightly higher than the figure of 40% quoted by Cross.
7. Swindells, Julia. *Victorian writing and working women.* Cambridge, 1985, p.101.
8. Bell, Currer. 'Bibliographical notice of Ellis and Acton Bell'. In: *Wuthering Heights* and *Agnes Grey*, new edition, (1850), p.ix.
9. *Saturday Review*, 13 December 1862.
10. Planché, J R. *Recollections and reflections.* London, 1901. p.307
11. The preface to the second edition of *Whitefriars* thanks the public for its interest in the author, taking three pages to explain why his identity has to remain a secret. *Whitehall*, the novel which followed, contains an elaborate account of the genesis of the three works so far published in the form of a preface by one 'Dr Johann Christian Ravenmann'. Briefly, he describes meeting a stranger with the name of 'Eidolon' (a Greek word which may be translated as 'ghost') who is in possession of a heap of manuscript papers. Eidolon has already published some of these as *Whitefriars*, and has recognised a connection with *Richelieu in love*: he invites Ravenmann to carry on the editorial work.
12. Tinesly, W. *Random recollection of an old printer.* London, 1900, vol.1, pp.92–93.
13. Contracts R–Z, ff.14, 16, 18. The archives of George Routledge and Sons are available on microfilm as part of Chadwyck-Healey's *Archives of British publishers*.
14. *The Matrimonial Vanity Fair*, vol.1, p.18.
15. Publication books 3, fol.17, 223, 643; 4, fol.525; 5, fol.556.

16. Royal Literary Fund. Letter from Routledge to Emma Robinson 9 August 1861. The archives of the RLF have been deposited on permanent loan in the British Library, Department of Manuscripts.
17. On 3 December 1864 Emma Robinson wrote to Bentley 'But if I were the publisher of *Dorothy Firebrace* I should depend more upon *advertisements* than *panegyrics*, with a well-known author.' The letter goes on to suggest the wording, and frequency of an ideal advertisement. Add.MS 46653, f.229).
18. Bentley papers. Add.MSS 46643, f.50.
19. Contracts R–Z, f.63.
20. RLF, 30 December 1869.
21. RLF, 31 May 1987.

Carole Holden

Nineteenth-century black American women's writing

In 1773 Phillis Wheatley's book of poetry *Poems on various subjects, religious and moral* was published in London, an astonishing achievement for the young black girl who had been brought as a slave from Africa to America in 1761 and purchased in Boston by John Wheatley when only seven or eight years old. The published volume includes an 'attestation', signed by a group of prominent citizens of Boston, which states that these citizens believed Wheatley to have written the poems herself. It is an indicator of the hard struggle that Wheatley had to get into print. None of Boston's publishers had credited her with the ability to have written the poems so, aged only eighteen, she had eventually endured an oral examination which resulted in her obtaining the attestation. This document was a key factor in attracting a publisher for the volume, although it had still been necessary for Wheatley, in the company of her master's son Nathaniel, to travel to England in 1773 where, with the aid of the Countess of Huntington and the Earl of Dartmouth, the poems were finally published. The British Library has two copies of this 1773 edition and numerous editions and reprints of Wheatley's writings have since appeared, culminating in a new, collected edition of her work which forms part of the *Schomburg Library of Nineteenth-Century Black Women Writers*.

Wheatley initiated a rich literary tradition which had already become firmly established by the late nineteenth century, a period of intense intellectual and publishing activity by women such as Frances Harper, Anna Julia Cooper, Ida Wells, Victoria Earle Matthews and many others who sought to respond to the demands of an increasingly racist era. The turn of the century saw publication of Pauline Hopkins' wonderful fiction and the wealth and diversity of writing by black women in America continued, and continues to flourish – through the 'Harlem Renaissance' writings of Jessie Faucet, Nella Larsen and Zora Neale Hurston, the urban fiction of Ann Petry and Paule Marshall, the poetry of Gwendolyn Brooks and Audre Lorde, through Alice Walker, Toni Morrison and many others who have carried on the tradition. For the purposes of this paper I have decided to focus on the nineteenth-century writings, partly because a fuller survey would be difficult in the space available, but also because I thought that the Library's holdings of this material might be less familiar (and less predictable) than for those of the later writings. In addition, while another Colloquium paper describes the English language collections in more detail, I have looked at these collections from a fairly narrow perspective and made some unexpected discoveries and found some surprising gaps.

I would like to begin by making a few general remarks which should help serve as pointers to some of the material that researchers interested in writing by Afro-American women might expect or, at least, hope to find within the British Library. First, it should be stressed that English language collections receive, through legal deposit, books and serials published in this country. In addition, many American publishers distribute their works in the UK and these are also deposited. This means that a substantial proportion of the literature, whether in the form of contemporary novels, reprints of earlier writings, literary criticism and biographies etc comes into the Library. Clearly, much of the literature is published in the United States and many of the important non-deposited items will be picked up in the selection process but the Library cannot hope to acquire all the works being published in this rapidly developing field. While compiling this paper, for example, I wished to consult several items (including an article in the journal *Sage*), none of which were held in Humanities and Social Sciences. However, the BL's Document Supply Centre had all the items in question and I was able to request and obtain them fairly quickly. Readers in the Bloomsbury Reading Room can similarly request material in this way.

Secondly, the amount of material that is now more readily available in this country has significantly increased and continues to increase as interest grows, not just in the contemporary work of writers such as Alice Walker and Maya Angelou, but in the rich history of writing by Afro-American women. Some years ago I wished to look at several of the works of Zora Neale Hurston. I was unable to find them in the bookshops but they were available to me in the Library. Now it is possible to buy many of Hurston's books in paperback editions published by Virago and these can, of course, also be found in the Library. Virago, Womens Press, Sheba and others have made available many of the important authors in the field and I note that Virago has recently published Mary Helen Washington's *Invented lives: narratives of black women 1860–1960*. The nineteenth-century writers have been re-examined and re-assessed in a growing number of studies, particularly by black women writers themselves. This examination has been made easier by the publication in 1988 of the *Schomburg Library of Nineteenth-Century Black Women Writers*, published by Oxford University Press under the general editorship of Henry Louis Gates Jr. Professor Gates has done a great service to scholars (and general readers) by initiating this invaluable collection which brings together in thirty volumes a vast array of material that clearly demonstrates the literary achievements made by black women during the nineteenth century. Material for 24 of the volumes was reprinted from holdings of the Schomburg Center for Research in Black Culture, part of the New York Public Library. Although the collection includes some well known works such as Frances Harper's *Iola Leroy* and Harriet Jacobs' *Incidents in the life of a slave girl*, there are also volumes of collected narratives and poetry and little known titles which will be reaching a wider audience for the first time. Each volume also has the benefit of an introduction written by a leading expert in the field.

When I first started to compile this paper I found the BL's holdings very uneven and unpredictable. While I discovered works by Ann Plato, Harriet Jacobs, Ida Wells, Octavia Albert, Pauline Hopkins and others, many voices were missing from our collections. In many instances the writers, like Wheatley, suffered indignities at the hands of publishers, their audience was limited, print runs were small and it is perhaps not surprising that their work did not find its way into the Library. However, there are also some notable omissions – Anna Julia Cooper and Frances Harper for example. Harper, as we shall see later, was a popular writer whose works enjoyed frequent reprinting and it is particularly puzzling to find her absent. It is interesting to note that some of these gaps were also discovered recently through the checking of an Afro-American Studies bibliography, one of a number of bibliographies commissioned by the American Trust for the British Library as part of its programme to strengthen the Library's American holdings for the period 1880-1950. Important works not found in the BL's collections are acquired in microfilm or reprint editions with ATBL funds. The later 'Harlem Renaissance' writings by women listed in the bibliography were, however, well represented. Fortunately, many of the significant gaps have now been filled by the addition to our collections of the aforementioned volumes of the *Schomburg Library of Nineteenth-Century Black Women's Writers*.

During the nineteenth century, black women expressed themselves on a variety of topics but certain subjects appear to dominate their writings – religion, social and political reform, education and family life – not surprising since it was these areas that were of most concern to their own lives. In many cases, elements of several, if not all, of these themes were to be found together. The strength of the church was particularly important and throughout most of the century religion and the call for political and social reform were fused in many of the writings. This fusion is clearly demonstrated in the remarkable religious essays of Maria Stewart, a freeborn northerner who grew up in Hartford, Connecticut. Making her first speech in 1832 to the Afric-American Female Intelligence Society in Boston, she was one of the first black women to lecture publicly for black advancement. The Afric-American Intelligence Society was one of a number of educational societies that were springing up in response to the needs of a small but increasingly articulate free black community. Such societies, together with the black churches, worked for the self-improvement of this community in the face of growing repressive legislation. Stewart, following a religious conversion, had decided to devote herself to the furtherance of her race and its women in particular. She urged these women to make full use of their abilities and to lead the struggle for freedom. 'How long shall the fair daughters of Africa be compelled to bury their minds and talents beneath a load of iron pots and kettles?'[1] Some of Stewart's speeches appeared in the *Liberator*, but they were collected together as the *Productions of Mrs Maria Stewart* and published in 1835. The BL does not have the original edition but the *Productions* appear in the volume of *Spiritual Narratives* in Schomburg.

A few years later, Ann Plato's *Essays; including biographies and miscellaneous pieces in prose and poetry* appeared, printed for the author in Hartford in 1841. This work, surprisingly, did find its way into the BL, a copy being purchased in 1868. Little is known about Plato although, like Stewart, she was a devout Christian. Her work is introduced by the Reverend James W C Pennington, a well-known abolitionist who was pastor of the Colored Congregational Church of Hartford where Plato was a communicant. Although mainly religious in theme, Plato's introspective writings are quite unlike those of the fiery Stewart and only occasionally do they touch on racial matters. In the essay *Education* Plato emphasizes the importance of education as a means of advancement and it is evident that she herself was well-educated. She notes that 'oral instructions' can only benefit one era so that books, 'the silent teachers' (p.27), need to be preserved as a means of passing on knowledge. Plato's work represents the first collection of essays to be published by an Afro-American. Only recently has it been reprinted for the first time since 1841, the reprint again appearing as a volume in Schomburg.

Personal narratives, both by former slaves and freeborn women, form an important and invaluable part of the literature of the nineteenth century. An example of the latter is a *Narrative of the life and travels of Mrs Nancy Prince*, published by the author in Boston in 1850, a copy of which is in the BL, an enlarged second edition appearing in 1853 (Schomburg collection). Prince describes her life as a 14-yeard-old servant in a religious northern household where her employers found no contradiction in holding daily prayers while at the same time exploiting their servants. She eventually married in 1824 and went to live in Russia where her husband was employed by the Czar. She describes life in Russia where 'there was no prejudice of color' (p.23) and contrasts it with the racism she again encountered in America when she was forced to return in 1833 due to ill health. She attended meetings of the Anti-Slavery Society in Boston and commented that, despite some changes having been made, much remained to be done although 'possibly I may not see so clearly as some, for the weight of prejudice has again oppressed me, and were it not for the promises of God, one's heart would fail' (p.42). Through her religious beliefs she never doubted that justice would ultimately prevail. Having become a widow, she was also to travel to Jamaica where she taught and worked with freed slaves.

Prince states that she wrote from a desire to support herself by her own endeavours, to remain independent. It is significant that, although she describes her travels, financial problems and sufferings etc, little of a personal nature is revealed. This is a notable trait which can be found in many such narratives. Lack of money led women such as Prince to 'sell' their stories in order to maintain their existences. Anthony Barthelemy, in his introduction to the volume of *Collected black women's narratives* in the Schomburg collection likens this to a 'literary return to the auction block' (p.xxxiv) where exposure in the market place signified humiliation, examination and sale. It was imperative for these writers that they should maintain possession and control of their own lives. They accordingly constructed their stories using language to both reveal and conceal.

Sadly, the Library has no copy of the original (and extremely rare) edition of *Our Nig* (1859), Harriet Wilson's novel set in the antebellum free north and largely based on her life as an indentured servant in New England. In the preface Wilson also states her reasons for publishing as being economic – the need to maintain herself and her child. It is significant that she appeals for support and patronage, not from a white northern audience, but from her 'colored brethren'. In this first novel by a black American, Wilson, like Prince, condemns the racism and hypocrisy in the north as the subtitle makes clear *Sketches from the life of a free black, in a two-storey white house, North. Showing that slavery's shadows fall even there.* Wilson uses and adapts the plot conventions of the sentimental novel in order to tell her story and Hazel Carby has argued that '*Our Nig* can be most usefully regarded as an allegory of a slave narrative, a "slave" narrative set in the "free" North'.[2] The work can, in fact, be seen as a link between the already well developed narrative tradition and the beginnings of black fiction. Like Prince, Wilson was not prepared to reveal everything and in the preface she says 'I do not pretend to divulge every transaction in my own life, which the unprejudiced would declare unfavourable in comparison with treatment in legal bondmen; I have purposely omitted what would provoke most shame in our good anti-slavery friends at home'. Towards the end of the book she adds 'Still an invalid, she asks your sympathy, gentle reader. Refuse not, because some part of her history is unknown, save by the Omniscient God. Enough has been unrolled to demand your sympathy and aid' (p.130). However, it does not appear that this sympathy and aid was forthcoming. The fact that Wilson was directly addressing the black community, together with her lack of ties to the abolitionists perhaps distanced her work from a white readership, but it also seems to have been ignored by its black audience, and went unnoticed for many years. It was rediscovered relatively recently by Henry Louis Gates Jr and reprinted, with an introduction and notes by Gates, in 1983. The BL has the 2nd edition of this reprint, published by Allison and Busby in Britain in 1984. Gates, in his introduction, notes that Boston in 1859 was a centre of abolitionist reform and that the black press at that time was eager to celebrate all black achievement. The fact that the publication of *Our Nig* went unnoticed 'remains one of the troubling enigmas of Afro-American literary history' (p.xxx).

Although many slave narratives appeared during this period (over one hundred separate narratives being produced before the Civil War), the majority were of male slaves and often gave scant attention to the lives of female slaves. Harriet Jacobs' *Incidents in the life of a slave girl*, published in Boston in 1861 (the BL has the 1862 London edition) is one of the last narratives to be published before the war and one of the few (and best known) surviving narratives by a woman. Jacobs wrote the book secretly at night while employed as a domestic servant, partly because of her household duties during the day, but also because her employer was pro-slavery and she feared his reaction to her writing. Jacobs, like Wilson, uses and adapts some of the conventions of the sentimental novel for her narrative. This would have made the work more acceptable to her intended white audience but, in addition, the usual conventions of the predominantly male narratives were inadequate to describe her experiences, particularly when she came to write about the sexual abuse and oppression she suffered at the hands of her white masters (an important motive in her fleeing the south was to try to protect her daughter from the sexual exploitation that she herself had suffered). In drawing attention to this sexual oppression and her vulnerability, Jacobs challenged the racist stereotypes of female slaves, often depicted as sexually wanton in the popular fiction of the day. Having compromised herself by revealing such intimate personal details, Jacobs wrote under the pseudonym of Linda Brent, as a means of self-protection, knowing that discovery would result in humiliation. Sexual purity was regarded as so important that she even refused to allow several of her white women friends to write a preface to her book for fear that their reputations would be tarnished by association with it (it was finally to be edited by L Maria Child). It was to the white women in the north that Jacobs addressed her work, wanting to make them aware not only of the suffering of the slaves in the south, but to urge them to help stop the hunting of fugitive slaves in the north.

Slave narratives were not only important in preserving the history of the slave generations for future generations but they also presented a positive and more accurate picture of life in contrast to the plantation myths generated by white novelists of the period. *House of bondage*, Octavia Albert's group narrative, appeared in 1890 and the desire to present an accurate portrayal of slave life was one of her motives for publishing the work. A committed Christian and scholar, Albert lived with her preacher husband in Louisiana. Former slaves would gather at the Albert home where they were given food, listened to readings from the Bible and were taught to read and write. Albert encouraged them to speak of their experiences as slaves and decided that their stories should be made available to a wider audience. Although there was by now a growing black middle class, Albert was well aware that the majority of blacks were poor, illiterate and unemployed. She considered this state to be a direct result of slavery and the presentation of the narrative was her way of trying to draw attention to and improve the situation. Having attended Atlanta University, Albert's ability as an interviewer and recorder makes *House of bondage* invaluable. The narratives originally appeared as a series of articles in the *South-Western Advocate* between January-December 1890, the book being published by popular demand at the end of the year after Albert's death. The Library has an 1891 printing of the work, purchased in July 1891.

As noted earlier, the last decade of the nineteenth century was a particularly active period for black women in America. Using all the literary conventions at their disposal, and against a background of increasing racism, they spoke out for their rights, challenging both racism and the traditional rôle of male dominance. In 1892 Anna Julia Cooper published her outstanding collection of feminist essays *Voice from the South*, a notable omission in the Library's holdings until we acquired the Schomburg collection reprint. In the introduction to the reprint Mary Helen Washington describes *Voice from the South* as 'the most precise, forceful, well-argued statement of black feminist thought to come out of the nineteenth century' (p.li). That it appreared at a time which saw the reversal of civil rights legislation and lynchings reaching a peak is even more astonishing. Cooper, a teacher with a degree from Oberlin College, recognised the urgency of education for her race and considered that its future lay in the development of men and women together. While racism inhibited both black men and women from obtaining an education, black women were doubly discriminated against. It was only through education that black women could hope to end their dependence on men. At the same time, the National Women's Suffrage Association was, in some instances, attempting to exclude black women from the fight for equal rights and Cooper criticised its leaders for their failure to take a stand against racism.

The difficulties in campaigning for equal rights for race together with equal rights for women, while the suffrage movement was predominantly white, was also addressed by Frances Ellen Watkins Harper, one of the most well-known women of the period. Harper had an international reputation as a writer, poet, lecturer and social and political reformer. She gave her first speech to a public meeting in New Bedford in 1854 on 'Education and the Elevation of the Colored Race', thus beginning a career as a lecturer which was to occupy a major part of her life. She spent most of her time campaigning against slavery during the antebellum years but was also a frequent contributor of articles to periodicals and, also in 1854, published her first collection of poetry, *Poems on miscellaneous subjects*. Harper was a popular poet; by 1858 this work had been enlarged and reprinted eight times. She married in 1860 and temporarily retired from the lecture circuit but, following the death of her husband in 1864, she once again devoted her energies to speaking on education and equality, particularly to black women's groups to whom she lectured free of charge. Harper also became increasingly active in the Women's Christian Temperance Union which, although not exclusively white, was segregated. She continued to write, often selling little booklets of her poetry after her speaking engagements. She published a number of works including *Moses: a story of the Nile* in 1869, *Poems* in 1871 (by which time *Poems on miscellaneous subjects* was in its twentieth printing), *Sketches of southern life* in 1872 and *Idylls of the Bible* in 1891. Her first and only novel *Iola Leroy, or shadows uplifted* appeared in 1892. In its treatment of such topics as slavery and reconstruction, religion and temperance, it appealed to a wide audience and was an immediate best-seller. Within one year *Iola Leroy* had already gone through five printings. The popularity of Harper's writings, together with the number of printings that they enjoyed make their absence from the Library's collections all the more inexplicable. Fortunately, the Schomburg collection contains not only *Iola Leroy* but also a volume of the *Complete poems of Frances E W Harper*.

Harper argued that a more diversified Afro-American literature was needed. Writers of the south such as Thomas Nelson Page and Joel Chandler Harris were becoming more popular and although, as we have seen, a variety of narratives were refuting the racist stereotypes depicted in these writings, they reached a very much smaller audience. Harper, already sixty seven years old by the time *Iola Leroy* was published, sought through the construction of a romantic novel – the most popular literary form of the day – to reach a wider audience, to change its views and to inspire both black and white to social and political action.

In 1893 Harper addressed the World's Congress of Women, assembled as part of the Columbian Exposition in Chicago, on 'Woman's political future'. The proceedings of this Congress are to be found in the BL. Speeches were also given by Anna Julia Cooper, Fannie Barrier Williams, Fannie Jackson Coppin, Sarah J Early and Hallie Quinn Brown although the Congress was very much a white women's forum. Afro-Americans were also notably absent from the Columbian Exposition itself, or rather, they were only included selectively as parts of exhibits with other ethnic groups, thus perpetuating and reinforcing the racist attitudes of the day. From the Haitian Pavilion Ida Wells, teacher, journalist and courageous campaigner against lynching, protested this exclusion of black Americans, giving out copies of the pamphlet that she had edited *The reason why the colored American is not in the World's Columbian Exposition*, a copy of which is in the library. We also have a copy of the *Open letter to President McKinley by Colored People of Massachusetts* (1899), which Wells presented to the President at the White House, following the lynching of a black postmaster in the south in 1898.

My last writer is Pauline Hopkins whose novel *Contending forces: a romance illustrative of Negro life North and South* was published in 1900, a fine copy of this work is in the BL. Hopkins, like Harper, saw the importance of fiction. It provided not only instruction and entertainment but could be used to change people's perceptions and bring about social and political reform. *Contending forces* was the first (and only) novel to be published by the Colored Co-operative Publishing Co of Boston. This venture had been set up in 1900 and began publishing the *Colored American Magazine* with the aim of 'uplifting and vindicating' the Afro-American. Hopkins devoted her energies of the success of the magazine, becoming its literary editor in 1903 until it was taken over in 1904 and came under the control of Booker T Washington. Three of Hopkins novels were published serially in the magazine and she also wrote numerous feature articles, biographical sketches and short stories. At present, the *Colored American Magazine* is not to be found in the Library but we hope to purchase a microfilm of it. Hopkins novels from the magazine are, however, available in a volume of the Schomburg collection.

In the preface to *Contending forces*, a story of a middle class black family in post-bellum Boston, Hopkins writes, 'In giving this little romance expression in print, I am not actuated by a desire for notoriety or for profit, but to do all that I can in a humble way to raise the stigma of degredation from my race' (p.13). She stresses the value of fiction as a preserver of manners and customs and as a record of growth and development from generation to generation and continues 'No one will do this for us; we must ourselves develop the men and women who will faithfully portray the inmost thoughts and feelings of the Negro with all the fire and romance which lie dormant in our history, and, as yet, unrecognised by writers of the Anglo-Saxon race' (p.14). That Hopkins herself was unable to make a living as a writer (she spent most of her working life as a stenographer) seems particularly unjust. Her novel received little attention, perhaps because the Colored Co-operative Publishing Co was unable to promote it widely and the circulation of her magazine fiction was small. Her writing has only recently started to receive the attention that it deserves and the improved availability of her work through the Schomburg collection reprints is to be welcomed.

Although it has not been possible to convey the full extent of the Library's holdings in this short survey, it will have at least indicated the richness and range of writing by black women in America in the nineteenth century. It is particularly disappointing that time did not allow a search of the periodical literature since much of the writing of the period is to be found in magazines. Although there are many gaps in the Library's holdings (some of which it is actively seeking to remedy) there is available a substantial amount of material of relevance not only to researchers of black women's writing but also to those interested in black literature and history, women's literature, feminism, US history and more.

References

1. *Productions of Mrs Maria Stewart*, p.16.
2. *Reconstructing womanhood*, p.43.

Bibliography

The following bibliography lists those titles mentioned in the paper. With the exception of Hazel Carby's *Reconstructing womanhood*, all Oxford University Press titles form part of the *Schomburg Library of Nineteenth-Century Black Women Writers*. Also included are some of the works used in the compilation of the paper. British Library press marks are given.

Albert, Octavia Victoria. *The house of bondage; or, Charlotte Brooks and other slaves, etc*. New York: Hunt & Eaton, 1891 [8156.aa.3]

Oxford University Press reprint (1890), introduction by Frances Smith Foster, 1988 [YC.1988.a.14523]

Bell, Bernard W. *The Afro-American novel and its tradition*. Amherst: University of Massachusetts Press, 1987 [YH.1988.b.1350]

Black women in nineteenth-century American life. Edited by Bert James Loewenberg and Ruth Bogin. Philadelphia: Pennsylvania State University, 1976 [x800/26470]

Brent, L (Harriet Jacobs). *Incidents in the life of a slave girl*. Edited by L Maria Child. London: Hodson and son, 1862 [12706.a.2]
Oxford University Press reprint (1861, Boston), introduction by Valerie Smith, 1988 [YH.1988.a.61]

Carby, Hazel. *Reconstructing womanhood: the emergency of the Afro-American woman novelist*. Oxford: Oxford University Press, 1987 [YH.1988.a.1050]

Chapman, Dorothy Hilton. *Index to poetry by black American women*. Westport, Conn: Greenwood Press, 1986 [2725.d.103]

Christian, Barbara. *Black feminist criticism: perspectives on black women writers*. New York: Pergamon Press, 1985 [Recently catalogued, awaiting pressmark]

Christian, Barbara. *Black woman novelists: the development of a tradition, 1892-1976*. Westport, Conn: Greenwood Press, 1980 [x950/4577]

Collected black women's narratives. Introduction by Anthony G Barthelemy. New York: Oxford University Press, 1988 [YC1988.a.14529]

Cooper, Anna Julia. *A Voice from the South*. Introduction by Mary Helen Washington. New York: Oxford University Press, 1988 [YC.1988.a.14522]

Harper, Frances E W. *Complete poems of Frances E W Harper*. Edited by Maryemma Graham. New York: Oxford University Press, 1988 [YC.1988.a.74]

Harper, Frances E W. *Iola Leroy, or shadows uplifted*. Introduction by Frances Smith Foster. New York: Oxford University Press, 1988 (YH.1989.a.62]

Hopkins, Pauline E. *Contending forces: a romance illustrative of Negro life North and South.* Boston: Colored Co-operative Publishing Co, 1900 [012703.h.47]
Oxford University reprint, introduction by Richard Yarborough, 1988 [YC.1988.a.14521]

Hopkins, Pauline E. *The magazine novels of Pauline Hopkins* Introduction by Hazel V Carby. New York: Oxford University Press, 1988 [YH.1988.a.63]

Joyce, Donald Franklin. *Gatekeepers of black culture: Black-owned book publishing in the United States, 1817–1981.* Westport, Conn: Greenwood Press, 1983 [2708.e.410]

Plato, Ann. *Essays; including biographies and miscellaneous pieces, in prose and poetry.* Hartford: printed for the author, 1841 [8404.aa.22]
Oxford University Press reprint, introduction by Kenny J Williams, 1988 [YC1988.a.14526]

Prince, Nancy. *A narrative of the life and travels of Mrs Nancy Prince.* Boston: the author, 1850 [1568/8628]

Stewart, Maria W. *Productions of Mrs Maria Steward. In spiritual narratives.* Introduction by Sue E Houchins. New York: Oxford University Press, 1988 [YC.1989.a.361]

Wells, Ida B (Barnett). *Open letter to President McKinley by colored people of Massachusetts, 1899* [8176.ee.18(3)]

Wells, Ida B (Ed). *The reason why the colored American is not in the World's Columbian Exposition.* Chicago, 1893 [8155.aaa.5]

Wheatley, Phillis. *The collected works of Phillis Wheatley,* Edited by John C Shields. New York: Oxford University Press, 1988 [YC.1988a.14519]

Wheatley, Phillis. *Poems on various subjects, religious and moral.* London: A Bell, 1773 [922.a.34/239.e.11]

Wilson, Harriet E. *Our Nig; or sketches from the life of a free black.* Introduction by Henry Louis Gates. London: Allison and Busby, 1984 [Nov.1988/2070]

World's Congress of Representative Women. A historical resumé ... of the World's Congress of Representative Women, convened in Chicago on May 15, and adjourned on May 22, 1893. Edited by May Wright Sewall. 2 vols. Chicago, 1894 [8415.h.36]

Eamon Dyas

Newspapers as source material for women's studies 1830s-1930s*

Women newspaper readers – early days

By the 1830s the basic format of the national daily newspaper, which was to last for most of the century, had been established. This usually consisted of advertisements, Parliamentary debates, foreign intelligence, military and naval news, legal news, sport, reviews, and so forth. The small fashion column consisted of the latest society events and fashions at Court with no other concession to female interests. This was despite the fact that women represented a significant proportion of the readership. Although no statistics exist on this matter, if the advertisements are any indication of readership it appears that women did indeed read the national press in sufficient numbers for advertisers to take them into account. Advertisements were directed at women as potential customers for products such as bedding, skin preparations, hair conditioners, quack medicines, etc and there are even advertisements specifically directed at women as potential investors in institutions like Benevolent Societies. Another indicator of female readership is the presence of advertisements placed in newspapers for female magazines. Throughout the 1830s titles like *Court Magazine & Belle* regularly advertised in the national press.

Although it can be assumed from this that women read newspapers it does not necessarily follow that women normally bought the newspaper. In most cases access to the newspaper was via a copy bought by a male member of the household. The purchasing readership was overwhelmingly male and the contents reflected this fact. Despite this however, there is much material in newspapers of the period which remains of value to anyone interested in women's studies.

Advertisements

The advertisements which point to the extent of female readership also offer an insight into aspects of women's experience at the time. Women were not only on the receiving end of advertisements. Throughout the period advertisements placed by women seeking employment regularly appeared in the newspapers. For instance, on one randomly selected day (2 July 1836) in just two newspapers (the *Morning Post* and the *Morning Advertiser*) we find adverts placed by women seeking positions as: maids,

---

*For reasons of space, the scope of this paper has been limited to newspapers only. Readers should note that popular magazines are dealt with in Cynthia White's definitive work *Womens magazines 1693-1968*.

housekeepers, governesses, tutors, lady's companions, and barmaids. A particularly good source for employment advertisements was the *Daily Chronicle*. From its inception as the *Clerkenwell News* in 1855 this paper carried extensive employment advertisements for and by women and from 18 February 1860 included a special category for *Servants and Girls*.

Financial dependence, widows and deserted wives

The social status of wives is also reflected in the advertisements. Examples of the following regularly appeared in the press throughout the early nineteenth century:

I, George Francis Grant Franks do hereby give notice, that I will not be answerable for any debt or debts that my wife, Martha Grant Franks may contract after this date.
July 25, 1836.
George Francis Grant Franks,
witness – Robert Ashley, No 16 Wade-street, Poplar.
(*Morning Advertiser*, 11 August, 1836)

The financial dependence of most women on their husbands during this time led to some surprising attitudes to widowhood among certain women. On the 11 March 1838 a weekly newspaper called *The Young Widow* was founded. It was edited by an anonymous female who used the paper to formulate a positive image of widowhood compared to the condition of women generally. In its third issue dated 25 February 1838, the editorial, having analysed the various states of women from spinsterhood to marriage, goes on to explain one of the positive features of widowhood in the following terms

In the happy condition of widowhood she arrives at a legal majority – the power of self-assertion and independence are acquired, and she becomes a bona fide member of the community, with all the rights and privileges incidental to citizenship ... When married she was treated like a child in money matters: the law gave her no control over property, and custom added so much to her pecuniary dependence upon her husband that this first exercise of her newly acquired rights could not but prove agreeable to her, and however much she might be expected to lament her loss, the Bank of England is not the place that she is bound to feel it most acutely.

The fact that wives were financially dependent on their husbands could lead to conditions of extreme hardship even amongst the upper classes. Some of these cases were chronicled in the newspapers. In 1852 the *Morning Advertiser* took up the case of Lady Mornington, a deserted wife, who, together with her two children, was compelled to sleep on the floor in the lodgings of a charitable carter and his wife. The *Morning Advertiser* published an editorial on the subject in its issue of the 28 May 1852 and called for a reform of the law which had compelled Lady Mornington to become a burden on the Poor Rates by entering a Workhouse. Only by this action could a warrant be issued against the husband as the person responsible for the up-keep of his family. However, it was another 18 years before Parliament got around to debating an ill-fated bill on the 'Disabilities of women' and another 12 years before any legislation was passed protecting the property rights of wives.

Divorce, railways and sexual harassment

Parliamentary debates are useful in gathering information on how politicians viewed issues affeccting women. Because these debates were usually reported *verbatim* in the newspapers, the reasoning and arguments of politicians remained undistilled and unaltered by editorial interpretation. One of the most important pieces of legislation affecting women in the nineteenth century was the 1857 Divorce Act. Besides the opportunities it offered women it also opened a whole new area for the newspaper editor. Before long most newspapers included a regular feature of reports from the Divorce Courts. As far as the editor was concerned such reports had all the ingredients to sell more newspapers: scandal, indiscretion and the lifestyle of the upper classes could all be expected to be revealed in such reports. So important was this in the drive to attract more readers that one particular publisher produced a newspaper entirely devoted to such reports. It was called the *Divorce Court and Breach of Promise Record* but it only survived the one issue dated 2 April 1864.

The development of railways opened up the opportunity for more people to travel further and faster than ever before. Women however, in seeking to take advantage of these opportunities found themselves exposed to new kinds of danger and harassment.

Increasingly, from the middle of the century onwards women were travelling alone on railway trains. An early report on what was to become an intractable problem was published in the *Observer* on 3 January 1864 under the title 'Outrages in railway carriages'. The report dealt with the experience of some women travelling alone on the Slough to Windsor line. Some years later reports were still appearing in the press on this same problem and letters were now being sent to the editors of newspapers. On the 18, 20 and 21 June 1870 the *Daily Telegraph* published such letters under the heading 'Scoundrels in railway trains'. *The Times* of 28 February 1888 carried a letter from 'A women who has to travel alone' on the subject of 'ladies only railway carriages'; an issue, incidentally, later taken up by '*Vote*' (1909-33), the organ of the Women's Freedom League. By 1904 the problem was proving to be as controversial as ever and the *Daily Mirror* of 9 June carried a full page article addressed to women who travelled on the railways. It was entitled 'Self defence with an umbrella: hints for women who travel alone'.

Judging by some of the letters to the editor, the harassment of women on railway trains was only one aspect of a more general problem. On 7 May 1870 there appeared a letter in the *Daily Telegraph* on the subject of 'Human beasts'. This letter was provoked by an editorial published in the paper on 5 May on the subject of sexual assaults. The letter recounted the experience of the sister of the writer who was, on several occasions, the subject of harassment. On 31 May, again in the same paper, there also appeared a letter on the subject of 'Annoying females' which complained about the harassment of women shop assistants as they left work for home each evening.

Women and work

The letter above is of interest also because it illustrates the growing number of independent working women at the time. The 1870s witnessed the arrival of journals specifically dealing with female employment. *Women and Work* ran from 1874 until 1876 and acted as a practical guide to employment for middle-class women. However it also included trades like compositing, sewing-machining, shoemaking, etc. Another paper of the 1870s performing a similar function was the *Women's Gazette*' which lasted from 1875 to 1879. This growth in female employment, together with the implications of the Married Woman's Property Act of 1882, meant that women were rapidly becoming a highly significant consumer group in their own right. As a result the press was becoming more interested in issues affecting women. In 1884, for instance, the *Pall Mall Gazette* published a series of articles on 'Women who work'. This twenty-part series included occupations such as cigar makers and dustwomen and, according to the index, in the first six months of 1885 no less that 42 articles/reports on women's issues were published in the paper. Women's increasing demand for work was also reflected in an article published in the *Daily Chronicle* on 6 June 1896 under the title 'The middle class working woman: wanted a national bureau'. The article reflected on the anarchic state of the employment market for women and reported on a case where one job attracted 700 applicants. In response to this, a letter written by an anonymous female appeared in the same paper on 11 July 1836. The writer apparently ran an employment agency for women and she recounts how on one occasion she had 990 applications for a single job. By 1900 the volume of women seeking employment was such that a specialist journal called *Women's Employment* was established. Unlike earlier attempts at such a journal, this one was to last for some time and did not cease publication until 1975.

Women and sport

Sport and outdoor activities were other areas where the traditionally passive image of women was being increasingly challenged. The extent of female involvement with these activities is mirrored by the arrival of new types of magazines specifically for women. The *Ladies' Kennel Journal* was founded in 1894 for those interested in dog-breeding. The involvement of women in the great cycling fashion at the turn of the century is reflected in journals such as the *Lady Cyclist*, founded in 1895 and *Wheelwoman* founded in 1896. The following journals devoted to women's sport were founded in the 1890's: *Sportswoman. An illustrated journal devoted to all ladies' sports* (1895), *Sportswoman's Field and Kennel World* (1898), *Sportswoman's World and Kennel Chronicle. A journal of sports for sportswomen* (1898), *Ladies' Field* (1898).

Later there are titles such as *Hockey Field. The official organ of the Ladies' Hockey Association* (1901) and *Women's Golf* (1907). Other sports, women's cricket, gymnastics, fencing, etc, regularly featured in such newspapers as *The Illustrated London News* and the *Daily Graphic* from about 1890 onward. By the 1920s the extent of female involvement in sport was beginning to cause concern among the medical establishment. The *Daily Express* of 20 April 1922 carried a report under the title 'Sport perils to women. Heading straight for extinction as a sex'. The report revealed the growing unease among the medical establishment on the effects of physical sport on women, and in particular adolescent girls. An indication of this concern was the setting-up of a Joint Medical Committee to investiage the implications of sporting involvement on women. Later in the decade a league to 'combat the growing physical and moral masculinity of women' was formed in Paris. Robert Lynd reported on this development in an article published in the *Daily News* of 11 January 1928.

Women readers and the new journalism

The desire to tap the growing purchasing power of women at the turn of the century was undoubtedly a factor in the development of what has come to be known as the 'new journalism'. Although much has been done on the effects of the 1870 Education Act on the development of the new journalism, the implications of the consumer power of women remain largely unexplored.

The format design associated with the new journalism was one that broke down the sombre and unbroken column structure of the traditional newspaper. This was achieved through a number of devices such as the use of illustrations, banner headlines, cross-column advertisements, cartoons, extensive paragraphing etc. Northcliffe, who is often credited as the leading architect of the new journalism, was only too aware of the importance of attracting the purchasing power of women. When he founded the *Daily Mail* in 1896 he insisted that it make itself attractive to women readers. Besides its 'Daily Magazine' page, Northcliffe directed that every page carry at least one story of potential interest to women. Most of the other newspapers quickly followed suit by including their own women's sections. The *Daily Chronicle* started a regular woman's Saturday column on 9 May 1896 with the title 'A Woman's fancies'. The *Star* began a daily woman's feature entitled 'Today's woman's world and fashion' on 27 May 1896. The *Daily Telegraph* started its Saturday 'Page for women' on 27 May 1899. Even *The Times* was not immune to the prevailing drive for women readers. When Northcliffe took over that paper in 1908 he quickly sent instructions that the paper needed to cater for women readers, 'otherwise the paper would not attract West End advertisers'. On 1 October 1910 *The Times* published what was intended as a regular weekly 'Womans supplement'. Although it did not last beyond 31 December, Northcliffe's influence meant that *The Times* continued to give an increasing amount of space to the activities and imagined interests of women.

The problem with all of these attempts at 'women's pages' however, was that they took their cue from the traditional women's magazines of the nineteenth century. Unsure as to how to relate to the emerging female market, newspapers decided to play safe and adopted a somewhat traditional interpretation of women's interests. There also appears to have been some confusion on the question of targeting. The *Star* was founded on the 17 January 1888 by T P O'Connor and was regarded as an example of the emerging new journalism. Initially the *Star* sought to reach a female readership through the intercessions of its male readers. Thus in the second issue dated 18 January 1888, it published a selection of female interest material entitled 'Show this to your wife', evidence that the paper was constrained by a fear of losing its male readership.

A woman's newspaper

The attempts to attract female readers were designed to extend the circulation into a new field, they were not intended to replace male readers with female readers. However, when Northcliffe launched the *Daily Mirror* on 2 November 1903 he was attempting to break new ground. The *Daily Mirror* was to be a paper 'written by gentlewomen for gentlewomen'. It was to be a woman's paper pure and simple and Northcliffe appointed Mary Howarth from the *Daily Mail* to be its first editor. Unfortunately it did not succeed. The readership levels, after an initial circulation of 265,217 fell away to a meagre 24,000 within a few months. On 26 January 1904 Northcliffe abandoned his project for a women's paper and turned the *Daily Mirror* into a popular picture paper. The extent to which Northcliffe's plans for a women's paper affected an uncertain industry can be gauged by the fact that in the same year (1903) that he launched the woman's *Daily Mirror* the following titles were registered as newspapers: *Lady's Daily Mail, Lady's Daily News, Lady's Mail, Lady's Post, Lady's Standard, Lady's Telegraph, Lady's Times*.

Presumably because Northcliffe's scheme with the *Daily Mirror* did not succeed, these titles never actually became newspapers but remained as registered titles. Northcliffe summed up the failure of the women's *Daily Mirror* in the following terms:

Some people say that a woman never really knows what she wants. It is certain she knew what she didn't want. She didn't want the *Daily Mirror*.

No newspaper ever started with such a 'boom' as that which marked the birth of the *Daily Mirror*. I advertised it everywhere, spending money lavishly. If there was anyone in the United Kingdom who was not aware that the *Daily Mirror* was to be started he must have been deaf, dumb, or blind, or all three. Had I had enough printing machinery I could have sold several millions of the first number.

The public made an excited rush for that first issue, but would have nothing to do with the second. Men didn't want a purely woman's paper. Woman feared that a woman's paper would be made up of articles written in a namby-pamby way. The woman's paper known as the *Daily Mirror* was a flat, rank, and unmitigated failure.

The new journalism and the women's movement

In terms of design the influence of new journalism can be seen in *Votes for Women* (1907-18), the organ of the Women's Social and Political Union, widely seen as the pioneer of popular journalism in the suffrage press. Besides design however, the new journalism represented significant developments in journalistic technique. Such people as W T Stead and Robert Blatchford heralded a style of investigative journalism which was to prove of great propaganda value to the Suffrage movement generally. W T Stead became the editor of the *Pall Mall Gazette* in 1883 and quickly developed a new socially conscious investigative style of journalism. His protracted campaign against child prostitution in 1885 represented a revolution in newspaper reporting and led to his imprisonment for three months. Stead was later to co-edit *The Link* (1888) with Annie Besant, and much of the style of her exposé in that paper of the Bryant and May's matchgirls' plight shows evidence of his influence. Another editor who used the technique of investigative journalism was Robert Blatchford, the editor of the *Sunday Chronicle* from 1885 to 1891. One of Blatchford's most famous campaigns was a series he published on the plight of the women chain makers of Crawley Heath. His social conscience cost him his job in 1891 and he went on to found the *Clarion* later that year. Blatchford also contributed to a woman's socialist journal called *Women Folk* which was published between 1908 and 1910.

Out of the factory

The effects of the dislocation of women workers after the end of the First World War is reported in various ways in the newspapers of the period. Initially, there was some optimism, as to the ability of the economy to accommodate not only the returning menfolk but a good proportion of the women workers also. This optimism is reflected in the *Daily Telegraph* of 7 December 1918. In a report on its 'Woman's Page' under the title 'Demobilisation' it gave an account of the restructuring and retraining efforts being put into equipping women employed during the war in government departments. With regard to the situation generally it quoted from an official from the Ministry of Labour as follows:

To those women dependent on their earnings it will be of some reassurance to know that progress is being rapidly made throughout the country by manufacturers in the process of re-starting peace industries. In one big London firm, for example, where several thousands of workpeople were employed on munitions, a change over is being undertaken to the manufacture of sewing machines. In this enterprise the whole of the employees will be retained and use made of the plant installed for shell making. Another London firm reports that they will probably employ more women and girls than during the war, while a firm of electrical engineers, also in London, state that of the small proportion of girls discharged some have been re-absorbed in dressmaking, others have been absorbed in the Post Office sorting for Christmas mail, others have been engaged as shop assistants for the holidays, and others, again, have returned to laundry work, or to positions they held before the war.

To facilitate this relocation of female labour the *Daily Express* announced in its issue for 7 December 1918 that it was offering free advertisements to women war workers seeking peacetime work. One of the problems which quickly became obvious was the reluctance of women to return to the type of work they held before the war. In a letter to the *Daily Express* published on 3 January 1919, a laundry proprietor, Charles Marshall, complained that:

The [laundry] industry lent the Government immediately war was declared about 150,000 women for munition work. Of these a large number are now discharged with an unemployment wage about 25s weekly. The result is these women will not return to work as long as the benefit exists.

On 7 January the paper carried a report on the reluctance of women war workers to return to their traditional jobs after being discharged.

The employment exchanges admit that very few women need be out of work at present if they would accept any employment that happens to be available. The 25s a week unemployment money is only paid out on the express condition that the recipient has not refused suitable employment.
   The difficulty is that only a small minority of the 500,000 ex-domestic servants and the 150,000 ex-laundresses who passed into the munition factories are registering at the employment exchanges under their old trades. They are registering as factory hands and want work in a factory – or 25s a week!

Back to the home

Almost as soon as the war ended the newspapers were beginning to devote more space to issues relating to motherhood and the home. An article by Mary Hinton in the *Daily Mirror* of 2 May 1919 reflects this new emphasis. The article was called 'Women return to the home life. The children's good time coming', and it concentrated upon the need for wives wherever possible to return to their domestic duties, particularly where children were involved. The psychology of nurturing was also apparent in an article published in the *Daily News* of 6 July 1920 entitled 'Baby's character. The parent's part in early training'. The change is graphically demonstrated by the Rowntree Cocoa advertisement prevalent at the time. In January 1919 it was using a drawing of a female land worker to sell the product. However, by March 1919 the image being used was a dutiful wife looking on as the returning husband greets his children. Evidence of this new interest in motherhood is also revealed in the advertisements where children were increasingly used as a means to sell products. The restrengthening of traditional responsibilities and preoccupations was further advanced by the First Annual Daily Express Woman's Exhibition. This was held between 12 and 29 July 1922 and although it included features on 'Vocations for women' and 'The evolution of the woman doctor' it was predominantly geared towards questions of beauty and the home with features like 'All about babies'. It was also during this period that children's features began to figure prominently in the newspapers. The *Daily Mail* 'Children's Corner' was started on 12 May 1919, Rupert Bear began in the *Daily Express* on 8 November 1920, and a daily feature entitled 'Tony Hoppit' began in the *Westminster Gazette* on 7 November 1921.

The new woman

It would be wrong to give the impression that newspapers precluded other ways of relating to women. It was very much in the interests of newspapers to cultivate the growing market represented by the expanding body of independent women. In 1919 an article entitled 'The woman newspaper reader' by Mary Agnes Hamilton was published in *Sell's Dictionary of the World's Press*; it states:

The woman reader is the great diamond-field of the up-to-date Newspaper, and a field as yet hardly explored. Publishers know well enough that their sales returns will be determined by the degree to which their wares do or do not appeal to women; newspaper men are feeling after the same truth. The questions of what will appeal to the women readers, and what will make sales go up, are nowadays almost the same. The 'new' readers that any paper can hope to attract are largely women.

Newspapers had, since the late nineteenth century, been struggling with the problem of knowing how to relate to women readers. The easiest option was to publish material along the traditional lines of beauty, home and motherhood. The problem with this approach was that it failed to acknowledge the other interests of women. The growing number of employed women from the latter part of the nineteenth century onward represented a body of opinion whose horizons, in many cases, went beyond the traditional. Newspapers were committed to gaining their allegiance if they entertained any ambition to increase sales. Thus we find that even after the First World War, when an increased emphasis was being placed on traditional values, the newspapers were also publishing articles and stories which reflected another dimension of women. The *Daily Telegraph* of 21 August 1920, for instance, published a report on the objections of the Women's Political and Industrial League to the Womens Employment Bill of that year, while the *Daily Express* of 5 July 1921 carried an article entitled 'Women Free Lances in Industry'. Women who became firsts at anything were also guaranteed publicity. Thus, a report on the first woman Presiding Magistrate, Mrs Ada Summers, Mayor of Stalybridge, appeared in the *Daily Express* of 1 January 1920 and the first woman Professor of Anatomy, Dr Mary Lucas Keene, appeared in the *Daily News* of 27 November 1924. Nor was all publicity relating to women restricted to the middle classes. The *Daily News* of 8 July 1920, for instance, carried a photograph of the woman leader of a strike by 1,000 men and women at the Van den Bergh margarine factory in Fulham.

Women's daily newspaper

The concern to attract female readers continued right through to the 1930s and can be seen in the newspaper trade papers of the time. For instance the *World's Press News* between August 1929 and 1934 carried some 26 articles on the woman newspaper reader. This concern reflected the growing competition for readers culminating in the great circulation battles of the 1930s. *The Times* introduced its first woman's page on 15 November 1937 in an effort to tap the female readership. Prior to that, in 1920 it had registered the title *Women's Times* but this was never published as a proper publication and was only introduced to protect the title. A recognition of the great potential female readership also led to some attempts in the 1930s to establish a woman's daily newspaper. Not since the ill fated days of the woman's *Daily Mirror* in 1903 had there been another attempt to establish such a paper. In the 1930s there were two. The first soundings for such a paper took place in 1930 but it was not until 3 March 1932 that a prospectus was published in the *World's Press News*. The title of the paper was to be *The Call* and it was the brainchild of Mrs Annie Colles, 'a journalist of 30 years experience'. A million £1 shares were to be issued to women only and no woman was allowed to purchase more than 200 shares. Although ownership was to be restricted to women the paper was to be operated by both men and women on an equal footing and a readership would be sought from both men and women. Despite its great plans *The Call* never actually got into print. One paper which did get printed was the *Woman's Daily Newspaper*. This was published by the Woman's National League of Unity but never got beyond its first issue dated 7 November 1938. Both these failures, together with the failure of the women's *Daily Mirror* in 1903, could be seen as a testimony to Northcliffe's statement on the difficulty of identifying a separate women's perspective in the area of a functioning general daily newspaper.

Using newspapers

One of the great problems with using newspapers is the dearth of indexes and finding aids available. Most of the newspaper indexes which have been published can be consulted on the open shelves in the Newspaper Library Reading Room at Colindale and a guide to these is available. Besides the published indexes there are also many 'hidden' indexes to both magazines and newspapers which would assist researchers, including women's studies' researchers. These indexes, rather than being published separately, were printed, usually every six months, and bound in with the volumes of their respective titles and stored in the closed access stacks. Because the catalogue does not include information on their existence, it is all very hit and miss whether the researcher finds these or not. However, staff at the Newspaper Library have made an effort to identify these and so far have located 821 titles in the collection which contain indexes. The following are some of these titles which are most likely to be of use to researchers pursuing women's studies. In each case the title is followed by place of publication and the period for which an index is available.

NEWSPAPERS

Church Times: an ecclesiastical and general newspaper
London.
Indexed: 1866; 1868-71; 1875-77; 1881-86; 1888-94.

Daily Graphic
London.
Indexed: Jan – Mar 1890; July 1891 – Mar 1897; July 1898 – Dec 1899; July 1900 – Mar 1903; July 1903 – Sept 1904; Jan – Dec 1905; April – June 1906; Oct 1906 – Mar 1907; July 1907 – Dec 1909; April – Dec 1910; April – June 1911; Jan – March 1912.

Graphic: an illustrated weekly newspaper
London.
Indexed: July 1870 – June 1874; Jan 1875 – June 1877; Jan 1878 – June 1883; Jan 1884 – Dec 1897; Jan – June 1899; Jan 1905 – Dec 1910; July – Dec 1911.

Guardian Newspaper [A Church of England newspaper]
London.
Indexed: 1846-54; 1856; 1862-63; 1866-1916.

Illustrated London News
London.
Indexed: May 1842 – June 1843; Jan – June 1844; Jan 1847 – Dec 1849; July 1850 – Dec 1854; Jan 1856 – June 1857; Jan – June 1858; Jan – June 1859; Jan – June 1860; Jan – June 1861; Jan 1862 – June 1866; July 1867 – Dec 1914; July 1915 – June 1916; 1919-32; 1934-39.
(In most cases the index only covers illustrations).

Illustrated Newspaper
London.
Indexed: March – Sept 1871.

Illustrated Times Weekly Newspaper
London.
Indexed: June 1855 – June 1860; Jan 1861 – June 1863; Jan – June 1869; Jan – June 1870.

Lady's Newspaper
London.
Indexed: 1847-54; July 1855 – Dec 1856; Nov 1862 – June 1863.

Lady's Own Paper
London.
Indexed: 1868-70.

Pall Mall Gazette: an evening newspaper and review
London.
Indexed: Feb 1865 – June 1868; Jan – Dec 1869; 9 May 1870 – Dec 1879; Jan 1884 – Dec 1888.

Pictorial Times: a weekly journal of news, literature, fine arts, and the drama
London.
Indexed: March – Dec 1843; Jan – Dec 1845; Jan – June 1847.

Press
London.
Indexed: 1855; 1859; 1862-65.

Public Opinion: a weekly journal embodying the opinions of the press on all the great topics of the day, political and social, home and abroad
London.
Indexed: Oct 1861-1906; 1911.

Tablet: a weekly newspaper and review [Roman Catholic]
London.
Nov 1868 – June 1881; Jan 1882 – June 1891; Jan 1892 – Dec 1916.

Times Weekly Edition
London.
Indexed: 1877-95.

MAGAZINES/JOURNALS

Enquire Within: ladies home journal
London.
Indexed: Oct 1890 – April 1891.

Ladies' League Gazette: the monthly journal of the Ladies' League for the defence of the reformed faith of the Church of England
London.
Indexed: March – Dec 1900; Jan – Dec 1902.

Listener
Indexed: Jan 1929 – Dec 1939.

New Statesman
London.
Indexed: 12 April 1913 – 2 Oct 1915; 8 April – 30 Sept 1916; 6 Oct 1917 – 28 Sept 1918; 5 April 1919 – June 1936; Jan 1937 – Dec 1939.

Queen: an illustrated journal and review.
London.
Indexed: Sept 1861 – Dec 1865; Jan 1868 – Dec 1871; July 1874 – June 1882; July 1885 – Dec 1894; July 1895 – June 1899; 1900-1914; July 1915 – Dec 1919.

Sketch: a journal of art and actuality
London.
Indexed: Feb 1893 – 5 April 1911; 11 Oct 1911 – 1 Jan 1913; 7 Jan – 1 April 1914; 7 Oct – 30 Dec 1914.
(Indexed every quarter).

Speaker: a review of politics, letters, science, and the arts
London.
Indexed: Jan – June 1890; Jan – June 1891; Jan 1892 – June 1893; Jan 1894 – June 1899.

Spectator: a weekly journal of news, politics, literature and science
London.
Indexed: 1830-36; 1839-54; 1856; 1862-64; 1866-85; 1887-1925; July 1926 – June 1927; July – Dec 1928; July 1935 – June 1937; Jan 1938 – Dec 1939.

Womans Herald
London.
Indexed: 1891-93. (List of interviews).

World: a journal for men and women
London.
Indexed: July 1874 – Dec 1892.

Young Gentlewoman: an illustrated monthly magazine
London.
Indexed: 1893.

Young Ladies' Journal: an illustrated magazine of entertaining literature, original music, toilet and household receipts, ets.
London.
Indexed: 1864-73; 1875-76; Jan – June 1890.

Morna Daniels

French resources for women's studies

Researchers into the history of women in France will find a number of useful tools on the open shelves of the Reading Room in the British Library's Humanities and Social Sciences Division. The *Subject Index* of the British Museum Department of Printed Books was begun in 1880, and continued in cumulations of five, ten, or in the first instance 20 years until 1975. The heading 'Women' yields a rich mine of useful titles, particularly in the early cumulations, and the sub-headings include sections on women in the professions, women and politics and women's health. If the researcher has the names of particular women in mind, these can be sought in the *General Catalogue* for listings of their works and cross-references to biographical material. The search can continue in the post-1975 microfiche *General Catalogue* and in the *Subject Index* which is established using the Precis system and is machine-searchable. However, French books were not subject-indexed by the British Library between 1975 and 1980 and subject-indexing was again partially abandoned in 1989.

In the Reading Room can be found the catalogue of periodicals and newspapers located at Colindale which is arranged in two sequences: by title, and a listing which groups publications by country. On the open shelves are many useful reference works, including the annual *Quid* published by Robert Laffont which includes a section of statistical information on women and a list of significant dates in the history of the women's movement. The open shelves of the Official Publications and Social Sciences Reading Room contain many statistical works useful for studies of women's conditions today, both in France and in the many Francophone countries of Africa and the Caribbean. French is still the language of the educated classes and of many official publications in former French colonies, particularly where one country embraces a number of tribes and languages. The British Library receives a number of statistical series from France, Belgium, Canada and Africa as well as census material. In France there is a Ministère des droits de la femme which has produced several guides for women.

When searching for older primary material on women, a useful work is the *Bibliographie des ouvrages relatifs à l'amour, aux femmes, au mariage...* par M le C D'I*** (Jules Gay) 4 ed, refondu par J Lemonnyer (1894-1900).

In the early days of printing, women sometimes inherited valuable type and presses on the death of their husbands, and continued to publish on their own account. The widow of Barnabé Chaussard published *Farce nouuelle des femmes qui font refondre leurs maris* in Lyons, 1550? [C.20.e.13(29)], one of a number of farces (in C.20.e.13) on the subject of marital strife. Jeanne de Marnef came from a dynasty of printers and published a number of books of poetry in Paris between 1545 and 1547. Denise de Marnef, from the same family, first published with her brother Jérôme. She then married two printers in succession, Ambroise Girault (died 1546) and Guillaume Cavellat (died 1576) who published many works with Jérôme. Denise then continued to publish with her brother again. An index of printers is provided in the Supplement to the *Short title catalogue of books printed in France . . . 1470-1600*, (London: British Library, 1986).

A defence of women was published by Henricus Cornelius Agrippa *De nobilitate & praecellentia foeminei sexus*, Coloniae, 1532 [4373.a.1]. It was translated by M de Gueudeville as *Sur la noblesse & excellence du sexe feminin . . .* Leiden, 1726 [1801.f.4-6] and by J d'Arnaudin as *De la grandeur et de l'excellence des femmes audessus des hommes*. Paris, 1713 [8416.aa.23]. A book that went into several editions was Jean de Marconville *De la bonté et mauvaistie de femmes*, 1566 [1081.f.13].

In the seventeenth and eighteenth centuries literary attacks on women were more common. *De l'excellence des hommes, contre l'egalité des sexes*, 1675 is attributed to F Poulain de la Barre [8043.bb.11]. Jacques Boileau in *De l'abus des nuditez de gorge*, Bruxelles, 1677 [12331.aaaa.43] blames women for inciting men to sin by their low neck-lines. *Imperfection des femmes tirée de la Sainte Écriture et de plusieurs auteurs*, Amsterdam, c.1700 [8415.aa.21] is in a similar misogynistic vein.

Many writers demanded a high moral standard from women, and extreme modesty, to atone for the sin of being a woman at all. P Hecquet attacks the disgusting idea of men assisting at childbirth in *L'indécence aux hommes d'accoucher les femmes, et l'obligation aux femmes de nourrir leurs enfans*, 1708 [1177.a.17]. It contains a back-handed compliment claiming that women midwives are better than male ones. Graillard de Graville in *L'ami des filles*, 1761 [1416.aaa.19(2)] urges girls to develop suitably feminine talents, and to seek a sensible marriage rather than marrying for love. P J Boudier de Villemert in *L'ami des femmes*, 1758 [721.b.36] criticises scholarly women, and urges them instead to marry, (breast) feed their children, and be virtuous housewives.

Another work of moral admonition is by J B Drouet de Maupertuis; *La femme foible, où l'on représente aux femmes les dangers auxquelles elles s'exposent par un commerce fréquent & assidu avec les hommes*. Amsterdam, 1775. [1094.d.21] Women writers could be as stern with their own sex. Madeleine de Puisieux, in her *Conseils à une amie*, 1750 [12510.aaa.2(2)] urges good conduct. Madame Galien pretends to be an anonymous male writer, M d*** on the title-page of her *Apologie des dames, appuyée sur l'historie*, 1737 [1174.d.11] which contains anecdotes of outstanding women. An anonymous but censorious male writer who produced *L'art de rendre les femmes fidèles* in 1703 (the BL holding is the 1713 edition press marked 8416.aa.9) was answered by Cornélie Wouters, afterwards Baronesse de Vasse in her *L'art de corriger et de rendre les hommes constans*, London and Paris, 1783. There are chapters on correcting jealousy, gambling, drunkenness, miserliness and unfaithfulness in husbands. A woman theologian could only be considered as a subject for comedy. G H Bougéant wrote *La femme docteur, ou, la théologie tombée en quenouille* (ruled by women). Comédie. Liège, c1730 [1607/4966].

The British Library has a large collection of pornographic works, most of them mild by modern standards. Some were bequeathed by Henry Spencer Ashbee in 1900, some by Charles Reginald Dawes, and a number of items in French were recently donated by Eric Dingwall, including some surveys of the 'low life' of Paris in the early twentieth century. P J Kearney compiled a catalogue, *The Private Case* (London: Landesman, 1981) in which about a quarter of the titles are in French including works by Restif de la Bretonne and the Marquis de Sade.

In times of revolution women rushed to the printing presses to claim their rights. Men too published appeals to women to play their patriotic part. But once peace returned, and the bourgeois status quo was restored, women were once again repressed. The Library has a fine collection of French Revolutionary tracts, and these include appeals by women for their rights. Examples are: R.409 tract 9 *Demande des femmes aux États-Généraux*; F.512(4) *Les femmes Françaises à la Convention Nationale*, (1795); F.378(6) *Les femmes Françaises à la nation* (1795); and FR.9(2) *Très-humbles remonstrances des femmes françaises* (1788). Three volumes of tracts are indexed as being on women: R.409, R.662 and R.443. Some are serious in tone. R.409(10) *Motions adressées a L'Assemblée Nationale en faveur du sexe* (1789) explains how women are exploited and asks for the abolition of dowries and freedom for nuns enclosed against their will. R.409(21) *Du sort actuel des femmes* (1791) complains of the inferior status of women in law, and tract 16 is a complaint from the 'courtisanes parisiennes à l'Assemblée Nationale concernant l'abolition des titres dèshonorans, tels que garces, putains, toupies etc., 'which are tainted with slavery. R.662 has many frivolous items, such as a directory of 'jolies libertine' and a list of 'notables cocus'.

The writer and noted feminist Olympe de Gouges was guillotined in 1793, for having claimed that women had a right to a place on the hustings, since they had a right to a place on the scaffold. The Convention suppressed women's clubs in that year, and feminist aspirations were doused. Napoleon had decidedly reactionary views on a woman's place, and under the Code Napoléon of 1804 women were entirely under the control of their husbands, the writing of a will being the only act they could perform without his permission. Single women had full civil rights, in theory. Olympe de Gouges is well represented in the *General Catalogue* under the heading Gouze, afterwards Aubry (Marie); plays by her are included as well as political works such as *Les droits de la femme* (1791) [F.932(14)].

Morals being somewhat relaxed during the Revolution, divorce was legalized, and tracts appeared in its favour: *L'art de rendre les ménages heureux* (ie by divorce) 1789 [FR207(3)]; *Le divorce, par le meilleur ami des femmes*, 1790 [F.535(7)]; A J U Hennet *Du divorce*, 1789 [879.b.19(1)]; *L'homme mal marié, ou, Questions à l'auteur Du divorce*, 1790? [F.535(8)]; and *Du divorce. Adresse à un grand prince qui s'est fait homme (le Duc d'Orléans)*, 1789 [FR207(4)]. In 1801, under Napoleon, Louis de Bonald wrote *Du divorce, considéré au XIX siècle*, 2nd edition, 1805 [8416.bbb.42]. Baron André Nougarede de Fayet wrote *De la législation sur le mariage et sur le divorce* in 1802

[7704.aaa.15(2)]. The Code Napoléon prohibited divorce, except of course for Napoleon himself, as did the legislation of the restored monarchy in 1816. A plea for divorce is *Plaidoyer en faveur du divorce*, par une femme, 1876 [8116.e.6(6)]. Divorce was not legalized again until 1884. The popular writer Marie-Antoinette de Riquetti de Mirabeau, who used the pseudonym Gyp, published *Autour du divorce* in 1886 [12491.0.7].

The possibility of divorce, and the demand that a husband's adultery should be punishable as well as a wife's, were only two of the demands of the movement for women's rights in the second half of the nineteenth century. Maria Deraismes (1828-94) was a leading figure, and the Library holds some of her feminist works, including *Eve dans l'humanité*, 1891 [8416.h.12]; as well as two dramatic works. Léon Richer (1824-1911), a radical freemason, was at the centre of the feminist group. He edited *L'avenir des femmes*, which was continued as *Le droit des femmes*. The Library holds only the issues from 1876-85 at PP.3643(1). The last page for 1876 lists the demands of the movement. The editors wanted to search for the natural fathers of illegitimate children and make them support their children, give wives rights over property in the home and over their children, and gain other civil rights for women.

In *La femme affranchie*, Bruxelles, 1860 [8415.aaa.42] Jenny d'Héricourt complains of the inequality of women in marriage, at work and in law. Only when they are taxed are women equal. Olympe Audouard wrote many books on her world travels and a number on women's rights: *La femme dans le mariage, la séparation et le divorce*, 1870 [8416.c.1(2)]; *Guerre aux hommes*, 1866 [12350.aaa.12]; *Lettre aux députés (les droits de la femme)*, 1867 [8050.h.4]

Hubertine Auclert (1848-1914) founded a group to demand the vote for women in 1876. A single issue of a periodical *Le vote des femmes* appeared at Troyes in 1884 under the pseudonym Sincère, [8052.aaa.12(2)], and Hubertine Auclert's book *Le vote des femmes* appeared in 1908 [08415.de.3]. The male viewpoint is reflected in *Ma femme vote* (a comedy in one act by E Leydet), Aix, 1894 [11740.e.25(12)].

There are several works on the vote for women in the 1911-15 cumulation of the *Subject Index*, including F Buisson *Le vote des femmes*, 1911 [08415.f.5]. J Barthélemy published *Le vote des femmes* in 1920 [08415.k.10], and A Toulemon *Le suffrage familial... le vote des femmes* in 1933 [08416.d.36]. In 1934 the Union nationale pour le vote des femmes published a report for their third congress *Problèmes nationaux vus par des Françaises* [08052.aa.30]. Women in France were not able to vote until 1945.

The 1881-1900 cumulation of the *Subject Index* contains many works on women's legal and social position in France and Switzerland at the time: *eg* M Provins *La femme d'aujourd'hui*, 1895 [8145.ff.8]; J Sagnol *L' Egalité des sexes*, 1889 [8416.h.8(6)] and a work on the Société nouvelle des femmes de France, 1894 [08275.e.30(7)]. There are several items on women at work, *eg* F de Donville *Les professions des femmes*, 1895 [8461.ff.9], and A de Mun *Le travail des femmes*, 1891 [8415.i.17(5)].

From earlier in the nineteenth century come some more general works on women, mostly in a condescending vein: Julien Joseph Virey *De la femme, sous ses rapports physiologique, moral et littéraire*, 1823 [08416.e.48]; Monpont, *Les défauts des femmes, leurs manies et leurs travers*, 1858 [08416.e.10] – this work is severe on blue-stockings, those who live in a world of novels, and those inclined to greed or avarice; Monpont *L'Art de gouverner les femmes*, 2nd edition, 1858 [12351.aaa.40(5)], and his *Les femmes coquettes, ou, La ruine des maisons. Actualité conjugale*, 1857 [12352.b.21].

L J Larcher wrote *Satires et diatribes sur les femmes, l'amour et le mariage, avec une réfutation*, 1860 [12354.aa.10] and *Le dernier mot sur les femmes* in 1864, [8145.a.55(5)]. V Rozier wrote *Les dons de la femme*, 1860 [12514.a.30]; and Édouard de Pompéry wrote *La femme dans l'humanité; sa nature, son rôle et sa valeur sociale*, 1864 [8415.cc.34]. Guides to the prostitutes of Paris used to be printed, such as the *Biographie des nymphes du Palais Royal et autres quartiers de Paris*, par Modeste Agnèse, l'une d'elles. (written by E M de Saint-Hilaire), 2nd edition, 1823 [Cup.365.aa.46].

A guide to feminist publications is Dzeh-Djen Li's *Le presse féministe en France de 1869 à 1914*, 1934 [11859.f.27]. Most of the periodicals for women listed in the *General Catalogue* under the heading 'Periodical Publications – Paris' are on the subject of fashion, and some include fashion plates of great artistry, eg *Journal des dames et des modes*, June 1912 – August 1914 [PP.5254.dc].

Revolution and war gave rise to many ephemeral periodicals including some published by or for women. Georges Sand published three issues of *La cause du peuple* in 1848 [1852.c.2(2)]. From the same year of revolution come several feminist publications now kept at the Newspaper Library, Colindale: one issue of *L'éventail-républicain. Journal des dames* [F.misc.456(64)]; *La République des femmes* no.1, 1848 [F.misc.464(15)]; *La politique des femmes . . . publié par les ouvrières*. n.1/2 June, 1846 [F.misc.456(76) 21/8/48, 28/1/49], which was absorbed by *L'Opinion des femmes* [F.misc.455(60)]. The period is covered by M Thibert *Le féminisme dans le socialisme francais de 1830 à 1850*, 1926 [08416.c.21].

Colindale has also some periodicals for women from the Franco-Prussian war of 1870, including *La tante Duchêne* 26/2–12/3 1870 [F.misc.504(28)]. There are a number of works by and about Louise Michel (1830-1905), the heroine of the Commune, listed under her name in the *General Catalogue*.

The 1916-20 *Subject Index* lists some works on the rôle of women in World War I. Colindale holds some periodicals for women which were launched during World War II: *Femmes françaises* 28/9 1944 – 9/11 1945 [MF.224.T]; *La femme. Hebdomadaire illustré des F.L.N*. March – June 1945 [F.misc.1216.T]; *Filles de France*, no.5, noël, 1944 [also at F.misc.1216.T]; and an imperfect set of *Marie-France*, 1/12/1944 – 14/6/1945. [F.misc.2001(3)], which was launched by the resistance group 'Rue de Lille' and continued after the war (though not held by the BL).

Frank marriage manuals are not an invention of the twentieth century. *L'Art de faire des garçons, ou, Nouveau tableau de l'amour conjugal* by Michel Cotelli appeared in 1760 [1173.c.1] with a chapter on erotic pleasure. J B T Serrurier wrote *Du marriage considéré dans ses rapports physiques et moraux* in 1845 [8415.g.35]. Auguste Debay's *Hygiène du mariage*, 1848 [7640.cc.4] went into many editions, and enlightened readers on aphrodisiac powders and liniments, and recommended red meat, exercise and erotic literature as remedies for a wife's lack of desire. Debay's *La Vénus féconde et callipédique*, 3rd edition, 1873 [7640.cc.2] expounds the fascinating theory that strong masculine men are likely to have sons, as are masculine, energetic women who exercise, eat red meat and drink red wine. Weak, inactive, 'feminine' women, who eat eggs and sweet 'weak' foods will have daughters. Debay also wrote a popular *Philosophie de mariage*, 7th edition, 1865 [7640.cc.5] on the history of marriage, with a study of marital happiness, adultery, etc. More theories on the sex of babies are ventured in *L'Art et la manière d'obtenir a son gré des garçons ou des filles*, 1900 [Cup.800.aa.23]. (Boys are conceived early in the monthly cycle, and particularly if the woman lies on her left side, and girls later in the month by those lying on their right.)

For the history of women's social position in the twentieth century, the reader is referred to the relevant cumulations of the *Subject Index*. The 1961-70 cumulation shows an increased number of books published on women, and includes three works on women in the French colonies of North Africa. There has been a relative explosion of publishing on women's rights and the history of women in recent years, including a series on *La femme au temps de . . .* published by Stock/Laurence Pernoud. Two feminist publishers are Des femmes and Régine Deforges.

The collections of the British Library have always been strong in literary works and literary criticism. These are relatively easy to trace under the names of individuals in the *General Catalogue*. A woman writer who was given a head start by the fact that her brother was King François I of France was Marguerite d'Angoulême who married Henri II of Navarre. She formed a centre of Renaissance learning and piety which inclined to Protestantism. The Library holds the first full edition of her *L'Heptameron des nouvelles*. . . B Prevost pour G Robinet, 1559, [C.7.a.14] and another 1559 issue at G.17750. First editions of her religious works are also held. The earliest edition of the *Mémoires* of the infamous wife of her grandson Henri IV, Marguerite de Valois, published in 1628, is at 6845.c.15.

The most famous French novel written by a woman in the seventeenth century is Madame de La Fayette's *La princesse de Clèves*, of which the first edition of 1678 is at 12510.df.4. Madeleine de Scudéry was another major novelist of the seventeenth century, though her novels were first published under the name of her brother, Georges. They were quickly translated into English. Even in the twentieth century a famous woman writer's reputation was hidden by a man: Colette's husband Henry Gauthier Villars, under the psuedonym Willy, took the credit for her early works, at first by himself and then jointly with her. The Library lacks any first or early editions, though it holds many modern editions and critical works.

Thus, although the British Library does not hold many ephemeral or periodical publications issued by the various groups seeking rights for women in France, many interesting monographs on women can be traced in its collections.

NOTE

All books mentioned in this paper are published in Paris unless otherwise stated.

Christine Burden

Holdings on women's studies in Italy

Although the women's movement came late to Italy there has been a large volume of material by and about women produced there since the late 1960s. The years from 1969-70 have been called the 'anni del nuovo femminismo'. Women's groups have mushroomed during these years. Many small groups have been set up, which respond to local needs. The relationship between feminism and politics is close; the Church, Socialism and Marxism have played a large part in shaping women's domestic and economic role. This local aspect of the women's movement is illustrated by Judith Hellman *Journeys among women: feminism in five Italian cities*. (Oxford: Polity Press, 1987).

At a national level, women's organisations are recorded in publications such as *DOC Italia* (Rome: Editoriale Italiana), *Guida Monaci* (Rome) and *Women's movements of the world*, edited by Sally Schreier (Harlow: Longman, 1988). Many, formed in the 1970s and 1980s, aim to reappraise and promote women's culture. They offer studies in various disciplines with women as the theme and have endeavoured to create a cultural and political climate within which women's cultural production can flourish. They also attempt to document the progress of women and attitudes to them. Some state funding is available to women's studies centres from the Ministero dei Beni Culturali and through local government.

One of the major institutions active in the field of women's studies is the Associazione Centro Studi 'Donnawomanfemme' founded in 1978. It maintains a library and organises exhibitions and lectures. In addition, it is now responsible for one of the major feminist journals *DWF: Donnawomanfemme* (first published in 1975) and collaborates in a publishing programme with the Cooperative Utopia. As a result of an initiative by the Associazione a network linking women's centres in Italy was set up in 1984, to facilitate the exchange of information.

The Centro di studi storici sul movimento di liberazione della donna in Italia, founded in 1979, promotes international cultural exchanges as well as maintaining an archive documenting the feminist movement in Italy and undertaking a publishing programme. Its *Bollettino* contains valuable bibliographical information.

Despite a late entry into the field, feminist publishing became established very quickly in Italy. During the 1970s the growth in women's groups was paralleled by the growth in publishing and by 1975 this literature was already being studied and recorded. Some titles have been produced by small, sometimes short-lived, specifically feminist publishers; others are the product of large, well-established, main-stream houses. There are no large-scale commercial feminist publishers.

The 'alternative' press in Italy is well organised but Anna Maria Crispino, in an article in *DWF* no.3 (autumn/winter 1986), criticising the lack of Italian representation at the Feminist Book Fair, wrote of the high cost of small print runs, the lack of access to booksellers, poor distribution, and limited resources for publicity. In her view these all contribute to what she calls the fragility of feminist publishing and the general invisibility of women's studies in Italy.

Publications fall into two main groups: studies on women (their being and their changing place in society), and works which are the expression of women's creativity. The British Library Humanities and Social Sciences Division holds three major women's studies bibliographies: *Donna e società industriale: bibliografia ragionata*, edited by Irene Barbero Beerwald. Turin: Editoriale Valentino, 1976; Banissoni, Maria, *Bibliografia sulla condizione femminile*. Rome: Bulzoni, 1978; Belforte, Francesca *La condizione delle donne: proposta bibliografica*. Livorno: Libreria Belforte, 1980.

Books about women held by H&SS cover a wide range of subjects. The most general are probably those on the rôle of women in society, both contemporary and historical: Agamben, Maria Federici. *Il cesto di lana*. Rome: SALES, 1957; Chianese, Gloria, *Storia sociale della donna in Italia (1800 – 1980)*. Naples: Guida, 1980.

More specifically, others deal with 'feminist' issues such as women's suffrage, the emancipation of women: ITALY. Comitato di Associazioni femminili per la parità di retribuzione, *L'emancipazione femminile in Italia: un secolo di discussioni 1861-1961: atti del convegno*. Florence: La nuova Italia, 1963; Sarti, Maria Alberta. *La lunga strada dell'emancipazione femminile* Fossano: Esperienze, 1978.

FEMINISM ITSELF: Gianeri, Enrico. *Storia del femminismo*. Milano, 1961; *L'Almanacco: luoghi, nomi, incontri, fatti, lavori in corso del movimento femminista italiana dal 1972*. Rome: Edizioni delle donne, 1978.

THE PSYCHOLOGY OF WOMEN AND MALE/FEMALE RELATIONSHIPS: Neera, *pseud* (Anna Zuccari, afterwards Radius). *Le idee di una donna*. Milan, 1904; Guiducci, Armanda. *La mela e il serpente: autoanalisi femminile*, 2nd edition. Milan: Rizzoli, 1974; Cavallo Boggi, Pina. *Immagine di sé e ruolo sessuale: analisi psicologica della condizione femminile*. Naples: Guida, 1978.

WOMEN AND WORK is a topic which recurs: Fano, Clelia. *La funzione sociale dell'operaia nel presente*. Reggio Emilia, 1906; Pieraccini, Gaetano. *Lavoro femminile casalingo ed estracasalingo*. Rome, 1953; Christé, Lucia. *Oltre il lavoro domestico: il lavoro della donna tra produzione e riproduzione* Milan: Feltrinelli, 1979.

THE LEGAL POSITION OF WOMEN: Bellomo, Manlio. *La condizione giuridica della donna in Italia*. Turin: Edizione RAI, 1970; Remiddi, Laura. *I nostri diritti: manuale giuridico per le donne*. Milan: Feltrinelli, 1976.

SOCIETY'S VIEW OF WOMEN AND ITS MANIFESTATIONS: Pellegrini, Elena. *La donna-oggetto in pubblicità*. Venice: Marsilio, 1977.

MATERNITY, SEXUALITY AND WOMEN'S HEALTH (including abortion) are major issues in Italian feminist publishing; the Library's holdings include the (in its day) scandalous *Le Italiane si confessano*, 2nd edition. Florence: Parenti, 1959.

BIOGRAPHIES OF WOMEN: Agostini, Piero. *Mara Cagol: una donna nelle prime Brigate Rosse*. Venice: Marsilio, 1980.

WOMEN AS SUBJECTS IN ART AND LITERATURE are more recurrent themes: Abete, Giovanne. *La donna in Manzoni e Leopardi*. Milan, 1942; Schiavo, Armando. *La donna nella scultura italiana dal XII al XVIII secolo*. Rome, 1950; *Il sesso, la donna, l'amore nella canzone italiana dal 1900 ai nostri giorni*, edited by Paolo Gatto. Messina: D'Anna, 1977.

THE CREATIVITY OF WOMEN themselves is much harder to document. There have been published studies on women's work in the cinema and on women artists: *Il gioco dello specchio: materiale per il cinema delle donne*, edited by Sheherazade. Florence: Usher, 1980; *Di fronte allo schermo: materiali per il terzo incontro dello specchio*, edited by Sheherazade. Florence: Usher, 1981; Rubino, Luciano. *Le spose del vento: la donne nelle arti e nel design degli ultimi cento anni*. Verona: Bertami, 1979.

However, the LITERARY WORK of women is harder to trace. The BL has Gastaldi, Mario. *Dizionario delle scrittrici italiane contemporanee*. Milan, 1957.

And ANTHOLOGIES such as: *Donne in poesia: antologia della poesia femminile in Italia dal dopoguerra a oggi* edited by Biancamaria Frabotta. Rome: Savelli, 1976; *La voce che è in lei: antologia della narrative femminile italiana tra '800 e '900*, edited by Giuliana Morandini. Milan: Bompiani, 1980.

THE CREATIVITY OF WOMEN has been studied by: Comerci, Mariella. *I profili della luna*. Rome: Bulzoni, 1982. Letters, autobiographies and diaries also fall into the category of self-expression, *eg*: Aleramo, Sibilla. *Diario di una donna*. Milan: Feltrinelli, 1979.

A further side to women's publishing is PUBLISHING FOR WOMEN, of which H&SS holds much less. It is reviewed in: Buonanno, Milly. *Naturale comme sei: un indagine sulla stampa femminile in Italia*. Rimini: Guaraldi, 1975 (which contains a bibliography) and Pezzuoli, Giovanni. *La stampa femminile come ideologia*. Milan: Il Formichiere, 1975.

The titles included in this paper are given for example only. A more extensive bibliography on H&SS holdings from Italy from 1900 onwards is deposited for consultation in the Italian Section of Collection Development (West European Branch).

Rosamond Eden

Resources for a study of the women's movement in Germany until 1945

The women's movement in German had its origins in the mid-nineteenth century, and gathered momentum through the activities and commitment of many remarkable women who worked within the framework of women's organisations and political parties. The culmination of these activities was the achievement of universal female suffrage in the wake of World War I. The years of the Weimar Republic and the Third Reich saw the gradual decline and defeat of the women's movement until its post-war renewal and revitalisation in the 1960s in the Federal Republic.

The British Library has a representative collection of both primary and secondary sources which I shall attempt to highlight. Research in the subject catalogues and through the bibliographies of many works listed here will doubtless reveal additional material.

Alongside recent general historical surveys such as *Geschichte der Frauenbewegung*, edited by Florence Hervé (1982); *Geschichte der Frauenbewegung* by Rosemarie Nave-Herz (1982); *Frauenemanzipation: Politik und Literatur der deutschen Sozialdemokratie zur Frauenbewegung 1863-1933* by Werner Thönnessen (1969) – also available in an English translation of 1973 – must be placed Daniela Weiland's indispensable and well-illustrated compendium of people, programmes and organisations *Geschichte der Frauenemanzipation* (1983). Useful works in English are Richard J Evan's *Comrades and sisters: feminism, socialism and pacifism in Europe 1870-1945* (1987), and *The Feminist movement in Germany 1894-1933* (1976).

Origins of the women's movement

For an analysis of the beginnings of the movement consult Margrit Twellmann's *Die deutsche Frauenbewegung: ihre Anfänge und erste Entwicklung 1843-1889* (1982), plus a separate volume on sources (*Quellen*, also published 1972).

By the late nineteenth century the question of women (die *Frauenfrage*) and their rôle in society was being much discussed in works such as Lily Braun's *Die Frauenfrage* (1901), and Luise Büchner's *Praktische Versuche zur Lösung der Frauenfrage* (1870) and *Die Frau* (1878). Also of interest are works by the radical feminist Hedwig Dohm – *Der Frauen Natur und Recht* (1876), *Emanzipation der Frau* (1874) and *Der Jesuitismus im Hausstand* (1873), the last of which contains the first written demand for votes for women – and by Luise Otto-Peters, considered by many to be the mother of the

German women's movement – *Das Recht der Frauen auf Erwerb* (1866). For a more detailed study of Peters' role in the movement see Ruth-Ellen Boetcher Joeres' *Anfänge der deutschen Frauenbewegung: Luise Otto-Peters* (1981).

Male attitudes to the problem are illustrated in Gustav Cohn's *Die deutsche Frauenbewegung* (1896), and in August Bebel's seminal *Die Frau in der Vergangenheit, Gegenwart und Zukunft* (1878) – the first work to attempt an investigation of the *Frauenfrage* from a socialist viewpoint.

Proletarian women's movement (Proletarische Frauenbewegung)

In Germany the impetus for women's rights came from the proletarian women's movement. Seeing the struggle for women's rights as part of the class struggle, it allied itself to the proletarian movement in general and to the Sozialdemokratische Partei Deutschlands (SPD) in particular. It was the SPD which introduced, as early as 1894, a bill for female suffrage, held its first women's conference in 1900 and was ultimately responsible for women being able to go to the ballot box at the elections of 1919. The rôle of the SPD in the furtherance of women's rights is reflected in one of the most important works of the movement, the journal for SPD women, *Die Gleichheit*, of which the Library has an almost complete set from 1892-1923. Clara Zetkin, leader of, and intellectual force behind, the proletarian women's movement, was its editor from 1892-1917, at which time she became disillusioned with the SPD's participation in the war effort and left to join the Kommunistische Partei Deutschlands (KPD). She remained active in the women's movement, serving as a KPD representative in the Reichstag. The BL has her *Ausgewählte Reden und Schriften* (reprinted 1957-60) and *Zur Geschichte der proletarischen Frauenbewegung Deutschlands* (1928, reprinted 1971).

Discussion of women's rights by the SPD can be found in the reports of their annual conferences (1887 onwards) and in Wilhelm Schröders *Handbuch der sozialdemokratischen Parteitage von 1863 bis 1909* (1910). The rôle of the Social Democrats in the women's movement and their relationship with other strands of the movement is discussed in Joseph Joos's *Die Sozialdemokratische Frauenbewgung* (1912). Lily Hauff's *Die deutsche Arbeiterinnen-Organisation* (1912) examines those organisations which were to play such an important part in the rise of a working class movement. For the movement in Austria see works by Adelheid Popp, its founder – *Autobiography of a working woman* (1912) and *Der Weg zur Höhe: die sozialdemokratische Frauenbewegung Österreichs* (2nd edition, 1930).

Important secondary works are: *Dem Reich der Freiheit sollst Du Kinder gebären: der Antifeminismus im Spiegel der Gleichheit 1891-1917* (1981) by Anna Freier. (Anti-feminism was always a problem even in a liberal organisation like the SPD; traditional and old-fashioned views of women and the family died hard, as did resentment of female competition in the labour market); *Reluctant feminists in German social democracy 1885-1917* (1979) by Jean H Quataert, and *Uns fehlt nur eine Kleinigkeit: deutsche proletarische Frauenbewegung 1890-1914* (1982) by Sabine Richebächer.

Bourgeois women's movement (Bürgerliche Frauenbewegung)

The bourgeois women's movement developed along both radical and moderate lines. Many members had been politicised initially through participation in professional organisations, such as the Allgemeiner deutscher Lehrerinnenverein (Association of German women teachers).

Prominent among the moderates were Helene Lange and Gertrud Bäumer who were responsible for the publication of the notable work on women's movements throughout the world, *Handbuch der Frauenbewegung* (5 vols, 1901-06). They also edited *Die Frau: Monatsschrift für das gesamte Frauenleben unserer Zeit* (1893-1944), of which the Library has a reasonably complete set. Also of interest are Lange's memoirs of a long career in the women's movement, *Kampfzeiten* (1928), and *Lebenserinnerungen* (1930).

The Helene-Lange-Archiv, now in the possession of the Berliner Frauenbund 1945 e.V., is a rich source of original material on the history of the bourgeois women's movement and the Bund deutscher Frauenvereine (Association of German women's organisations), which had been established in 1894 as an umbrella organisation for the different women's groups. A guide to the archive has been published recently – *Findbuch der Archivalien des Helene-Lange-Archivs* (1987).

The radical stream of the movement is represented by Minna Cauer (see her *Leben und Werk*, 1925); Käthe Schirmacher (see Hanna Kruger's *Die unbequeme Frau: Käthe Schirmacher im Kampf für die Freiheit der Frau und die Freiheit der Nation, 1865-1930*, 1936); and Lida Heymann (see her *Frauenstimmrecht und Völkerverständigung*, 1919). Heymann and her great friend and fellow activist, Anita Augspurg, went into exile during the 1930s. Their memoirs make fascinating reading – *Erlebtes – Erschautes: deutsche Frauen kämpfen für Freiheit, Recht und Frieden 1850-1940* (1972).

Important secondary works are: *Die bürgerliche Frauenbewegung in Deutschland, 1894-1933* (1981) by Barbara Greven-Aschoff; *Wir wollen unser Teil fordern: Interessenvertretung und Organisationsformen der bürgerlichen und proletarischen Frauenbewegung im deutschen Kaiserreich* (1987) by Doris Beavan and Brigitte Faber; and the compilation, *Die bürgerlichen Parteien in Deutschland* (1968) which includes a chapter on the bourgeois women's movement.

The First World War

1914 witnessed the increasing involvement of women in the workforce by way of the Nationaler Frauendienst (National Women's Service), founded by the Bund deutscher Frauenvereine to provide assistance, both industrial, medical and social, to a nation at war. German women were also closely involved in international peace movements both during and after the war, and especially in the Women's International League for Peace and Freedom, many publications of which are in the Library. Works which deal with this period include Paula Mueller's *Wir Frauen und der Krieg* (1915); Luise Zietz's *Die sozialdemokratischen Frauen und der Krieg* (1915); *Geschichte des Vaterländischen Frauen-Vereins, 1866-1916* (1917), *Kameradin: junge Frauen im deutschen Schicksal, 1910-1930* (1936); and *Die Deutsche Frau in der sozialen Kriegsfürsorge*, edited by Gertrud Bäumer (1916).

Weimar Republic and the rise of national socialism (1919-33)

Votes for women became a reality in 1919, and, after the elections to the National Assembly on 19 January, 37 women, out of a total of 310 women candidates, took their seats. However, female suffrage did not result in the triumph of socialism, rather the reverse. The Social Democrats were entitled to feel betrayed by those for whose political rights they had fought. The rôle of women in the rise of national socialism is a contentious issue – on the one hand they are considered to be responsible for bringing Hitler to power, attracted by his charismatic personality and his emphasis on family life as the heart of a strong and ordered society, on the other hand they are seen as victims of a system which was inherently hostile to women's rights.

The political rôle of women during this period is discussed in Gabrielle Bremme's *Die politische Rolle der Frau in Deutschland* (1956); Käthe Kern's *Frauen, entscheidet euch!* (1931); Sylvia Kontos's *Die Partei kämpft wie ein Mann: Frauenpolitik der KPD in der Weimarer Republik (1979)*; Erik Ernst Schwabach's *Die Revolutionisierung der Frau* (1928); and Christl Wickert's *Unsere Erwählten: sozialdemokratische Frauen im Deutschen Reichstage und im Preussischen Landtag, 1919 bis 1933* (1986). Other useful, more general, works are Hugh Puckett's *Germany's women go forward* (1930), and *Mutterkreuz und Arbeitsbuch: zur Geschichte der Frauen in der Weimarer Republik und im Nationalsozialismus* (1981).

Third Reich, 1933-45

The Nazis saw themselves as the promoters of equal rights for women but only as long as those rights were exercised strictly within the female domain. Women were not excluded from the labour market, but home and family had to come first, and they were to be denied a political rôle – there were no women Nationalsozialistische Deutsche Arbeiterpartei parliamentary candidates. Instead, participation was encouraged in the various women's groups founded by the party, under the overall control of the NS-Frauenschaft (NSF). Under its leader, the most powerful woman in the Third Reich, Gertrud Scholtz-Klink, the NSF aimed to integrate as many women as possible into the Nazi framework and to mobilise them for motherhood and active public service – apart, of course, from those political and economic concerns which were the affairs of men. The Bund deutscher Frauenvereine, unable to co-operate, dissolved itself in 1933 rather than be compelled to join the NSF!

Essential reading for this period is Scholtz-Klink's own account published in 1978, *Die Frau im Dritten Reich*, in which she reflects on what she saw as the 'positive' aspects of Nazi rule and its benefits for women – compare this with her contemporary account, *Verpflichtung und Aufgabe der Frau im nationalsozialistischen Staat* (1936). The official Nazi view of the rôle of women is also advanced in one of Joseph Goebbels's publications *Signale der neuen Zeit* (1934) which includes a section on

German womanhood. Party publications aimed at women include: *Frauen schaffen für Deutschland* (1938), *Frauenkultur im Deutschen Frauenwerk* (1935); *Hilfswerk Mutter und Kind*, (1936), *Nationalsozialistische Frauenschaft* (1937); and *Nationalsozialistische Mädchenerziehung* (1935, 1943). For men *SS-Mann und Blutsfrage* (1941) makes chilling reading in its emphasis on choosing a mate of the correct (Aryan) blood stock. Other interesting source material can be found in *Frauen um Hitler* (1983) by Henriette von Schirach who was one of Hitler's circle; *Die deutsche Frau und der Nationalsozialismus* (2nd edition, 1933) by Guida Diehl, a prominent woman Nazi; *Eine stumme Generation berichtet: Frauen der 30er and 40er Jahre* (1982, contemporary accounts of everyday life in the 1930s and 1940s); *Familie und Frau im neuen Deutschland* (1936, a sociologist's view by Karl Beyer); *Deutsche Frauen an Adolf Hitler* (2nd edition, 1934, an over-enthusiastic and idolatrous compilation!); and Ruth Gaensecke's *Die Frauenbeilagen der deutschen Tageszeitungen im Dienste der Politik* (1938).

Contemporary views by outsiders are provided by American sociologist, Clifford Kirkpatrick, in his *Woman in Nazi Germany* (1939) and *Nazi Germany: its women and family life* (1938), and by Katherine Thomas in her *Women in Nazi Germany* (1943).

There are also a number of recent works in English which look at women in the Third Reich, notably Claudia Koonz's well-researched and comprehensive guide *Mothers in the fatherland: women, the family and Nazi politics* (1987), which includes an interview with Gertrud Scholtz-Klink dating from 1981. See also two works by Jill Stephenson, *The Nazi organisation of women* (1981), and *Women in Nazi Society* (1975).

Other more general publications in German include Hannelore Kessler's *Die deutsche Frau: nationalsozialistische Frauenpropaganda im Völkischen Beobachter* (1981), and Dorte Winkler's *Frauenarbeit im Dritten Reich* (1977).

Georg Tidl's *Die Frau im Nationalsozialismus* (1984); Renate Wiggershaus's *Frauen unterm Nationalsozialismus* (1984); and *Frauen im deutschen Faschismus* (1982) by Annette Kuhn and Valentine Rothe.

Der Bund deutscher Mädel in Dokumenten (1984), a well-illustrated collection of contemporary documents, provides a good account of life in this most popular of young women's organisations.

One unexpected side effect of the Third Reich was an upsurge in the number of admissions of women to universities with official encouragement to train for the professions. Thus many professional and middle class women who had supported the women's movement before 1933 were able to live with national socialism. Gertrud Bäumer's *Krisis des Frauenstudiums* (1933) is a timely plea for equal educational opportunities for women. More recent works include Jacques R Pauvel's *Women, Nazis and universities: female university students in the Third Reich, 1933-1945* (1984) and a chapter in *German democracy and the triumph of Hilter* (1971) on women and the professions in Germany, 1930-1940 by Jill McIntyre.

Women in the resistance

For all those who collaborated and participated actively in Nazi organisations there were also many brave women who participated in resistance and underground movements. Many died in concentration camps, were driven into exile or simply 'disappeared'. Many were Jewish or political and religious dissidents. Works to be consulted include: Gerda Szepansky's *Frauen leisten Widerstand, 1933-45* (1983); Erich Klausener's *Frauen in Fesseln: Hoffnung in der Finsternis: von Mut und Opfer katholischer Frauen im Dritten Reich* (1982) and the editorial compilations *Seit 1848: Frauen im Widerstand, Frauen im Faschismus, 1933-45* (1977); *Frauen unterm Hakenkreuz* (1983) and *Frauen – KZ Ravensbruck* (1982). For a very personal account of one woman's struggle for survival read the bestseller *The past is myself*, by Christabel Bielenberg (1968, reprinted 1984). For a history of the Jewish women's movement see Marion A Kaplan's *Die jüdische Frauenbewegung im Deutschland* (1981).

In conclusion, while commending the depth of the Library's resources, the attention of researchers should be drawn to the major bibliographic tool in this field *Die Frauenfrage in Deutschland: Strömungen und Gegenströmungen, 1790-1930: sachlich geordnete und erläuterte Quellenkunde*, edited by Hans Sveistrup and Agnes von Zahn-Harnack (1934), continued from 1937-80 under the auspices of the Deutscher Akademikerinnenbund (Association of German women academics). Its coverage is now worldwide and further volumes will appear on an irregular basis, making it an indispensable reference source.

Brigid Haines

Women's studies in West and East Germany

'Women are no longer looking for equality but for new forms of living.' *Christa Wolf*

In the two Germanies the many issues which fall under the umbrella of women's studies have probably never been so important as they are today, both in terms of the volume of published output and in terms of the creative power and intellectual vigour of the work being produced. The British Library is a good source of material in this area because of the breadth of its general collecting policy, and because of its strong holdings of serials and of imaginative and academic literature. This short paper can only provide a general indication of what this material includes: readers are referred to the catalogues and in particular to the subject indexes for further information. I have, however, looked in more detail at two central issues, namely feminist linguistics, and women's writing in East Germany.

General bibliographies of women's studies in the two Germanies include *Thema: Frau: Bibliographie der deutschsprachigen Literatur zur Frauenfrage 1949-1979*, by Ulla Bock and Barbara Witych (Bielefeld, 1980). This is a useful bibliography on all aspects of women's studies. Of particular interest is the list, on p.262, of feminist magazines and periodicals. See also *Bibliographie: Frauenforschung über Frauenarbeit in Produktion und Reproduktion 1979-1984*, edited by Beate Collin and Irmgard Schulz (Bielefeld, 1986).

The West German situation

The current women's movement in West Germany sprang up in the 1960s and has been heavily influenced by the American model.

The movement consists of many diverse groups which have campaigned for such causes as equal pay, equal rights, childcare and changes to the abortion laws, the notorious Paragraph 218, and to the *Berufsverbot* which restricts entry to civil service jobs, including the teaching profession, for those active in left wing politics. Groups have also set up publishing companies, such as *Frauenoffensive*, discussion groups, homes for abused women, lesbian collectives and so on. Many women are active in anti-nuclear and environmental groups, especially the Green Party.

Herrad Schenk's *Die feministische Herausforderung: 150 Jahre Frauenbewegung in Deutschland*, 2nd edition (München, 1981) gives a summary of the new women's movement, relating it to the historical perspective. It is particularly strong on feminist theory. Alice Schwarzer's excellent *So fing es an!: 10 Jahre Frauenbewegung* (Köln, 1981) charts the main events of the seventies and reviews many important books.

Women's rights in West Germany are far advanced but in other areas, particularly childcare and career development, support for women's needs is sadly lacking. Women are seriously underrepresented in the professions and, in 1985, earned only 65% of the average income. The authors of a recent report in *Brigitte*, quoted in *Die Zeit*, no.43, 21 October 1988, wrote 'We have created a society in which the good mother is still tied to the picture of the housewife, and yet at the same time having a job is, both for men and women, seen as necessary for fostering a sense of identity'. *Die Zeit* comments 'Interesting and professionally employed, or motherly and at home – well, which is it to be?' This dichotomy is at the heart of West German, and indeed, of western society.

General statistical information about women's social conditions and women's groups in West Germany can be found in *Die Situation der Frau: Trendbeobachtungen über Rollen- und Bewusstseinsänderungen der Frauen in der Bundesrepublik Deutschland*, by Gerhard Schmidchen (Berlin, 1984).

Courses in women's studies are now taught at several West German universities and the following publications list archives and other bibliographic sources: *Frauenforschungs- und Frauenstudieninitiativen in der Bundesrepublik Deutschland*, by Clemens Bärbel (Kassel, 1983), and *Frauenarchive und Frauenbibliotheken*, edited by Karin Schatzberg (Göttingen, 1985).

A particularly important work here is *German feminism: readings in politics and literature*, edited by Edith Hoshino Altbach et al, (Albany, 1984). This is a remarkably comprehensive anthology in English of important texts in the German women's movement. Topics covered include abortion, Turkish women in Berlin, motherhood, housework, the Lesbian Action Centre in West Berlin, women in politics and the trade unions, and women in adult education. These reflect the spectrum of published research into women's topics. Theoretical articles include 'The function of sexuality in the oppression of women', by Alice Schwarzer (editor of the influential journal *Emma: Zeitschrift von Frauen für Frauen*), 'Towards a methodology for feminist research', by Maria Mies, and 'Literature and politics', by Jeanette Clausen. The creative writers who have contributed are also among the most influential: Verena Stefan, Elfriede Brüning, Irmtraud Morgner, Sarah Kirsch, Helga Novak, Jutta Schutting, Elfriede Jelinek, Christa Wolf, Maxie Wander, Margot Schroeder, Christa Reinig and Jutta Heinrich.

A similarly useful collection of articles on feminist topics can be found in the special feminist issue of *New German Critique*, 13, 1978. One scholarly periodical worth a particular mention is *Feministische Studien*, which has special issues on topics such as social studies, science, the history of the women's movement and war.

Linguistics

Alternative feminist thought is making inroads into all the major academic disciplines, including literary theory, medicine, sociology, psychoanalysis, theology, history, philosophy, education, law, linguistics and classical studies.

In all of these it is stimulating lively debate. Women's issues have for too long been a 'blind spot', as Professor Annette Kuhn, Chair of Women's History at the University of Bonn, claims. She herself taught history for twenty years 'without noticing that women did not appear at all in it'. I will outline briefly how feminist scholarship has contributed to the understanding of one discipline, namely linguistics.

Twentieth century philosophy and thought have been dominated since Wittgenstein by the relationship between language and reality. The implications of the view that language forms the basis of all human thought and communication are only now being thought through. Socio-linguistics is part of this debate and deals with the nature of spoken language and in particular the language of minority and oppressed groups. One branch of this is feminist linguistics which looks at women's use of language as opposed to men's and also at the perceived bias against women in the structure and vocabulary of many languages, which serves ultimately to dominate the collective unconscious and keep power in male hands.

Language is central to feminism, because if language forms consciousness and structures reality, then it can and will be used as an instrument of oppression. Promoting awareness of this, even if attempting to change it is seen as too ambitious, becomes an urgent priority.

The contribution of West German scholars to both sides of this international debate has been considerable. A very influential book on this subject is *Gewalt durch Sprache: die Vergewaltigung von Frauen in Gesprächen*, edited by Senta Trömel-Plötz (Frankfurt am Main, 1984). This contains articles which analyse situational language use in schools and universities, in medicine and in radio and television broadcasts, exploring women's unequal position in speech. Also important are *Das Deutsche als Männersprache: Aufsätze und Glossen zur feministischen Linguistik*, by Luise F Pusch (Frankfurt am Main, 1984), which explores the issues of gender and power in the German language in particular, and *Frauensprache: Sprache der Veränderung*, by Senta Trömel-Plötz (Frankfurt am Main, 1982).

Other recent articles on women and language are 'Sprache und Geschlecht', by Gisela Schoenthal in *Deutsche Sprache*, 13, 2/85, which has a good bibliography on the subject, 'Sprache und Geschlecht: die sprachliche (Selbst)darstellung von Frau und Mann', by Otmar Käge, in *Wirkendes Wort*, 33, 1984 (which begins with an enigmatic quotation from Karl Kraus: 'language decides everything, even the women question'!), and 'Sexismus und Häufigkeit', *Deutsche Sprache*, 4/81. It is interesting to note here that men are contributing to the debate as well as women.

The question of women's language also occurs in the domain of women's writing, where the German language is often felt by women writers to be an unsuitable tool. Verena Stefan, author of one of the most influential novels of the West German women's movement, *Häutungen: autobiographische Aufzeichnungen* (München, 1975), spoke for many women when she wrote 'Language fails me the moment I attempt to devise new experiences'.

The position of women in East Germany

There is supposedly no need for a women's movement in East Germany, since the question of women's equality has been 'solved' with the advent of socialism which seeks freedom from oppression for all people, not just women. Western feminism is often rejected in that country as 'a bourgeois attempt to achieve superficial liberation through a battle of the sexes' (Patricia Herminhouse), which diverts attention from the real issues.

It is true that women's lives are in some material ways often better in East Germany than they are in the west: women make up 50% of the workforce (compared with only 38.2% in West Germany), employers are legally bound to draw up a plan for the positive advancement of women, a *Frauenförderungsplan*, the level of childcare provision is high, maternity leave is generous, women are granted up to thirteen weeks per year of paid sick leave to care for sick children, there is abortion on demand and so on.

Many of these advantages do, of course, also benefit the state – women's labour is vital for the economic health of the country, for instance, and providing childcare facilities is a way of retaining women in the workforce – nevertheless matters of principle are important too: despite a falling birth rate, contraception is legal and is seen as a woman's right.

But despite these advantages, firmly entrenched attitudes and prejudices ensure that women do not take leading positions in GDR society, and that their lives are still more dominated by domestic responsibilities than are those of their men: studies have shown that women still do about 80% of the household chores despite going out to work as well. Apart from early attempts at alternative types of communities, the nuclear family is still the official organizational principle in the GDR. The state uses the family as a stabilising element and alternative lifestyles are frowned upon.

For a good summary of women's position in GDR society, both in the family and in the society as a whole, see *GDR Society and Social Institutions: facts and figures*, by G E Edwards (London, 1985); *Die Frau in der DDR: Ideologie und konzeptionelle Ausgestaltung ihrer Stellung in Beruf und Familie*, by Friedel Schubert (Opladen, 1980); and *Die gesellschaftliche Stellung der Frau in der Deutschen Demokratischen Republik: ein Auswahlverzeichnis*, by Barbara Jokisch et al (Leipzig, 1986). There are also chapters on women in *The GDR under Honecker 1971-1981*, edited by Ian Wallace (Dundee, 1981), and in Ian Wallace's useful general bibliography *East Germany: the German Democratic Republic* (Oxford, 1987).

Women's writing in East Germany

Many critics would contend that the most significant and innovative literature in German to have appeared anywhere since the mid 1960s has come from the GDR, and a considerable amount of it is by women. These writers have expanded the initially confining limits of socialist realism and deal seriously with twentieth century issues such as the nuclear threat, German feelings of guilt about the Holocaust, identity, the rôle of the individual in society and the effect of socialism on interpersonal relationships. They are increasingly reintroducing the private sphere and the validity of personal experience into the agenda of GDR writing.

Their work is important both within the GDR, since literature has become 'an arena for the discussion of controversial issues which find no place in the national press' (Chris Weedon), and outside it, since it reflects the high level of cultural and political debate in that country.

A seminal work was Maxie Wander's *'Guten Morgen, du Schöne': Frauen in der DDR: Protokolle* (Berlin, 1978). This consisted of frank and open interviews with ordinary women and started a new trend of documentary literature about everyday life in the GDR. Other important works have included *Blitz aus heiterem Himmel*, edited by Edith Anderson (Rostock, 1975), an anthology of stories on the theme of sex change and gender roles; Irmtraud Morgner's *Leben und Abenteuer der Trobadora Beatriz nach Zeugnissen ihrer Spielfrau Laura: Roman in dreizehn Büchern und sieben Intermezzos* (Berlin, 1974), which gives a realistic view of modern life through the eyes of a medieval female troubadour who comes to the GDR seeking an escape from the patriarchal structures of medieval life; and Brigitte Reimann's *Franziska Linkerhand: Roman* (Berlin, 1974), whose heroine, an idealistic young architect, rejects traditional women's rôles and seeks to serve the community, only to realise the high personal cost of this approach.

The single most influential writer is Christa Wolf, who has been awarded many prizes both at home and abroad. Her powerful, partly autobiographical novel *Kindheitsmuster* (Berlin, 1977), is an attempt to explore and come to terms with German fascism and to answer the question 'how have we come to be as we are?' Memory and language are powerful themes. Her latest work, *Störfall: Nachrichten eines Tages* (Berlin, 1987), was written in the immediate aftermath to the Chernobyl nuclear accident, and reflects on the dominance of science and technology and on the nature and worth of artistic statements in the modern world.

There are several excellent anthologies which give a taste of GDR women's writing, namely *Die Frau in der DDR: an anthology of women's writing from the German Democratic Republic*, edited by Chris Weedon (Oxford, 1988): *Die Heiratsschwindlerin: Erzählerinnen der DDR*, edited by Ingrid Krüger (Darmstadt, 1983); and an important new volume of poetry, *Wenn wir den Königen schreiben: Lyrikerinnen aus der DDR*, edited by Jutta Rosenkranz and Hanna Castein (Darmstadt, 1988).

Conclusion

Finally I would like to mention the United States organisation called 'Women in German', whose journal, *Women in German yearbook: feminist studies and German culture* (held in the library of the Institute of Germanic Studies at 29 Russell Square), contains many useful articles. A similar organisation, called 'Women in German Studies', or WIGS, was set up in Britain in 1988 and will meet annually to discuss developments and hear papers.

In both West and East Germany, women are increasingly finding a voice, or rather many voices, and articulating their worries, as well as their hopes and aspirations, more and more confidently. As Christa Wolf wrote in the quotation which begins this paper, the emphasis in the women's movement has moved away from the search for equality, to a questioning of the nature of society, of gender and of language, and a proposal for new forms of living in which each individual can 'live as a complete human being'.

Janet Gilbert

Dutch resources

The Dutch collections of the British Library include a wide range of materials dealing with the history and development of the women's movement in the Netherlands, as well as many contemporary analyses of the rôle of women in past and present society. In this paper I shall concentrate mainly on items published in the Netherlands in the last fifteen years, during which time the ineradicable influence of feminism has stimulated a boom in the publication of works by, for and about women and the women's movement. This period coincides approximately with a rise in government awareness of the need for well-defined policies for equal opportunities in Dutch society, and also with the first steps towards establishing university programmes of women's studies in the Netherlands. This brief survey cannot hope to provide much more than a general indication of the Library's holdings in this field: readers are referred to the Library's subject catalogues and to the detailed bibliographies in the items mentioned.

Early history of the women's movement

The 'first wave' of Dutch feminism swept the Netherlands around the turn of the century, as more and more women gained access to secondary and university education and turned their attention to the fight for the suffrage and for the rights of women. In the latter years of the nineteenth century various organisations, such as 'Arbeid adelt' (1871), the 'Vrije Vrouwn Vereeniging' (1889), and the 'Vereeniging voor Vrouwenkiesrecht' (1984), were set up throughout the country to raise awareness of women's rights at work, in the home and in society in general, and many of these groups worked in close contact with international organisations; for instance, the International Congress for Women's Suffrage in 1908 was held in Amsterdam. A comprehensive overview of the position of Dutch women during the last two hundred years, with excellent coverage of the early twentieth century, is found in *Van moeder op dochter: de maatschappelijke positie van de vrouw in Nederland vanaf de Franse tijd*, edited by W H Posthumus-van der Goot, herself a leading feminist, and Anna de Waal (Nijmegen, 3rd ed, 1977).

The early struggle for women's rights with regard to work reflected the different problems experienced by the middle class and by working class women, encompassing as it did both the question of the right of women to take paid employment and hence to gain financial independence, and the fight against the exploitation of those women who were forced to work long hours in menial, lowly paid jobs. In 1898 a major exhibition, the *Nationale Tentoonstelling van Vrouwenarbeid*, was staged in The Hague, encouraging even greater interest in the rôle of women and their work. The theme of women's labour in the late nineteenth and early twentieth centuries is explored in *Vrouwenarbeid in Nederland 1870-1940* by Marjolein Morée and Marjan Schwegman (Rijswijk, 1981). Some of the works of Clara Meijer-Wichmann, a prolific early writer on feminism and the labour movement, and co-author of an encyclopaedia on women and women's labour, have also recently been republished under the title *Vrouw en Maatschappij* (Nijmegen, 1978). *Vrouwen rond de eeuwwisseling*, edited by Aukje Holtrop (Amsterdam, 1979), offers evocative portraits of some of the leading members of the early women's movement, such as Betsy Perk, Wilhelmina Drucker, Roosje Vos, Mina Kruseman and the remarkable Aletta Jacobs, as well as an informative account of the movement around 1900. The latter two women are described further in, respectively, *Mina Kruseman 1839-1922: portret van een militante feministe en pacifiste*, edited by Margot de Waal (*De Engelbewaarder* 12, Amsterdam, 1978), and *Lieve Dr. Jacobs: brieven uit de Wereldbond voor Vrouwenkiesrecht, 1902-1942*, edited by Mineke Bosch and Annemarie Kloosterman (Amsterdam, 1985).

The year 1913 saw a second major exhibition in The Hague, entitled *De Vrouw 1813-1913*, which also generated much comment. Mia Boissevain, one of the driving forces behind the 1913 exhibition, whose memoirs were published as *Een Amsterdamsche familie* (Diepenveen, 1967), offered an illuminating appraisal of the situation in 1915:

> How is the women's movement getting on in [the Netherlands]? Is it backward as in German, partly militant as in England, or victorious as in the Scandinavian countries? Let me answer you at once by saying it is neither backward, nor militant, nor yet victorious; it is simply what anyone with a knowledge of the national character would expect it to be, that is, thorough, earnest, slow-going but steadfast (*The Woman's Movement, a general view of the Netherlands*, no.24 (The Hague, 1915) p.3).

Dutch women at last attained the right to vote in 1919. The first women member of Parliament had been elected to the Tweede Kamer, the lower house, by the male vote in 1918, and was shortly followed by five other women in 1922, while the first women member entered the Eerste Kamer, or upper house, in 1937.

The mid-twentieth century: different priorities

The achievement of universal female suffrage did not, of course, mean that activities by women came to a halt. Many organisations within the women's movement, such as the Wereldbond voor Vrouwenkiesrecht, directed their efforts towards campaigning for peace and against fascism in the period between the wars. In general, however, the movement played a less important rôle in the Netherlands, as the Dutch grappled with the economic problems leading to the Depression of the 1930s and then had to face the anguish of war. Els Blok assesses the position of women in these years of crisis in *Uit de schaduw van de mannen: vrouwenverzet 1930-1940* (Amsterdam, 1985) and argues that many women were committed to fighting for the right to work, for decent working conditions, and against poverty, while maintaining their opposition to the threat of war and fascism.

The rôle of women in the war-time Resistance in the Netherlands is described in *Kinderwagens en korsetten: een onderzoek naar de sociale achtergrond en de rol van vrouwen in het verzet 1940-1945* by Bob de Graaff and Lidwien Marcus (Amsterdam, 1980), who note that women were frequently used as couriers because they could hide weapons in their prams or disguise themselves as expectant mothers by padding their corsets with important documents. Marjan Schwegman's *Het stille verzet: vrouwen in illegale organisaties, Nederland 1940-1945* (Amsterdam, 1980) also looks at illegal war-time organisations and suggests a connection between the responsibilites and activities of women at this time and the later emergence of discontent with their more traditional function in the household. The diaries and letters of Etty Hillesum, published recently in *Het verstoorde leven* (Amsterdam, 18th edn, 1986), *Het denkende hart van de barak* (Haarlem, 1982) and *In duizend zoete armen* (Weesp, 3rd edn, 1984), cast a unique light upon some of the problems facing women in the 1940s and in particular Jewish women during the German occupation. Fourteen Dutch women who survived incarceration in the concentration camp of Ravensbrück recall their experiences and talk of the lasting effects in *Terug in de tijd: Nederlandse vrouwen in de jaren '40-'45*, edited by Dick Walda (Amsterdam, 1974).

During the years immediately following the war, the issues of the women's movement were anything but prominent as attention was focussed upon rebuilding the country. Some women entered into paid employment outside the home, and in *Loonarbeid van vrouwen in Nederland 1945-1955* (Nijmegen, 1978), Els Blok describes the attempts of women to gain some financial independence in the turbulent post-war years. The vast majority of women, however, slipped back into the accustomed rôle of homemaker. A recent anthology of extracts from diaries of women for all walks of life, *In verloren minuten: dagboeken en herinneringen van vrouwen 1896-1979*, edited by Annette Mevis (Weesp, 1985), includes several evocative memoirs of this period. Incidentally, this book was published in commemoration of the fiftieth anniversary of the founding of the Internationaal Archief voor de Vrouwenbeweging in Amsterdam in 1935 by Wilhelmina Posthumus-van der Goot, Johanna Naber and Rosa Manus. The Dutch government now subsidises the upkeep of the building where the *Archief* is housed, and the collections, which include the papers of Aletta Jacobs, are accessible to researchers.

The 'second wave'

In the late 1960s, the 'second wave' of feminism (referred to by some as the 'permanent wave') reached the Netherlands. It stemmed from a growing awareness of dissatisfaction with the traditional position assigned to women in society, and a new willingness to express openly this lack of fulfilment, and hence a radical reappraisal of the rôle and abilities of women. This question of frustration was addressed in a seminal article by Joke Kool-Smit entitled 'Het onbehagen bij de vrouw', which was published in the influential periodical *De Gids 130* (1967). In the context of the socio-economic and cultural developments of the 1960s, her arguments struck a resounding chord in many women and inspired among some a determination to improve the existing situation. In 1968 the pressure group Man Vrouw Maatschappij was founded, followed by the establishment of a second organisation 'Dolle Mina' (named after Wilhelmina Drucker) in 1969. These two groups contributed a great deal to the growth and vigour of the women's movement over the next few years. This early history of the 'second wave' is discussed in the excellent *Sociale atlas van de vrouw 1983*, edited by Corrine Oudijk (*Sociale en culturele studies 3*, 's-Gravenhage, 1983).

Publications such as '*Margriet weet raad*': *gevoel, gedrag, moraal in Nederland 1938-1978* by Christien Brinkgreve and Michel Korzec (Utrecht, 1978), an analysis of the startling changes in both questions and answers in the advice column of the women's magazine *Margriet* over the years, reflect the degree of social upheaval due to implications of the 'second wave' for all women in every aspect of their lives. By the early seventies the feminist movement was expanding rapidly in a number of directions. Throughout this period many individuals and groups allied themselves with single important social issues, such as the campaign for abortion on demand, known as Wij vrouwen eisen and the attempts to encourage in girls, parents and teachers an awareness that correct and informed choices about their schooling and careers is just as important for girls as for boys. This latter campaign, Marie, word wijzer, is subsidised by the government: *see*, for instance, *Om er wijzer van te worden: vrouwen over onderwijs voor vrouwen* ('s-Gravenhage, 1975). Such broadly-based struggles drew together women from political parties, the trade union movement, the more traditional women's groups and churches, as well as those who had no particular affiliation but wished to express their support for equal rights and better opportunities for women.

The Dutch government responded to the social turmoil and to the groundswell in public opinion by setting up the Nationale Adviescommissie Emancipatie in 1974, just before the commencement of the International Women's Year. The Emancipatie Kommissie (EK), as it came to be known, was planned as a temporary body to advise the government about initiating and administering coherent policies concerning equal opportunities. Apart from its quarterly reports, *EK-signalen*, it also issued separate publications on various important topics, such as the comparative study *Emancipatiebeleid in het buitenland: overzicht van structurele voorzieningen voor emancipatiebeleid in zestien westerse landen* (Rijswijk, 1979). One of the founding members of the EK, Sienie Strikwerda, was recently honoured with a collection of essays entitled *Doen we mee of blijven we aan de kant staan?*, edited by Mary Michon (Baarn, 1986).

Anders geregeld (Den Haag, 1978), an official inventory of laws and regulations which allowed discriminatory treatment of people according to their gender or their marital status, was the first step in the continuing investigations into legal reform. As part of the ongoing review of legislation, such clauses were scrapped during the consitutional reforms of 1982.

In 1981 the Emancipatieraad (ER) was installed in place of the EK, with the task of ensuring the implementation of government policy on equal opportunity in all its activities and all its departments. The government is obliged to request advice from the ER on proposals which may affect the position of women, while the ER is also empowered to issue its own reports on the government's policies on women and on issues relating to equal opportunity, and the Library has collected many of these *Adviezen, Adviesbrieven, Studies* and *Achtergrondstudies*, as well as the ER's information bulletin *Kwartaal nieuws*. The ER's recommendations for the 1990s are stated in *Emancipatieondersteuningsbeleid in de jaren negentig* (Advies no.11/63/88, Den Haag, 1988).

The equal opportunity policies of the government are also reflected in the work of individual ministries and government departments, many of which also issue reports on various issues concerning women. A valuable bibliography of such national and international publications is *Emancipatie van de vrouw: een keuze uit de literatuur over de positie en de emancipatie van de vrouw, het emancipatiebeleid en enkele daaraan verwante onderwerpen* (Den Haag, 1984).

The question of the provision of adequate child care facilities is addressed in a number of official reports, including *Werk en kinderopvang* (Den Haag, 1988) and *Kinderopvang en arbeidsparticipatie van vrouwen* by Dies Wilbrink-Griffioen, Ineke van Vliet and Anne Elzinga (Den Haag, 1987). Health and social services for women within the existing national structures were considered by the committee Project vrouwenhulpverlening, which made its recommendations in *Slangengodin & Co* (Den Haag, 1986): government progress is outlined in *Vrouwenhulpverlening: voortgangsrapportage 1987-1988* (Rijswijk, 1988). Various statistical publications examine specifically the position of women in society: for instance, *Beroepsarbeid door vrouwen in Nederland: een benadering vanuit de plaats van de vrouw in gezin en huishouden* by A B Berends and A C Boelmans-Kleinjan (*Monografieën volkstelling 1971*, no 7, 's-Gravenhage, 1979), and *M/V: mannen en vrouwen naast elkaar... een vergelijking tussen 1975 en 1985* ('s-Gravenhage, 1987), as well as *Emancipatie in cijfers* ('s-Gravenhage, 1983-1987). The *Sociale atlas van de vrouw 1983* (see above) also presents a thorough examination of the position of women in contemporary Dutch society, including some statistical information.

About 20% of the members of the Dutch Parliament are women, and in 1981 they established the Kamerbreed Vrouwen Overleg, an informal all-party group which meets monthly to discuss women's issues and which also aims to encourage the participation of women in national politics. *Vrouwen en het Binnenhof*, edited by Aneeke Groen (*Reeks Parlementaria 7*, 's-Gravenhage, 1985), includes interviews with members of the KVO and briefly discusses the history of women representatives in both houses, a subject also tackled by Marie-Louise den Bandt in *De rol van de vrouw in de Nederlandse politiek* (Den Haag, 1972), while *Vrouwen in het landbestuur: van Adela van Hamaland tot en met Koningin Juliana*, edited by C A Tamse ('s-Gravenhage, 1982)

reviews the history of Dutch women in positions of political authority. In view of
the still relatively small number of women in national politics, Agnes Koerts offers a
guide to the machinery of Dutch political life in The Hague, including a history of
the feminist lobby, in *Onze vrouw in Den Haag: machten, spelers, spel, lobby*
(Amsterdam, 1985).

Women's studies

Dutch universities reacted to the growing strength of the women's movement and
the increasing demands for a less male-dominated approach to education by
introducing departments of women's studies (often inter-faculty groupings) from the
late 1970s onwards; on the history and development of women's studies see
Historiography of women's cultural traditions, edited by Maaike Meijer and Jetty Schaap
(Dordrecht, 1987). The studies focus on the analysis of the subordinate position of
women in society, and on the work and rôle of women in a broader social context.
In the Netherlands, a country where strong emphasis is placed on research in the
social sciences and debate on sociological issues, women's studies have assumed great
significance, and much important work on all aspects of feminism and the activities
of women in both a national and an international context is published here. For
instance, Els Diekerhof, Mirjam Elias and Marjan Sax explore the problems of
discrimination facing Dutch women journalists from the nineteenth century to the
present day in *Voor zover plaats aan de perstafel: vrouwen in de dagbladjournalistiek, vroeger
en nu* (Amsterdam, 1986). Johanna van Doorne-Huiskes, *Vrouwen en beroepsparticipatie:
een onderzoek onder gehuwde vrouwelijke academici* (Utrecht, PhD thesis, 1979), discusses
the means by which married women graduates can be encouraged to take on
responsible positions at work, a question tackled further in *Women in small business:
focus on Europe* edited by Rik Donckels and Jane N Meijer (Assen, 1986), who stress
the strains of combining business and family. Trudie Knijn and Carla Verheijen also
take up the theme of the responsibilities and conflicts of motherhood for women in
contemporary Dutch society in *Tussen plicht en ontoplooiïng: het welbevinden van moeders
met jonge kinderen in een veranderende cultuur* (Nijmegen, 1988). *The changing position of
women in family and society: a cross-national comparison*, edited by Eugen Lupri (Leiden,
1983) includes a chapter on women in the Netherlands during the early 1980s; see
also *Vrouwen en maatschappij...*, by A G Weiler *et al* (*Annalen van het Thijmgenootschap*
72/2, 1984).

In a wider context Dutch women have made numerous important contributions
to feminist discussion in general. The noted feminist sociologist Anja Meulenbelt
examines the biological, psychological and conditioned differences between women
and men in *De schillen van de ui. Socialisatie: hoe zijn we vrouwen en mannen geworden*
(Amsterdam, 3rd edn, 1986), and follows this up with *De ziekte bestrijden, niet de
patient: over seksisme, racisme en klassisme* (Amsterdam, 1986). Trudie Knijn's work on
the rôle of mothers (see above) is complemented by *Unravelling fatherhood*, edited by
Knijn and Anne-Claire Mulder (Dordrecht, 1987), while the need for more female
input in administrative authorities is stressed in *Female designing in social policies*, edited

by Marieke Renoù and Janneke van Mens-Verhulst (Dordrecht, 1987). Ilana Goldman's works, *Bijdrage tot een algemene theorievorming over de vrouw in de huidige westerse maatschappij* (Utrecht, PhD thesis, 1983) and *Vrouw en beroep in de westerse samenleving: een psychoanalytische beschouwing* (Baarn, 1986), concentrate on the general framework of western society and women's position in it. *Women's language, socialization and self-image*, edited by Dédé Brouwer and Dorian de Haan (Dordrecht, 1987), examines the problems and the development of gender differences in the use of language.

The effects of feminism on disciplines such as history and literature in the Netherlands cannot be ignored. The interest in women's studies has led to a complete reappraisal of the rôle and image of women in the past. *Both Middeleeuwers over vrouwen*, edited by R E V Stuip and C Vellekoop, 2 vols (Utrecht, 1985), and *'t Is kwaad gerucht, als zij niet binnen blijft: vrouwen in oude culturen*, edited by Fokkelien van Dijk-Hemmes (Utrecht, 1986), call into question modern pre-conceptions about women in earlier societies. The negative image of women towards the end of the Middle Ages is considered in Lène Dresen-Coenders, *Het verbond van heks en duivel: een waandenkbeeld aan het begin van de moderne tijd als symptoom van een veranderende situatie van de vrouw en als middel tot hervorming der zeden* (Baarn, 1983), and also in *Tussen heks en heilige: het vrouwbeeld op de drempel van de moderne tijd, 15de/16de ereuw* (Nijmegen, 1985).

The creativity of women in oral literature is highlighted in *Ik zing mijn lied voor al wie met mij gaat: vrouwen in de volksliteratuur*, edited by Ria Lemaire (Utrecht, 1986), who also stresses the rôle of literature and literary studies in programmes of women's studies. Elly de Waard has edited two collections of feminist poetry, *Op weg naar het onbekende* (Amsterdam, 1986), and *De nieuwe wilden in de poëzie* (Amsterdam, 1987), while Christine d'Haen has released an anthology of poems in Dutch about women, *Ik ben genoemd meisje en vrouw: 500 gedichten*... (Tielt, 1980). The Library's collections also include essays and works of fiction, drama and poetry by the major contemporary women writers, such as Andreas Burnier, Renate Rubenstein and so on.

The influence of feminist theory on theology has been particularly noticeable in the Netherlands. At the Catholic University of Nijmegen from 1983 to 1986 Catharina Halkes held the first Chair in Europe in Feminism and Christianity: the title of her inaugural lecture is *Vrouwen – mannen – mensen* (Baarn, 1984), and she later published *Met Mirjam is het begonnen: opstandige vrouwen op zoek naar hun geloof* (Kampen, 1986). Other works in the Dutch collections in this field include Sieth Delhaas, *Feministische theologie: een dwaalweg* (Amersfoort, 1986), and a plea for the ordination of women priests, *Prudentes sicut serpentes: enige 'serpentinen' rond de toelating van de vrouw tot het ambt*, by A J de Groot (Nijmegen, 1985). A collection of essays, *Zij waait waarheen zij wil: opstellen over de Geest*..., edited by Riet Bons-Storm et al (Baarn, 1986), was presented to Catharina Halkes on her retirement.

The future

Since the onset of the 'second wave' of feminism over twenty years ago, the early radical ideas concerning equal rights and equal opportunities for women have been adopted and encouraged in most areas of contemporary Dutch society. The British Library's collections reflect the history and background of these far-reaching changes, as well as including representative examples of current developments in women's studies and of discussions of social issues affecting women. The plans and recommendations of the Stimuleringsgroep Emancipatie-onderzoek in *Met het oog op 2000: vrouwenstudies* ('s-Gravenhage, 1988), and the inaugural lecture *De belasting van de bevrijding*, delivered late in 1988 by Christien Brinkgreve, the new professor in women's studies at the Catholic University of Nijmegen, are a clear indication that women contemplate the future of women's studies with intelligence and enthusiasm.

Tom Geddes

Scandinavian publications since the mid-1970s

The Nordic countries have an exemplary record on the status of women in the political and intellectual sphere and in the field of public social policy and employment. To cite just a few facts: Finland was the first European country to introduce women's suffrage (in 1906) and the first country to elect women to parliament (in 1907); Iceland has a woman president; Norway has a women prime minister; in Sweden about one third of the seats in parliament and on local councils are occupied by women, and almost a third of cabinet ministers are women; in Norway over a third of cabinet posts are held by women; Denmark first ordained women clergy in 1948. All five countries are among the most advanced in the world on equal rights for the sexes; all have generous conditions of maternity and paternity leave in employment and full nursery provision for all who require it; and nowadays most would probably agree that legislative provision leaves little to be desired. Viewed from the outside, Scandinavia can be seen as a model to all in most matters affecting the situation of women; from within the respective countries, there doubtless still seems much work to be done. Some of this feeling is shown in the publications of recent years – but these publications are also in themselves evidence of the healthy state of women's studies in those countries.

The British Library's Scandinavian collections are rich in material relating to women and women's studies in both earlier and modern periods, but since space does not permit a full coverage here, the following survey is restricted to the last decade or so, a period which corresponds to the tremendous growth in relevant publishing that has followed the 'new' women's movement since the late 1960s, but presents only a sample of the total material acquired. It is complemented by a closer examination of Norwegian women writers by Barbara Hawes, to exemplify literary production.

The post-1975 British Library subject catalogue includes at present 315 books from Scandinavia under the simple term *women*; if this term is 'truncated' in a computer search to include all phrases beginning *women('s)*, then the number of titles found expands to 455. Apart from the 'controlled vocabulary' of the Library's subject indexing system, one can also search on-line for the Scandinavian words for 'women' appearing in book titles: such a search (excluding Finnish) produces 480 titles. Allowing for the overlap, the total is 550, but to this would have to be added an unknown quantity of books on related subjects, in non-Scandinavian languages or with oblique titles. A full search on all relevant subject terms could well increase the total by half as much again, and that just for 1976-87. Such figures exclude women literary writers and most secondary literature on them.

It would not do justice to the collections to try to delimit this presentation to particular trends. Instead, the sample, which does not pretend to be evaluative, will start with bibliographies and serials, and go on to cover literature, language, the arts, history, politics, the women's movement, society, inter-personal relations, and topics not specifically related to Scandinavia. References will normally be to titles (in the original language to allow access to full details in the BL catalogue) rather than to authors, since the titles are more informative. An English versions is appended in square brackets where the meaning is significant or not obvious from the context. Much academic work in the Scandinavian languages or Finnish includes an English-language summary, but this fact will not normally be mentioned here, nor will the presence of often invaluable bibliographies. The general coverage of recent resources from Scandinavia may serve as a complement to some of the more specific presentations relating to other countries in this Colloquium and as an indicator of a similar range of material that can be found from many other areas. Users of the Library's subject catalogue should however be aware that many books from France, Germany and the USA were not entered in the subject catalogue in the late 1970s and early 1980s, and that this catalogue is in abeyance for all foreign books from mid-1988.

For bibliographical works, it seems useful to mention a fairly comprehensive selection of recent titles – but here as elsewhere it should be remembered that the British Library collections also contain older material, and indeed that the concept of women's studies is by no means a new one in Scandinavia: Albert Thura's *Gynæceum Daniæ Litterarum* was published in Altona, then under Danish rule, as early as 1732. This Latin work, a bio-bibliography of Danish 'women of letters', mentions a total of 180 names. By contrast, one of the most useful current bibliographies is *Ny litteratur om kvinnor/New literature on women*, a quarterly publication, international in scope and including journal articles as well as monographs. It is based on the humanities and social sciences intake of Gothenburg University Library, whose women's studies collections are described in *Bibliotheca feminarum: om de kvinnohistoriska samlingarna i Göteborg*. Relating specifically to Sweden is *Kvinnor och kvinnohistoria i Sverige: förteckning över bibliografier* [Women and women's history in Sweden: list of bibliographies], which complements bibliographies of bibliographies from other countries, such as those of Patricia Ballou, Margrit Eichler or Maureen Ritchie. There are several bibliographies from Denmark: *Kvindeforskning og kvindelitteraturen* [Women's literature and research on women] covers women writers and women's studies in Scandinavia as a whole; on Danish material in particular are *Danske bøger om kvindesag* [Danish books on the women's question], *Kvinders historie: annoteret litteraturliste* [Women's history: annotated book list], *A selection of recent Danish feminological publications* (exhibition catalogue compiled by Jette Drastrup & N Koch), and KVINFOs *bibliografiserie* [Bibliographical series from KVINFO, Centre for Interdisciplinary Information on Women's Studies], comprising various subject bibliographies on topics such as literature, language, periodicals, and even one on men. Norwegian bibliographies include *Kvinnesak og kjønnsroller 1965-1974* [The women's question and sex roles]; *Kvinnerelevante artikler i norske tidsskrifter* [Articles relating to women in Norwegian periodicals], and *Forskning om kvinner... 1975-81* [Research on women]. From Finland, *Naistutkimuskirjallisuutta* [Literature on women's studies], although based on the holdings of Oulu University Library, is a bibliography which provides a good general coverage of both Scandinavian and international material. A short and incomplete bibliography of material in English appeared under the title 'Women in Scandinavia' in *Scandinavia Review* (New York), 1977, no.3.

In the literary field, the following bibliographies are worth noting: *Dansk kvindelitteratur 1970-79: bibliografi over kvindelige forfatteres lyrik, romaner, noveller og dramatik* [Danish women's literature... poetry, novels, short stories and plays]; *Kvinnan inom svenska litteraturen intill... 1893* [Women in Swedish literature to 1893] (a recent facsimile); *Kvinnliga författare 1893-1899: biobibliografi över svensk och finlandssvensk skönlitteratur* [Women writers: bio-bibliography of Swedish and Finland-Swedish literature]; *Kvinnliga författare*, a bio-bibliography of Finland-Swedish women writers to 1892 intended to complement the above facsimile. These last two emanate from longer-term women's literature projects at Uppsala and Turku respectively.

Other specialised bibliographies include: *Vold, voldtægt, incest... artikler, bøger og film i Danmark* [Violence, rape, incest... articles, books and films in Denmark]; *Graviditet, fødsel... en annoteret bibliografi* [Pregnancy, birth... an annotated bibliography]; *Women and mathematics, science and engineering... annotated bibliography; Litteratur om kvinder i u-lande* [Literature on women in developing countries]; and *Women in Tanzania: an analytical bibliography*.

Serials comprise journals, monographic series, and annuals. Those mentioned here are among the ones devoted exclusively to women's studies, although many others also include relevant material. Denmark has two English-language titles, *EWL-European women's law* and *European women's studies in social sciences*, both monographic series which began in 1982; and *Serie om kvindeforskning*, which covers a wider range of women's topics (also entitled *Women's studies series*, since some individual volumes are in English). Journals range from the more academic *Forum for kvindeforskning* to the more popular *Kvindespor*. General series include *Kvindestudier*, an annual volume of articles on 'interdisciplinary feminology' based on lectures for university extension courses; *Skriftserie fra Arbejdsgruppen for kvindestudier* (a monograph series from a study group at Odense University); and *Årbog for kvindeforskning* (a yearbook of research published by the Centre for Women's Studies at Copenhagen University). There are two further titles in the sphere of law: *Kvinderetlig skriftserie* [Women's law monograph series] and *Årbog for kvinderet* [Women's law yearbook]; and two on Third World questions: *U-landskvinden* [Women in developing countries], and *KULU-bladet*, from a women's committee on developing countries.

An English-language series from Norway is also on law: *Working papers in women's law*, from Oslo University; in Norwegian, *Kvinneretslige studier* [Studies on women's law] was a separately published series which now forms part of the *Institutt for offentlig retts skriftserie* [Monograph series for the Department of Public Law]. The Secretariat for Women's Studies of the Norwegian Research Countil (NAVFs sekretariat for kvinneforskning) publishes a series of working papers (Arbeidsnotat) on various topics, of which the BL has acquired a selection.

Recent English-language serials from Sweden are *Göteborg women's studies* and *Uppsala women's studies*, which began in 1986 and 1987 respectively. *Kvinnovetenskaplig tidskrift* is an academic quarterly from Lund that began in 1980. At a less academic level are *Kvinnotidningen Q*, of which the BL holds a short run in the 1980s, and *Kvinnobulletinen*, which defines itself as a socialist-feminist journal and contains some rather 'popular'-level polemic as well as more serious political articles. A selection from that journal in the decade 1970-80 has been published in book form under the title *Gråt inte, kämpa* [Don't cry, fight].

One periodical above all others must be singled out: *Hertha* began life in 1859 under the title *Tidskrift för Hemmet* [Home journal], changing to *Dagny* in 1886, and taking its present title in 1914 from a novel by Fredrika Bremer (1801-65), who is best known outside Sweden for her impressions of women's conditions in the USA (*The homes of the New World*, 1853). *Hertha* is published by the Fredrika-Bremer-Förbund, a long-established association in the Swedish women's movement. The Library's holdings run from 1859 to 1926 and resume again from 1975. It describes itself as the longest-running journal of its kind, and can indeed have few contenders for longevity and commitment to the women's cause.

Women literary writers should be proportionately as well represented in the BL collections as in their own national literatures, and no attempt will be made to list them here. Norwegian writers are the subject of a separate brief presentation, together with some relevant secondary literature. Before passing to literary studies from Denmark and Sweden, however, attention should be drawn to a recent Norwegian book on female characters in the Icelandic sagas, *Skjebneveven* [Web of fate].

Danish literary history includes *Dansk kvindelitteratur 1885-1920* [Danish women's literature], *Det moderne gennembruds kvinder* [Women of the modern (literary) breakthrough], *Danske kvindelige forfattere* [Danish women writers], *Undertrykkelse, oplevelse og modstand i den nye kvinderoman* [Repression, experience and resistance in the new women's novel], *Lysthuse* [Summer-houses] (on Scandinavian women writers), and *Den bristende uskyld* [Disappearing innocence] (on female characters in nineteenth century Scandinavian drama). *De knuste spejle: billeder og modbilleder i kvindelitteratur* [Cracked mirrors: pictures and reflections in women's literature] is a critical investigation of both fiction and non-fiction, and *Digternes damer* [Writers' ladies] is a volume of essays on women in literature. *Kvindelitteratur og kvindesituation* [Women's literature and situation] looks at various aspects of literary production, and *Kvindeoffentlighed 1968-75* [Women in public] links women's literature and the women's movement in Denmark. Studies of individual authors include three in the 1980s on Karen Blixen (made better known abroad by the film of *Out of Africa* than by the English biography), Marie Bregendahl, Thit Jensen, and on female characters in the works of Holberg and Nexø.

Mothers – Saviours – Peacemakers: Swedish women writers in the twentieth century is a useful English-language presentation of recent Swedish literature; *Kvinnornas litteraturhistoria* [A women's history of literature] presents Swedish women writers in a two volume collection of specially commissioned essays written by women. On Scandinavian literature there is *Kvinnor och skapande* [Women and creativity], a festschrift collection of essays; and on Swedish literature *Kvinnomedvetande* [Female consciousness], investigating the portrayal of women, family and class, *Det underordnade jaget* [The subordinated self] on women's autobiographies, *Ämnar kanske fröken publicera något?* [Are you thinking of publishing something, Miss?], summarised in English as 'Female and male in short stories of the 1880s'. Individual author studies include monographs on Victoria Benedictsson, Karin Boye, Anne Charlotte Leffler, and Moa Martinson. One should also point to a slight increase in English translations of women writers in recent years, partly due to the advent of feminist presses in Britain and the USA. Recent Swedish examples are books by Margareta Bergman, Karin Boye, Margareta Ekström, Moa Martinson, Selma Lagerlöf; and from Finland-Swedish Solveig von Schoultz, Edith Södergran and Märta Tikkanen (though the relative success of one book by this last author, *Manrape*, had perhaps less to do with literary merit than with the subject matter and a subsequent film). At a more popular level the socially-committed detective stories of the Swedish wife and husband team Maj Sjöwall and Per Wahlöö are well known; and among children's writers in translation are Astrid Lindgren (Pippi Longstocking and much else), Barbro Lindgren, Elsa Beskow and the Finland-Swedish writer Tove Jansson (the Moomin characters). For children's and 'popular' literature, the BL may not necessarily hold all the original language works by a particular author, though there may be a representative sample; for more serious literature, one should expect to find all original works in the collections.

For Finland, attention should be drawn to two poetry anthologies, *Suomalaisen naisen viisautta* [The wisdom of Finnish women], a compilation extending to over 500 pages; and at half that length *Du tror du kuvar mig liv? Finländska kvinnors lyrik genom tiderna* [You think you can suppress life in me? Finnish women's poetry through the ages], which brings together Swedish-language poetry and Finnish poetry in Swedish translation. Two very recent studies of Finland-Swedish literature are *Från Fredrika Runeberg till Märta Tikkanen*, subtitled 'freedom and dependence in Finland-Swedish women's literature', and *Hur flickor blir kloka: om flickuppväxt i nyare finlandssvensk litteratur*, on adolescent girls in Finland-Swedish literature.

The growth of interest in sociolinguistics has led to a number of books on women and language, including *Kvindesprog* [Women's language], from Denmark, dealing with the socio-psychological aspects of oral language; *Språk og kvinneundertrykking* [Language and the suppression of women], from Norway; and the Finnish *Isosuinen nainen* [The loud-mouthed woman], essays on sexual differences in the spoken and written language. Relevant articles and bibliographies will also be found in the annual publication *Språk i Norden* [Language in Scandinavia].

Women artists are the subject of *Kvindelige kunstnere*, on European women painters, composers and writers of the sixteenth and seventeenth centuries; *Kvinna och konstnär*, also on individual women from all of Europe, 1600-1970; *Danske kvindelige kunstnere*, on Danish women artists of the nineteenth and twentieth centuries; *En oversigt over ca. 1000 kvindelige bildende kunstnere*, a survey of 1000 Danish women artists whose work appeared in a two and a half year period following International Women's Year in 1975. *Kvinner ved staffeliet* [Women at the easel] and *Kvinners bilder* [Women's pictures], are both on Norwegian artists up to 1900; and *Kvinne & kunstnar* also deals with Norwegian artists. Swedish artists form the subject of *Kvinnor som konstnärer* [Women as artists] and *Kvinnliga konstnärer i Sverige* [Women artists in Sweden]. There are books on the representation of women in art, for example in the paintings of Carl Larsson.

Architecture features in *Bygga och bo på kvinnors villkor* [Build and live according to women's demands], *Boligrammer – menneskeværd: en kvinderapport* [A framework for building – human values: a women's report], and *Women's expressions on the environment*, about the work of women architects, planners and artists in Denmark. Books on the cinema include *Suomalaisen elokuvan naiskuva* [Women in Finnish films], *Billeder af en ny virkelighed?* [Images of a new reality?], about female characters in films (internationally), and *Film af/om kvinder* [Films by/about women] (a catalogue also international in scope). Three relevant books on music are *Kvinnor i rockhistorien* [Women in the history of rock], on British and American soloists and groups, *Kvinner komponerer*, on Norwegian women composers, and *Borgerliga kvinnors musicerande*, on nineteenth-century women musicians in Sweden.

Turning to the media, women journalists over the last 150 years are the subject of *Kvinner i norsk presse* [Women in the Norwegian press], and Swedish journalists from 1690 to 1975 that of *Pennskaft* [Penholder]. *Äntligen ord från qwinnohopen* [Words at last from the women] presents research on the eighteenth-century Swedish magazine press for women, *Kvinder: klasser og ugeblade* [Women: class and the weeklies] deals with Danish women's magazines, *Blikfang: om kvindæstetik og dameblade* [Eyecatcher: on women's aesthetics and women's magazines] has a more international perspective, and *Kvinne i ramme* [Women framed] analyses sex rôles in magazine advertisements. The possibly sexist bias of current affairs reporting in Finland is investigated in *Kvinnlig och manlig journalistik: nyhetsvärdering ur jämställdhetssynvinkel* [Male and female journalism: news evaluation from the viewpoint of equality].

In the historical field there is a substantial English-language book on Denmark: *Women in Denmark yesterday and today*; a general historical presentation can also be found in the two-volume *Kvindfolk: en danmarkhistorie fra 1600 til 1980*, and *Kvindeværd: kvindelighedens teori og socialhistorie* [Women's values], a discussion of theoretical approaches to women's situation, including an examination of Marxist theories. Material on the Middle Ages includes *Kvindeskikkelser ... i Danmarks middelalder* [Female figures in mediaeval Denmark]; *Kvinder i middelalderen*, conference papers on women in mediaeval Scandinavia; *Aspects of female existence ... women in the Middle Ages*, conference papers mainly in English and not limited to Scandinavia; *Den frugtsommelige abbedisse* [The pregnant abbess], on women and power in Europe. *Satans store port* [Satan's great gate] deals with women and children in fourteenth-century Denmark, and *Kvindekår ... i reformationens århundrede* is a study focussing on the town of Ribe in the sixteenth century. Bringing us up to date is *Det besatte køn:*

kvindelighedsdannelse fra Reformationen til i dag [The obsessed sex], on the concept of femininity. For the modern period, there are general studies: *Kvindekøn... 1880-1980* [The female sex]; studies of the working classes: *Arbejderkvinder... i københavn ca.1870-1906* and *Arbejderkvinder i Danmark... 1924-1939*; and also a social history of women in Copenhagen 1880-1920, *Rent og urent* [Clean and unclean]. The Second World War provides the specific circumstances for *Kvinder i modstandskampen* [Women in the Resistance] and *Sigtet for spionage* [Charged with spying], on women imprisoned by the Gestapo. Two other items of interest are a facsimile reissue of *Den danske Kvindes Historie... 1701-1917*, and a book published in Sweden on women in the chronicle of the mediaeval Danish historian Saxo Grammaticus, *Kvinnor och män i Gesta Danorum*.

From Sweden, studies of the mediaeval period include *Kvinnans ekonomiska ställning*, papers summarised in English under the general title of 'The economic conditions of women in the medieval North'. *Häxornas Europa 1400-1700* is a collection of essays on the persecution of witches, written by specialists from around the world. Swedish history is covered in *Kvinnans rättsliga... ställning... 1750-1976* [Women's legal status], *Konsten att blifva en god flicka* [The art of being a good girl], a collection of essays on women's history, and *I kvinnoled*, a twentieth-century social history on the transmission of values in family life. Monographs on particular topics include women's sport (*Kvinnoidrottens utveckling i Sverige*), working-class women (*De få vara tacksamma...* [They ought to be grateful]), and domestic servants (*Från tjänstehjon till hembiträde*, summary in English entitled 'From household drudge to domestic servant'). *Handbok i svensk kvinnohistoria* provides a good overall introductory coverage, while *Manliga strukturer...* [Male structures and female strategies] has the distinction of being a festschrift presented to the first professor of women's history in Sweden, and indeed in Scandinavia.

Norway has produced books ranging from the Viking period (*Vikingkvinnen*) to the Occupation (*Dømte kvinner*). On modern history, two recent books have been entitled *Kvinner selv* [Women themselves], one describing itself as the hidden history of Norway, the other a collection of seven essays on various topics. *Kvinnenes kulturhistorie* attempts a world-wide cultural history in two volumes, useful and well-illustrated if at times verging on the popular. *Kvinnfolkarbeid* deals with the employment of women in the period 1875-1910. From Finland there are books on the war years: *Yhteinen tulikoe* [A common ordeal], a collection of personal experiences written by women; and on the rôle of women in society: *Vapautta naisille!* [Freedom for women!]; a collective biography summarised in English as 'The influential Finnish woman' (*Suomalaisia vaikuttajanaisia*); and a substantial volume of European history in a Swedish translation from the Finnish (*Evas döttrar* [Daughters of Eve]). A full coverage of the history of women's employment in Iceland is provided by *Vinna kvenna á Íslandi i 1100 ár*.

Current politics are the subject of *Kvinnan i politiken* (from Sweden) and *Kvinder og politik* (from Denmark). *Utvalgt til Stortinget* [Elected to Parliament] adopts a more historical approach to Norwegian politics, while *Gro* affectionately takes the prime minister's first name as the title of a study of her first years in office. *Welfare state and woman power: essays in state feminism* is an English-language work from Norway of more general interest. The Nordic Council of Ministers has published a book on women in national and local politics in Scandinavia under the title *Vi har ventet længe nok* [We have waited long enough]. Party politics are represented by *Framåt systrar!* [Forward, sisters!] from Sweden's Centre Party. *Women in political 'movement'* and *The Swedish woman in political life* are two English-language items from Sweden, the latter simply an 8-page leaflet in the Swedish Institute's prolific series *Current Sweden*, but a useful introduction nevertheless.

As we have seen from the serials mentioned above, there is ample material on law. One of the most recent books is in English from the Norwegian University Press: *Women's law: an introduction to feminist jurisprudence*. Denmark gives us *Women's law in Scandinavia* and *Equality legislation in a comparative perspective — towards state feminism? Ligestillingslovgivning* is a comparative study of European equal opportunity laws, and *Kvinder i retslivet* looks at discrimination against women in the Danish legal system.

In moving from history, politics and law to contemporary society, it might be opportune to single out a few of the many books on the women's movement as such. *Likhet eller särart* [Similarity or difference], with English summary, is an analysis of the ideas of the women's movement from America in the 1960s to Sweden in the '80s. *Studier i den svenska kvinnorörelsen* has an English summary entitled 'Studies on the Swedish women's movement'; *Jämställdhet eller emancipation* [Equality or emancipation] is a Swedish title from the Department of Women's Studies at Åbo University (Turku, Finland) which looks at strategies in the women's movement; *Bak slagordene* [Behind the slogans] deals with the new movement in Norway; *Kvindeoffentlighed 1968-75* investigates the rôle of women writers in the movement in Denmark, where earlier developments are examined in *Bidrag til den danske kvindebevægelses historie 1870-1900*. *Kvindebevægelsens hvem — hvad — hvor*, the who/what/where of the women's movement, tries to cover a number of topics and a rather arbitrary selection of countries from the developed and developing world; it is held only in its first (1975) edition, but is still of historical interest. *Kvindehåndbogen* is a directory of groups in Denmark, and *Vi kan, vi behövs!* [We can, we're needed!] deals with associations in Sweden. There is a steadily increasing number of books looking back to the early women's movement (*Kvinnokrav* on the period 1902-21 and *Kvinnor i facklig... kamp* on political demands between 1880 and 1920 may serve as examples) and on individual activists (Fredrika Bremer, Adolphina Fridolin, Ellen Key, Agneta Klingspor, Aasta Hansteen).

Books on women in contemporary society that do not fall into other categories are too diverse and numerous to allow any really representative sample (Denmark and Sweden about sixty each, Norway thirty and Finland a dozen in the period under consideration). A number of English-language titles deserve inclusion for their linguistic accessibility: *Sex roles in transition, Equality is the goal, Swedish women on the move, Women in Denmark in the 1980s, Side by side... equality... in Sweden, Strategies for integrating women into the labour market, Capitalism and patriarchy, On the social mobility of women in the Scandinavian countries, Social mobility... women in France and Sweden, Women and decision-making, Cultural identity: immigrant women in Sweden*. There are several books on this last subject, including *Invandrade kvinnor i Norden* [Immigrant women in Scandinavia]. Employment issues range from the general to particular work environments (*Kvinnor och arbete* [Women and work], *Kvinder på fabrik* [Women in factories]), from part-time employment (*Deltid – kvindetid*) to the effects of technical advances on housework (*Teknologiens Tommeliden*) or pension provision (*Omkring de særlige pensionsregler for kvinder*). One alternative to employment is crime, of course, and this is covered in *Kvindekriminalitet* from Denmark, with Sweden providing a sequel on conditions in women's prisons: *I de fördömdas värld*. There is a number of books on education, ranging from *Børnehave* (nursery schools in Denmark) through *Piger i gymnasiet* (girls in Danish secondary education) and *Kunnskap uten makt* [Knowledge without power] on Norwegian women in education as both pupils and teachers, to *Kampen om katedern* [Battle for the (teacher's) rostrum] on what the author describes in her English summary as the feminization of the teaching profession in Sweden in the second half of the nineteenth century. The church has been much written about recently, particularly the subject of women priests: *Myten om madonnan* [The myth of the madonna], which sees the problem in a historical perspective of repression, is but one example. *Naiset eivät vaienneet* (with English summary) discusses the contribution of women evangelists to the Finnish pentecostal movement. Moving back to the more general, a new biographical work is to be published regularly from 1988: *Vem är hon? Kvinnor i Sverige*, a 'Who's who?' of women in Sweden (the 1988 volume contains over 600 pages).

There are very many books on personal relationships between the sexes, from rape and incest (*eg Våld mot kvinnor* [Violence against women]), to women's sexual feelings and experiences (*Den svenska kvinnorapporten*, or its Norwegian equivalent *Kvinners seksualitet*), lesbianism (*Homofile*, on male and female homosexuality in Norway), sex rôles (*Manlig, kvinnlig, stressad* [Male, female, stressed]), perception differences between the sexes (*Två världar* [Two worlds]), and on femininity (*Kvindens naturer*).

Finally to non-Scandinavian topics: for space reasons only books in English will be mentioned by title here; otherwise just an indication of subject will be given. There is a wealth of material from Scandinavia on developing countries: *Women in Tanzania, The peripheral centre: Swedish assistance to Africa in relation to women, Women in Africa and development assistance, Tanzanian rural women, Women's programmes in Zimbabwe, Women of Namibia, The village woman in Ghana*, and *An annotated bibliography on female genital mutilations in Africa*. In Scandinavian languages there are books on women in Angola, Botswana, the Congo, and Vietnam; in Japan, China, the Soviet Union, Poland, Albania and in West European countries. The other most prolific non-Scandinavian field appears to be that of literature, where Finland has produced *Women's suffrage and fiction in England 1905-1914*, and Norway *Two women characters in Čechov's work*, and books on women in Russian and European literature. From Denmark there are studies of English and American literature (Charlotte Brontë, Sylvia Plath, black women writers); German literature: women in Fontane and Böll; Russian literature: women in Dostoevsky. Books from Sweden include women in science fiction and in the works of Heinrich Mann and Heinrich Böll, and *The portrayal of women in the fiction of Henry Handel [ie Ethel Florence] Richardson* and *Portraits of women in . . . Virginia Woolf and E M Forster*.

The limited period under review has produced at least 20 Scandinavian conferences on aspects of women's studies whose published proceedings are in the BL. It is beyond the scope of this present survey to give details of them or of the more permanent centres of research on women's studies in Scandinavia. A list of the latter can be found in *Kvinnovetenskaplig tidskrift*, 1988, no.1, which might be of use for those who wish to make contact with Scandinavian colleagues. It is hoped that this cursory overview will help to stimulate awareness and use of the Scandinavian research represented in the British Library collections.

Barbara Hawes

Norwegian women writers

The four best-known names in Norwegian literature are Ibsen, Bjørnson, Kielland and Lie. These four authors were all writing in the second half of the nineteenth century and they were all men. However, in the last ten years or so, with the growing interest in women's studies, it has become more common to find reference to another 'four greats' in Norwegian literature. These four are women writers and are evidence of an equally fine literary tradition. They are Camilla Collett (1813-95), Amalie Skram (1846-1904), Sigrid Undset (1882-1949) and Cora Sandel (1880-1974). In this brief survey (restricted to the nineteenth and twentieth centuries) an attempt has been made to show how rich that tradition is and to what degree the British Library holdings provide source material for those interested in this subject.

Primary sources

For the reader without Norwegian linguistic skills the range of material is necessarily limited. Of the four women writers listed above, three have had works translated into English. Sigrid Undset's fame as a Nobel prize winner in 1928 ensured that most of her work has been translated into English and the Library has a comprehensive collection of these translations, numbering 22 in total (including some multiple editions). She is best known for her multi-volume historical novels, particularly *Kristin Lavransdatter* (1920-22) and *Olav Audunsson* (1925-27), but also for works set in contemporary times such as *Jenny* (1911). In these works, but also more directly in a collection of essays *Et kvinnesynspunkt* (1919) [A woman's point of view] she deals with the problems of personal responsibility, particularly as it affects women.

The work of Cora Sandel is also well represented in translation. The 'Alberte' trilogy, *Alberte og Jacob, Alberte og friheten, Bare Alberte* (1926-39) [*Alberte and Jacob, Alberte and freedom, Alberte alone*], is perhaps the best known but Sandel was also a prolific short story writer and some of these stories are available in translation, such as *Kjøp ikke Dondi*, translated as *The Leech*. Originally published in the 1960s by Owen, these translations have in the last ten years been republished by The Women's Press. As a recent critic has pointed out, Sandel's work has much in common with contemporary feminist thinking, its message being that 'to enhance private happiness necessitates political action'.

Of Amalie Skram's work only two titles have been translated, one *Professor Hieronymus* (1895) and the other *Forraadt* (1892) [*Betrayed*]. The former was translated in 1899, very close to its original date of publication. The latter has been translated more recently (1986) and published by Pandora, again reflecting the more recent interest in women's literature. Both are to some degree autobiographical and caused a scandal when they originally came out by their frank discussion of sexuality and double standards. Many of Skram's best known novels, such as the four volume work *Hellemyrsfolket* (1887–98) [The people of Hellemyr], have not as yet been translated. However, to bring this survey up-to-date, a translation of *Constance Ring* (1885) was published last year by The Seal Press (USA) and will be acquired shortly.

For those British Library users able to read works in the original language there is a very substantial collection of works by Norwegian women writers. Foremost among these are the novels and autobiographical works of Camilla Collett, who is usually regarded as the pioneer not only of Norwegian women's literature but also of the wider women's movement within Scandinavia. There is a complete set of her collected works. Her *Amtmandens Døttre* (1885) [The Governor's daughters] is a classic in Norwegian literature being one of the first to discuss the lot of women brought up with marriage as their only aim. A thorough analysis of this novel is also held, entitled *Women and literature – Camilla Collett – Amtmandens Døttre and the critics*.

Nor is it just the 'classics' which are to be found. There is a considerable number of women writers from this century whose works have been acquired. Within the limited space available it is only possible to mention a few. The authorship of Torborg Nedreaas (1906–), although not complete, is well represented. Her best known works are short stories and novels, notably the trilogy *Trylleglasset, Musikk fra en blå brønn* and *Ved neste nymåne* (1950–71) [The magic glass, Music from a blue well, At the next new moon] but the Library also holds examples of her articles and plays. As with many other Norwegian women writers there is a strong political message in her work and a recurrent theme is how the vulnerable and inarticulate (and for Nedreaas this means particularly women) cope with everyday life. Again it is encouraging to note that within the last year translations of two of Nedreaas' novels *Musikk fra en blå brønn* [*Music from a blue well*] and *Av måneskinn gror det ingenting* (1947) [*Nothing grows by moonlight*] have been published by the University Press of Nebraska.

To turn to another genre, poetry, the works of the poet Halldis Moren Vesaas (1907–) are representative of what is best in this literary form, and seven of her poetry collections are held, among them *I ein annan skog* (1955) [In another forest], as well as two autobiographical pieces. The work of short story writer Bjørg Vik (1935–), one of Norway's most popular contemporary literary figures, is also well covered, with ten short story selections, one of which, *En håndfull lengsel (1979)* [*Out of season and other stories*] has been translated into English. *Kvinneakvariet* (1972) [*An aquarium of women*] has also recently (1987) been translated and is published by Norvik Press.

In addition to works of individual writers, a number of anthologies are available, such as *Kvinner i nynorsk prosa* [Women in New Norwegian prose] and, covering an earlier period, *Fra gamle dager: memoarer, dagboker, salmer og dikt av kvinner ca. 1660-1880* [From the old days: memoirs, diaries, hymns and poems by women].

Other Norwegian women writers of repute whose work is held include Astrid Hjertnaes Andersen, Nini Roll Anker, Magnhild Haalke, Aasta Hansteen, Ingeborg

Hagen, Inger Hagerup, Ebba Haslund, Gunvor Hofmo, Liv Koltzow, Cecilie Løveid, Vigdis Stokkelien, Marie Takvam, Merete Wiger and Dikken Zwilgmeyer.

Secondary sources

Most secondary source material in this area is in Norwegian. There are two comprehensive bibliographies, *Dette skrev kvinner* [This is what women wrote] and *Norske kvinnelige forfattere til og med 1900* [Norwegian women writers to 1900]. There are also a number of general works on the subject, the most comprehensive of these being: *Gjennom kvinneøyne: Norske kvinners litteraturkritikk og reaksjon på litteratur 1880-1930 & 1930-1980* (2 vols) [Through the eyes of women: Norwegian women's literary criticism and reaction to literature]; *Et annet språk: analyser av norsk kvinnelitteratur* [Another language: analyses of Norwegian women's literature]; and *Frihet til å skrive: artikler om kvinnelitteratur fra Amalie Skram til Cecilie Løveid* [The freedom to write: articles on women's literature from Amalie Skram to Cecilie Løveid]. Two very recent (1988/1989) acquisitions deserving special attention are: *Kvinners spor i skrift* [Women's legacy in literature] which describes itself as 'a supplement to Norwegian literary history' and aims to provide an outline of women writers in Norway from medieval times to the present day; and the first volume of *Norsk kvinnelitteraturhistorie* [Norwegian women's literary history].

For the English reader *Mothers and daughters as portrayed by Norwegian women writers from 1854 to the present day* provides an interesting and readable introduction to the subject. The number of books devoted to just one author is somewhat limited and tends to cover better known writers such as Undset and Collett and to be found only in Norwegian.

One of the most valuable but often more elusive sources of secondary material is journal articles. Bibliographical access to this type of material can be found by a number of approaches including the use of tools such as the *MLA annual bibliography* and the bibliography in *Norsk litteraer årbok* [Norwegian literary yearbook]. The journals which often cover relevant material include *Basar, Edda, Kontrast, The Norseman, Norsk litteraer årbok, Norwegian-American Studies, Scandinavian Review, Scandinavian Studies, Scandinavica, Vinduet,* – all held by the Library. Even in journals published in Norway, such as *Edda*, articles are often written in English and are undoubtedly the best way of keeping up-to-date on the subject. Three illustrative examples will suffice: Janet Rasmussen's 'Feminist criticism and women's literature in Norway: a status report', in *Edda* (1980); Nancy Ramsey's 'Cora Sandel and *Alberte*', in *Norseman*, 15 (1957); Carla Waal's 'The Norwegian short story: Bjørg Vik,', in: *Scandinavian Studies*, 49 (1977).

For reasons of space this presentation has been a limited one and it is important to point out that much valuable and interesting material has been omitted. Nor has it been possible to give a fair picture of the *quality* of the literature available. However it will have given some indication of the extent of the collection in the comparatively small area of Norwegian women's literature, and thus of the resources that may similarly be assumed to exist for other Scandinavian and indeed other European languages.

Janet Zmroczek

Women in the Soviet Union from 1917 to the present: sources for research

Interest in Soviet women began early in the development of women's studies because the Soviet experience presents a view of the question of women's rôle in society which is startlingly different to that of the capitalist west. However, the discovery that many aspects of inequality are replicated in an avowedly socialist state helped in the realisation that women's lives and problems have fundamental similarities regardless of the prevailing state ideology.

Discussion of the 'woman question', which had begun in nineteenth century Russia, blossomed in the intellectual ferment of the revolutionary period largely because of the efforts made by remarkable women like Aleksandra Kollontai. However, from the early 1930s onwards Stalin's assault on all areas of social and private life saw an erosion of the rights women had gained. Whilst lip service was paid to the concept of sexual equality and the facilitation of full participation by women in public life, under Stalin the subject was virtually closed. It was not until the 1960s that serious discussion began to abound once more. An interest has remained, but the discourse has never regained the intensity and fire of the early revolutionary period.

This paper presents a brief analysis of the major developments of the period 1917-1928, identifying key areas of interest relating to women's rôle in society, followed by a thematic treatment of them down to the present.

The survey offers an introduction to the findings made during the compilation of a bibliography of approximately 450 items which will be expanded and made available in the future. All items cited are held by the British Library. The study concentrates on monographs although recognising the potential for a further study of journal articles.*

The British Library collections are a remarkably rich source of materials for the study of Soviet women. They have been systematically acquired by donation, by purchase and by exchange; exchange playing the major rôle in current acquisitions. Material published in the Soviet Union is supplemented by a growing number of western publications, particularly from the United States.

---

*At the time of writing I had found no single authoritative bibliography on Soviet women; however in the interim period I have found a bibliography entitled *Women in Russia and the Soviet Union, December 1984*. Ottawa: Carleton University, 1985 compiled by Tova Yedlin and Jean Wilman, and a *Supplement* compiled by Janet Hyer and published in 1987 or 1988. However, I have not as yet seen these works and am thus unable to offer comment.

Sources used for this paper include printed catalogues such as the New York Public Library *Dictionary Catalog of the Slavonic Collection*, the British Library's *General Catalogue of Printed Books* and various *Subject Indexes*, the British Library online databases available on BLAISE-LINE, eg the H&SS file and the BNBC files, Soviet printed bibliographies such as the *Ezhegodniki*, abstracting journals such as *The American bibliography of Slavic and East European studies* and finally the bibliographies in monographs. Two excellent examples are to be found in Gail Warshofsky Lapidus' *Women in Soviet society* (Berkeley, 1978) and the post-1917 selection of Richard Stites' bibliography in *The women's liberation movement in Russia 1860-1930* (Princeton, 1978). These two works provide authoritative historical reviews of women in the Soviet Union and form part of the large body of literature offering a general historical overview which has been published in both the Soviet Union and the west from the 1920s onwards. Of the Soviet publications, often rather blandly propagandistic in style and content, the more interesting general works include P M Chirkov's *Reshenie zhenskogo voprosa v SSSR (1917-37 gg)*. (Moskva, 1978) and *Zhenshchiny strany sovetov: kratkii istoricheskii ocherk* (Moskva, 1977).

The Revolutionary Period 1917-28

The decade following the Revolution of 1917 was an era of ground-breaking experimentation and attempts to remodel society. High priority was attached to the question of the new Soviet woman and her rôle. A large body of legislation was passed on equal pay, marriage, custody of children, abortion and divorce laws. Useful sources include works in English: *Marriage laws in Soviet Russia: complete text of the first Code of Laws ... dealing with civil status and domestic relations* (New York, 1921) and Rudolf Schlesinger's valuable work of 1949 *The family in the USSR: documents and readings* (London, 1949).

Legislation was, of course, not enough in itself: action and organisation were necessary to promulgate the desired changes. Mobilization of the mass of unpoliticized women in both town and country was a mammoth task, undertaken with vigour by a dedicated core of women led by Inessa Armand (1874-1920) and Aleksandra Kollontai (1872-1952). Armand was a close associate of Lenin and a long-standing Communist organiser of working women. In 1919 she became the first leader of the Women's Department of the Russian Communist Party (Bolshevik), known as the Zhenotdel. Items in the Library's collections by Armand, written under the pseudonym Elena Blonina, include examples of revolutionary political-educational pamphlets such as *Pochemu ia stala zashchitnitsei Sovetskoi vlasti* (Moskva, 1920), a strikingly clear and simple exposition of the advantages which the Soviet system was bringing for ordinary working women, written in the form of answers to questions asked by a group of as yet politically uncommitted textile workers. Works about Armand include a collection of memoirs, *Pamiati Inessy Armand* (Moskva, 1926), edited by N K Krupskaia. Armand's internationalist approach to the question of women's liberation inspired the First International Conference of Communist Women held in 1920 to coincide with the second meeting of the Comintern. The report of the Conference, *Otchet o pervoi mezhdunarodnoi konferentsii kommunistok* (Moskva, 1921) was not published until after Armand's untimely death from cholera. Kollontai succeeded her as director of the Zhenotdel.

The aim of the Zhenotdel, which was set up in 1919 as a result of the First All-Russian Congress of Working Women, was to bring women out of the home and into the labour force and full participation in public life. Kollontai described how and why the Congress was organised in the handbook *Kommunisticheskaia partiia i organizatsiia rabotnits: posobie dlia propagandistok* (Moskva, 1919). The Zhenotdel's initial work involved publishing pamphlets, leaflets and other propaganda material and establishing regional and town women's committees. Examples of propaganda literature of this type can be seen in the series *Rechi i besedy agitatora* and *Raboche – krest ianskie listovki* of which the Library has extensive holdings. However, this work reached in the main only the literary, politically-aware women and consequently mass agitation began which entailed going to the people. The main method of working was the delegate's assembly. Workers or peasant women would elect delegates from amongst their number who would attend the assemblies. The assembly served as a school for political education after which the delegate would participate in various areas of public life, first as an observer and later, it was hoped, as a fully-fledged activist.[1]

It was her duty to spread what she had learnt amongst those who elected her. These methods of working are described in detail in various instructional materials published for women agitators, for example, the *Sbornik instruktsii otdela TS.K.R.K.P. po rabote sredi zhenshchin* (Moskva, 1920), one of the British Library's collection of fascinating primary materials from this era. Other items include reports of work done, for example, *Otchet otdela TSKRKP po rabote sredi zhenshchin za god raboty* (Moskva, 1921), and early issues of the Zhenotdel's theoretical journal *Kommunistka*. According to Lapidus' figures[2], participation in Zhenotdel activities rose from 150,000 delegates in 1924 to 2,500,000 in 1928.

The Zhenotdel was of particular significance in Muslim areas of Central Asia. A western work based on personal observations made in the area is Fannina W Halle's *Women in the Soviet East* (London, 1938), translated from the German. An invaluable modern academic approach is Gregory J Massell's penetrating study *The surrogate proletariat: Moslem women and revolutionary strategies in Soviet Central Asia 1919-29* (Princeton 1974). His work shows how 'Moslem women came to constitute, in Soviet political imagination, a structural weak point in the traditional order: a potentially deviant, and hence subversive stratum susceptible to militant appeal, in effect, a surrogate proletariat where no proletariat in the real Marxist sense existed'.

Russian sources on the subject include early works such as V Kasparova's *Raskreposhchenie zhenshchiny Vostoka* (Moskva, 1926), and modern studies such as B B Palvanova's *Emantsipatsiia musulmanki* (Moskva, 1982). Many women, both indigenous and Russian Bolshevik activists, were murdered for their attempts to change traditional Muslim society.

The Soviet approach to the question of women's rôle in the new socialist society was intricately bound up with the question of the family and childcare. Women had to be drawn into productive labour, yet maternity was to be encouraged for demographic purposes. Thus the solution was envisaged early on of socialised housekeeping and institutionalised childcare. As Minister of Social Welfare, Kollontai was responsible for these matters. Her position regarding the equality of women and their emancipation from the family is stated clearly in *Sem'ia i kommunisticheskoe gosudarstvo* (Moskva, 1920), published in the same year in English in London by the Workers' Socialist Federation under the title *Communism and the family*. Many popular pamphlets were produced on the subject of the family in the Communist state including Ekaterina Arbore-Ralli's *Mat' i ditia v Sovetskoi Rossii* (Moskva, 1920); Z I Lilina's *Ot kommunisticheskoi sem'i, k kommunisticheskomu obshchestvu* (Petrograd, 1920); and V A Bystrianskii's *Kommunizm, brak i sem'ia* (Leningrad, 1921).

Much attention was paid to the need for protective labour legislation for working women during pregnancy and for nursing mothers. In 1920 the First All-Russian Congress on the Protection of Motherhood and Infancy was held. Papers presented can be consulted in *Materialy pervogo Vserossiiskogo Soveshchaniia po okhrane materinstva i mladenchestva* (Moskva, 1921) and V Lebedeva's *Okhrana materinstva i mladenchenstva* (Moskva, 1921).

Also worthy of note is Alice Withrow Field's *Protection of women and children in Soviet Russia* (London, 1932), a work based on careful research and full of interesting data. It also has a useful bibliography. Lebedeva was a Bolshevik doctor and ex-revolutionary who headed the Matmlad, the Commission for the Protection of Mothers and Infants, attached to the Commissariat of Health. In 1919, at the First All-Russian Conference of Women Workers, she came forward with the statement 'when a woman gives life to a child she performs work every bit as important as that of the engineer who constructs roads'.[3]

Aleksandra Kollontai shared this view of motherhood as social reproduction which she expounded in her work *Obshchestvo i materinstvo* originally published in Petrograd in 1916. However she looked deeper than many other pronatalists and identified work and sexuality as the essential elements of the new Soviet woman.[4]

Kollontai campaigned for sexual liberation and an openness in relationships which brought widespread criticism and ultimately damaged her political career and the projects with which she was associated.

Her works are well known in the English-speaking world because of numerous translations ranging from the 1920s Workers Socialist Federation pamphlet mentioned above to Falling Wall Press publications of the 1970s and Alix Holt's edition of *Selected writings of Alexandra Kollontai* (London, 1977). Noteworthy biographies include Cathy Porter's *Alexandra Kollontai* (London, 1980) and Barbara Evans Clements' *Bolshevik feminist* (Bloomington: London, 1979). Kollontai's imaginative literature, portraying the ideal new Soviet woman and her problems, has also reached a wide audience, probably the most famous work being *Liubov' pchel trudovykh* (Moskva, 1923) translated by Cathy Porter as *Love of worker bees* (London, 1977).

Finally, for an interesting overview of some of the concerns and issues important during the first twenty years of Soviet power the reader might consult N K Krupskaia's *Zhenshchiny strany Sovetov – ravnopravnyi grazhdanin* (Moskva, 1938).

The next phase: the reinstatement of the family and women's work

In 1928 the First Five Year Plan was launched marking Stalin's rise to power and a distinct change in the social, political and intellectual climate. The rapid development of industry and the forced collectivisation of agriculture necessitated a massive influx of women into the paid labour market.

By 1939 women constituted 41.6% of the paid labour force. For an early academic approach to this era, Susan Kingsbury and Mildred Fairchild's *Factory, family and women in the Soviet Union* (New York, 1935), is to be recommended. It includes statistical material and a bibliography. Participation in productive labour was no longer an element of emancipation but a prerequisite for the economic success of the Soviet Union. However, provision of communal services to ease the family burden of the working woman was not given high priority and their development was slow despite evidence from the Workers and Peasants Inspectorate which noted

'Every day 36 million hours are expended in the RSFSR for cooking alone... collective cooking of the same amount of food would require one-sixth of this time and would release over 4 million housewives for productive labour'[5]

The family was enshrined once again in legislation which strengthened it as a unit and consequently deprived women of much of their new found independence in the interests of providing a secure bulwark to weather the storm of industrialisation and collectivisation.

Nevertheless the Soviet Union still worked to capitalise on the advances made in the emancipation of women. Published sources over the entire Stalin period are generally triumphant in tone. An excellent example of the writing of the era is B N Serebrennikov's *The position of women in the USSR* (London, 1937). In 1936 new family laws[6] included the abolition of legal abortions. Serebrennikov states that because of improved economic conditions women no longer need abortions: 'The new law prohibits abortion in the interests of women's health and further strengthening of healthy family and conjugal relations' (p.23). *Soviet Women* (Moscow, 1939), an album which constitutes a fine example of socialist realist principles in photography, presents an attractive and revealing view of women in the 1930s and their rôle in the political priorities of the day. There is a dual emphasis – on women at work in what were previously male-dominated areas and on women as mothers.

This idea is perpetuated throughout the Stalin period in works such as N V Popova's *Zhenschiny strany sotsializma* (Moskva, 1947), N G Bilshai-Pilipenko's *Sovetskaia demokratiia i ravnopravie zhenshchin v SSSR* (Moskva, 1948), and V L Bilshai's *Reshenie zhenskogo voprosa v SSSR* (Moskva, 1956), whose very title emphasises the fact that the woman question has been laid to rest, solved.

As in the west, women were called upon to take over from men in all spheres when the Soviet Union entered the war in 1941. Their rôle both at the Front and in keeping the economy and society running is the subject of a number of works such as L I Stishova's *V tylu i na fronte: kommunistki v gody Velikoi Otechestvennoi voiny*

(Moskva, 1984); V S Murmantseva's *Sovetskie zhenshchiny v Velikoi Otechestvennoi voine 1941-1945* (Moskva, 1979); and some western works such as Bruce Myles' *Night witches: the untold story of Soviet women in combat* (Edinburgh, 1981).

The 1960s thaw and the resurgence of the 'woman question'

It was not until the 1960s, in the generally more liberal atmosphere of the post-Stalin thaw, that the question of women once again came to prominence and attention began to be paid to the problems women faced in trying to cope with the dual burdens of home and family, hindered by inadequate services, poor housing conditions and mismanagement of the production of food and consumer goods and the retail system. A telling sign of the new spirit at large was the publication, originally in the journal *Novyi mir* (November 1969 p.23–51) and later translated into English and published in *Spare Rib*, of Natalia Baranskaya's short story *Nedelia kak nedelia* [A week like any other], in which a struggling young mother describes her life in terms of a constant battle to fulfil her rôle as wife, mother and scientific worker. This story, along with a collection of others by the same author, have recently been published by Virago in translation by Pieta Monk[7].

A large body of literature has been devoted to this theme, both Soviet and western. It can be seen as a major preoccupation of the new Soviet sociologists in the 1960s and 1970s. A representative selection of their works includes standard sociological studies such as E E Novikova and Z A Iankova's *Zhenshchina. Trud. Semia: sotsiologicheskii ocherk* (Moskva, 1978), and A G Kharchev and S I Golod's work based on surveys undertaken in Leningrad and Kostroma, *Professional'naia rabota – zhenshchina i semia* (Leningrad, 1971). An economist's approach can be seen in N M Shishkan's *Sotsialno-ekonomicheskie problemy zhenskogo truda* (Moskva, 1980), whilst great attention is still paid to protective labour legislation and the rights of women at work *eg* V N Tolkunova's *Pravo zhenshchin na trud v SSSR* (Moskva, 1980), and T E Chumakova's *Trud i byt zhenshchin: sotsialno-pravovye aspekty* (Minsk, 1978). A useful guide to legislation can be found in *Okhrana truda zhenshchin: spravochnik po zakonodatelstvu*, (Moskva, 1978), edited by A A Abromova, and N I Danchenko's *Pravovaia okhrana truda zhenshchin v SSSR* (Kiev, 1985). Of the western works *Women, work and family in the Soviet Union* (New York; London, 1982) introduced by Gail Warshofsky Lapidus is to be highly recommended. Others include Michael Paul Sachs' *Women's work in Soviet Russia: continuity in the midst of change* (New York, 1976), *Work and equality in Soviet society* (New York, 1982), and Alistair McAuley's *Women: work and wages in the Soviet Union* (London, 1981).

Dissent

It is notable by omission that the issue of women's sexuality and any discussion of alternatives to the traditional family structure have been given a back seat and only surfaced in the publications of dissenting women in the 1970s and early 1980s.

These feminist writings are a clear expression of dissatisfaction with the status quo and they reveal the shortcomings of state facilities for childbirth, childcare and many aspects of women's everyday lives. They have made a strong impact in the west. For the first time women in Western Europe and the United States could read for themselves of feminist consciousness among their Soviet sisters in *Zhenshchina i Rossiia: almanakh zhenshchinam o zhenshchinakh* (Paris 1980), also translated into English and published in London by Sheba Feminist publishers in the same year under the title *Woman and Russia*. This almanach is a collection of writings voicing many disparate views, some expressing a strong religious element. The first item is an interview between Julia Voznesenskaya and Tatiana Goricheva in which they discuss the importance they attach to spiritual regeneration as a basis for women's liberation and opposition in Eastern Europe. In 1980 the women who had participated in preparing the Almanach founded a feminist club and journal which they called *Maria*.

The journal was translated and published in Paris as *Maria: journal du club féministe 'Maria' de Leningrad* (Paris, 1981), the year in which four of the editors of *Maria* were expelled from the Soviet Union. Their later writings can be examined in *Women and Russia: feminist writings from the Soviet Union* (Oxford 1984), edited by Tatiana Mamonova, one of the four; and in Voznesenskaya's novels: the vibrant *Women's Decameron* (London, 1986) and her latest work *The Star Chernobyl* (London, 1987).

Women and the Party

On the subject of women's involvement in official political life in the Soviet Union, there has always been a problem of tokenism, of women being pushed into supposedly female spheres of activity, for example areas involved with welfare, education and childcare. Krupskaya recognised this tendency even in the 1920s. In the Stalin era some women were involved in political life, an interesting example being Praskovia Angelina[8] who became a Deputy to the Supreme Soviet after setting up the first Women's Tractor Brigade. Her views on participation in political life can be found in her book *O samon glavnom* (Moskva, 1948), written in response to a request for information from the American compilers of a new universal biographical dictionary. There are books on the Soviet Women's Committees such as A S Stoiakina's *Zhenskie sovety* (Moskva, 1962) and studies of women in the trade unions, for example E E Novikova's *Sovetskie zhenshchiny i profsoiuzy* (Moskva, 1984). An interesting Western study is Genia K Browning's *Women and politics in the USSR: consciousness raising and Soviet women's groups* (Brighton, 1987).

Women in the non-Russian Soviet Republics

As noted earlier, women played an important rôle in the Party's plans for breaking down traditional lifestyles and societies in the non-Russian republics. There is a large body of Soviet literature about these non-Russian women which dates particularly from the 1960s and early 1970s. Titles like *The women of Soviet Uzbekistan* (Tashkent,

1962); *Velikii Oktiabr' i raskreposhchenie zhenshchin Severnogo Kavkaza i Zakavkazii 1917-1936* (Moskva, 1979); and Z S Tatybekova's *Zhenshchiny sovetskogo Kirgizstana* (Frunze, 1967) abound. Other interesting works include a report of an Uzbek Women's Congress *Vtoroi s' ezd zhenshchin Uzbekskoi SSR, 1961* (Tashkent, 1962), and a study of the rôle of Uzbek women in World War II, M IUldasheva's *Zhenshchiny Uzbekistana – frontu* (Tashkent, 1982).

Magazines and journals

An enlightening source of information on the rôle of women in Soviet Society are the journals and magazines written specifically for women. While the Library's collections of these journals are not particularly strong they merit some mention. Besides the Zhenotdel organ *Kommunistka*, the Library holds copies of the peasant women's magazine *Krestian'ka* for the late 1940s and part of the 1950s; *Soviet Woman* in its English version from 1946 onwards; and an interesting monograph about the history of the journal *Rabotnitsa* [The working woman] by A V Artiukhina, *Vsegda s vami* (Moska, 1964). These journals are often a fascinating source for examining the way in which the perceived characteristics of the ideal Soviet woman were in fact constantly subject to change in order to accord with the latest exigencies of Party policy.

Statistical sources

Hard data about women in the Soviet Union can be obtained from various statistical handbooks in the Official Publications and Social Sciences collections. There are odd copies of *Zhenshchiny i deti v SSR: statisticheskii sbornik* (Moskva) for the 1960s and a set of the annual *Zhenshchiny v SSSR: statisticheskie materialy* (Moskva), complete from 1981 with a few odd copies from the 1960s and 1970s. Legal materials include the aforementioned *Marriage laws of Soviet Russia*, etc, and Schlesinger's *The family in the USSR*, along with G M Sverdlov's *Sovetskoe zakonodatel'stvo o brake i sem'i* (Moskva, 1949) and a Soviet publication in English *Soviet legislation on women's rights: a collection of normative acts* (Moscow, 1978). Also of interest are the texts of the RSFSR constitution of 1918 and the three successive Soviet constitutions of 1924, 1936 and 1977.

Soviet fiction

A useful source for the lives of Soviet women and how they are perceived by society, which constitutes an important area of study in itself, is the field of imaginative literature. The British Library has an extensive and comprehensive collection of Soviet fiction in the original Russian and in translation. Various studies of women in Soviet fiction have been published. An early example is E I Petrova and N A Stoliar's *Rabotnitsa i krest'ianka v po-oktiabr'skoi khudozhestvennoi literature* (Moskva, 1926). The best known work is Xenia Gasiorowska's *Women in Soviet fiction 1917-64* (Madison, 1968).

General works

To conclude, there are a large number of general works on the subject of Soviet women, mainly dating from the 1970s and 1980s when the influence of women's studies was already being felt in the west. Some examples of these later works are:

Mary Buckley's *Soviet social scientists talking: an official debate about women* (London, 1986) *Moscow women: thirteen interviews* by Carola Hansson and Karin Liden (London, 1984, originally published in Sweden); *Soviet sisterhood: British feminists on women in the USSR* (London, 1985), a thought provoking review of women's rôle in contemporary Soviet society edited by Barbara Milland; and Susan Bridger's *Women in the Soviet countryside* (Cambridge, 1987).

A number of comparative studies have also marked the growth of interest in the subject. These include Hilda Scott's *Does socialism liberate women? Experiences from Eastern Europe* (Boston 1975); Alena Heitlinger's *Women and state socialism: sex inequality in the Soviet Union and Czechoslovakia* (London, 1979); Margaret E Leaky's *Development strategies and the status of women: a comparative study of the United States, Mexico, the Soviet Union and Cuba* (Boulder, 1986); and *Women in Eastern Europe and the Soviet Union*, edited by Tova Yedlin (New York, 1980).

A selection of the numerous Soviet works from this period include: *Sovetskaia zhenshchina – sotsial'nyi portret* (Moskva, 1978) by the leading sociologist Zoia Alekseevna IAnkova; N Vishneva-Sarafanova's *Soviet women – a portrait* (Moscow, 1981); and N A Egorova's *Zhenshchina v sovremennom mire* (Erevan, 1976).

The future

There are, as yet, no books on the implications of Gorbachev's far-reaching reforms for women's issues, but it is clear from various of his speeches (as for example the *Political report of CPSU Central Committee of the 27th Party Congress of the CPSU* (Moscow, 1986) that he is at least aware of the issues involved. It remains to be seen whether the new spirit of glasnost will lead to a new flowering of literature by and about Soviet women and the vital issues in their lives.

References

1. The Zhenotdel activist was identified by her red headscarf. A famous portrait of a 'delegatka' was painted by G G Riazhskii whose series of paintings of the new Soviet women are an interesting visual resource (*G G Riazhskii*, Moscow, 1952).
2. Lapidus, *op cit.* p.65.
3. Halle, F. *Woman in Soviet Russia.* London, 1933, p.149.
4. *See*, for example, *Novaia moral' i rabochii klass.* Moskva, 1918.
5. Kingsbury, S. and Fairchild M, *op cit.* p.202.
6. *See* the above work edited by Schlesinger.
7. Baranskaya, Natalia. *A week like any other.* London, 1989.
8. *See* A O Slavutskii's biography *Praskovia Angelina.* Moskva, 1960.

Discussion

In the subsequent discussion a number of points were raised:

The importance of women as journalists (*eg* Harriet Martineau, leader writer for the *Daily News* in the 1850s and 1860s); the pressing need for the Library to produce short analytical bibliographies (conventional catalogues and indexes often use words in ways which obscure the rôle of women); a *Checklist of nineteenth-century women writers* will be published by the British Library; the need to emphasise the experience of women as well as feminist activity.

The following participants took part in the discussion: Jane Carr (BL, Marketing and Publishing); Rosalind Delmar (writer and lecturer); David Doughan (Fawcett Library); Brigid Haines (BL, St Pancras Planning); Rosemary Seton (School of Oriental and African Studies library); Dorothy Sheridan (University of Sussex Library); Ilse Sternberg (BL, Collection Development, English Language Branch).

Penelope Tuson

Suffragettes and saris: resources for women's studies in the India Office Library and Records

In March 1985 the Inner London Education Authority organised the 'London Women's History Week.' The programme consisted of a wide range of events for primary and secondary school students and one of its aims was to advertise the resources available in London's museums, galleries and libraries. The India Office Library and Records, with its recently established Education Service, agreed to hold a small seminar for sixth-form history students.

The best known materials in our collections at the time were those relating to the *memsahib*, the Englishman's wife, mother and daughter and her domestic and social life in pre-Independence India. The resources presented a valuable detailed and intimate record of one particular group of women in one particular historical context and they were widely exploited although not always understood. We nevertheless felt that it was important to move away from the female Raj stereotype and look for materials on women in different rôles – working women, politically-active women, fighting women, both European and Asian, their relationships with each other and with the male and predominatly European imperial administration in India.

The results were predictable. Searching for documentary material on women and their rôle in the Independence movement it became increasingly and depressingly clear that here was another group of active and energetic women who had suffered and fought for their own personal freedom and for that of their country, but whom the standard history books had yet again consistently ignored or at least relegated to minor rôles on the sidelines of the main event. Equally predictable was the discovery that within the thousands of files and volumes in the IOLR there was an enormous amount of completely un-exploited material on women but it was rarely indexed and almost always hidden behind another subject.

Since 1985 an ever-widening range of material has been explored, particularly by history teachers working at secondary school level. There is still much more to be found and this paper illustrates, through the careers and lives of some very different women, the main research areas from 1857 until Independence. It does not attempt to cover the earlier period or to deal with resources on the women of South Asia outside their relationship with the British Emprire.[1] It describes the tip of an iceberg.

The India Office Library and Records

The India Office Library and Records is the national centre for source material on the British involvement with India and with surrounding Asian countries for the period c.1600-1947. The Library holds more than 100,000 books in European languages and 250,000 in Asian languages together with journals, newspapers, prints and drawings, and oriental manuscripts. The official archives comprise the records of the East India Company (1600-1858), the Board of Control (1784-1858), the India Office (1858-1947), and the Burma Office (1937-48). The archives are, of course, British and official, largely created by western imperial administrators who were, without exception, men. They are supplemented by a large and growing collection of private papers, comprising letters, diaries and other records of British administrators and their wives and daughters, as well as both male and female members of the medical and teaching professions, missionaries and business people; they include the papers of a few Indian women who achieved some political or professional prominence under imperial rule.

The printed books, manuscripts and private papers offer readily accessible material for women's studies; the official archives present a formidable research problem but probably offer the highest rewards. The women discussed below have been chosen to illustrate the scope of the resources. The bibliography lists the most useful guides to the collections as well as a small selection of monographs which have drawn on the materials.

Women in battle: the rebellion of 1857 and the Rani of Jhansi

The rebellion of 1857, or the 'Indian Mutiny' as it was traditionally called, provides an eminently suitable starting point for a survey of sources on women because it was the first politico/military event in the history of British Indian relations in which women were involved, albeit unwillingly, in large numbers.

Hundreds of women, both Indian and British, were caught up in the fighting in India during 1857. At Cawnpore and Lucknow, scenes of the most notorious events, men, women and children were besieged for several months before the dwindling numbers of survivors were relieved by British forces. Even though the uprisings were restricted to a relatively small area of the subcontinent as a whole, the European inhabitants were nevertheless terrified and harsh precautionary and retaliatory measures were taken by the British authorities. Both sides were responsible for acts of great heroism and great savagery and passions and prejudices were aroused on a scale never before experienced in British Indian history. Because the experiences of women were felt to represent a wider attack on British honour, they were for once of great interest to the British public and there was a huge demand for both official and unofficial accounts of the events.

Most of these accounts are extremely subjective. The majority of the British writers, the administrators, soldiers and historians, were of course, male. The British women were, on the whole, passively involved in their traditional rôles as waiting wives and mothers, as innocent victims and as objects of pity and outraged pride on the part of the men who justified their own barbaric acts of revenge by the depth of their womenfolk's humiliation. Nevertheless, many women recorded their personal experiences in diaries and memoirs which predictably concentrate less on the savagery and bloodshed and more on the private grief and domestic tragedy. Twenty-three year old Katherine Bartrum is typical. Married to a surgeon at the tiny outstation of Gonda, she spent her time in besieged Lucknow 'fully occupied in nursing' and tending the sick and dying. Her letters to her father describe first the death of her husband at the relief of the Residency and then, only three months later when the rebellion was over and she was on her way home, the death of her small son.[2] Other accounts simply describe the endless and tedious business of dealing with everyday deprivations. Boils, lice, rats, overcrowding and arguments about washing were all subjects of great importance to Maria Germon. In the struggle to maintain a semblance of normality, death seemed to be no more noteworthy than the dinner menu[3]:

Wednesday, August 19th. No news – after breakfast Mrs Harris sewed up Mrs D's baby in a clean table cloth first having dressed it in a clean night dress and linen cap and crossed its arms on it breast and the little thing was carried away to the hospital to await its burial at night – the day passed as usual.
Thursday, August 20th. No news again. The night had been very quiet – as I was sitting at the front door making a petticoat a European was shot at the gun in our garden, right through the head – Mr Cunliffe was wounded. I had a very bad boil on my hand for which I made an *attah* poultice – our dinner this day was stew – *dal* and rice and *chupattees*. We were told before going to bed that Johannis' large house was to be blown up at day-break.

However, not all the women were confined to the besieged towns. Some of them escaped and occassionally in circumstances more reminiscent of the fictional adventures of heroines of school-girl novels of the 1950s than of Victorian England.[4]

On the Indian side, the ordinary waiting wives, mothers and children were not written about by the British. But, in a strange reversal of traditional male/female rôles, Indian womanhood was represented in the person of Rani Lakshmibai of Jhansi, whose kingdom had been annexed by the British in 1853 and whose military the political prowess provided formidable opposition to the British both on the battlefield and in the council chamber. The Rani aroused strong feelings in those who fought against her and the official records, by their very nature, present the British point of view. However, her death in battle in June 1858 is recorded vividly and with great admiration by G B Malleson in the third volume of his and Sir John Kaye's *History of the Indian Mutiny 1857-1858*[5]:

Amongst the fugitives in the rebel ranks was the resolute woman who, alike in council and on the field, was the soul of the conspirators. Clad in the attire of a man and mounted on horseback, the rani of Jhansi might have been seen animating her troops throughout the day.

When inch by inch the British troops pressed through the pass, and when reaching its summit Smith ordered the hussars to charge, the rani of Jhansi boldly fronted the British horsemen. When her comrades failed her, her horse, in spite of her efforts, carried her along with the others. With them she might have escaped but that her horse, crossing the canal near the cantonment, stumbled and fell. A hussar, close upon her track, ignorant of her sex and her rank, cut her down. She fell to rise no more. That night her devoted followers, determined that the English should not boast that they had captured her even dead, burned the body.

Material on the rebellion and its background may be drawn from virtually all categories of East India Company archives. These sources and other, additional, records are comprehensively described in Rosemary Seton's *The Indian 'Mutiny' 1857-58: a guide to source material in the India Office Library and Records* (London: British Library, 1986). Individual private accounts of 1857 written by women are listed in the appendix.

A clash of cultures: Cornelia Sorabji and the social reform movement

Cornelia Sorabji, Indian barrister and social reformer, was born at Nasik in the Bombay presidency in November 1866, the fifth daughter of the Reverend Sorabji Karsedji, a Christian convert from the Parsi community. She was the first woman student admitted to the Deccan college, Poona, from where, in 1886, she graduated with a first class degree. Students with such a qualification were entitled to a scholarship at a British university but Sorabji was turned down because of her sex. She taught English literature at Ahmedabad and then, with the help of friends in England, obtained a 'substitution scholarship' to Somerville College which had opened nine years earlier. She read the Bachelor of Civil Law course and was given permission in 1892 to sit the examination, the first woman ever to do so. In 1923 she was called to the bar and subsequently practised in Calcutta until 1929.

In the meantime, however, Cornelia Sorabji had created for herself a rôle as protector of the rights of women landholders in Bengal, Bihar, Orissa and Assam; in particular she worked on behalf of Indian women living in *purdah*. Her experiences as a lawyer and her involvement with social services, infant welfare and district nursing are described in her two autobiographical works, *India calling: the memories of Cornelia Sorabji* (London, 1934) and *India recalled* (London, 1936). After a visit to the United States in 1929 she settled in London, turning more to writing and visiting India only during winters.

As well as her published works, the India Office Records holds the Cornelia Sorabji collection[6]. This contains letters, diaries and papers covering all aspects of her life and career from 1882 until her death in London in 1954.

Cornelia Sorabji's career is an interesting illustration of the inherent conflict which existed within the social reform movement from the early nineteenth century onwards. The British reformers and missionaries were, on the whole, determined to impose their own western religious and moral values on the subcontinent. At the same time, the early Indian social reformers were generally western-educated and influenced. Attempts to abolish *sati*, female infanticide and child marriage were regarded by the conservative and orthodox elements of Indian society as the thin end of the imperial wedge and were deeply resented. After the shock of 1857 British attitudes changed and the attempt to reform Indian society along western lines was largely abandoned. Nevertheless the Indian intellectual élite continued to be English-educated and women in particular maintained close contacts with their European counterparts.

Information on missionaries and social reformers may be found in their own private papers and published works as well as in the official archives.[7] Material on social reforms specifically relating to women – education, property rights, marriage etc – is located in Parliamentary Papers and other official publications (IOR: V), in India Office departmental records (particularly Public and Judicial, IOR:L/P&J) and in the Proceedings of the Indian administrations (IOR:P).

The women's movement in India

The women's movement in India was a logical and inevitable development out of the social reform movement and its leaders included both Indian and British women. It encompassed a large network of national and local women's organisations many of which maintained records of proceedings and sponsored their own publications. The aims and objectives of the movement may be traced through three major organisations:

1. THE WOMEN'S INDIAN ASSOCIATION, was founded in Madras in May 1917 by Mrs Dorothy Jinarajadasa, a notable social reformer, and it was supported by Irish suffragette and Home Rule campaigner, Margaret Cousins. Its first President was Annie Besant and its aims and objectives included education for all, abolition of child marriage and votes for women. Thirty three branches were formed in the first year and by 1927 it had over 4,000 members. The official journal of the Association, *Stridharma*[8] was published in English, Tamil and Telugu and distributed to several countries.

2. THE NATIONAL COUNCIL OF WOMEN IN INDIA was formed in 1925 as a branch of the International Council of Women. Its general aims were to raise the status of Indian women by removing social and legal disabilities and it mobilised public opinion through seminars, conferences and meetings. It played a significant part in the campaign for women's suffrage but its influence was limited in that its members were mostly English-educated, drawn from the official and aristocratic classes, and its journal, the *NCWI Bulletin* was published in the English language.

3. THE ALL INDIA WOMEN'S CONFERENCE was founded in 1927. It was the most important and powerful of the women's organisations and had international links, particularly with women's groups in England. Its leading founder member was Margaret Cousins who had already been involved in the WIA. Although the AIWC began with an interest in educational reform it gradually widened its scope to include political activities and became closely involved with the Independence Movement.

The struggle for Independence: Vijaya Lakshmi Pandit

Vijaya Lakshmi Pandit played a prominent part in the Indian Independence movement, as did her father, Pandit Motilal, her daughters, Nayantara, Rita and Lekha, her husband, Ranjit Pandit, her brother, Jawaharlal Nehru and her niece, Indira (Nehru) Gandhi.

Mrs Pandit was imprisoned three times for her political activities: first in 1932 when she spent a year in Lucknow Central Jail for her part in Gandhi's Civil Disobedience campaign, the second time in 1940 when she spent nine months in Naini Central Prison, and finally in 1942 when she was arrested with other prominent political leaders but released after ten months because of ill-health. During the years leading up to Indian Independence she established herself both as a politician and social reformer. Between 1937 and 1939 she was the first woman Minister of Local Self Government and Health in the United Provinces, a post which she was to hold again from 1946-47. Between 1940 and 1942 she was President of the All India Women's Conference and Save the Children Fund Committee. In 1946 she led an Indian delegation to the United Nations General Assembly and in 1954 she was the first woman to be elected President of the Assembly. She was appointed Indian Ambassador to Moscow in 1947, to Washington in 1949 and Indian High Commissioner in London in 1955. In 1964 she became Governer of Bombay.

It is an interesting reflection on the historiography of British India that in spite of her career in politics, Mrs Pandit is invariably referred to as her brother's sister. The scholarly and respectable documents on *The Transfer of Power* in its 12 volumes refers to her in only 17 out of 7500 documents and then almost always in the context of 'sister of...' Even the left-wing writer Tariq Ali in his book *The Nehrus and the Gandhis* only gives her a cursory mention in his list of politicians as 'Jawaharlal's younger sister', although experienced feminist historians will not necessarily find this any more surprising.[9] There is, however, plenty of material in the official archives on the activities of women in politics although it is not often properly indexed. Particularly useful are the series of India Office Public and Judicial Department files (IOR:L/P&J) which include papers on the imprisonment of Indian women political leaders – the Nehrus, the Gandhis, Sarojini Naidu, Kamaladevi Chattopadhyaya – and some interesting correspondence with their supporters in England – Agatha Harrison, Margaret Corbett Ashby, Maud Dickinson, Vera Brittain and others – who continually lobbied the India Office on their behalf. The official sources should be supplemented and balanced by the personal correspondence and published works of the women themselves, many of which are held by the Library,[10] and by newspapers and political journals such as the *Bulletin of the Indian Women's Movement* which regularly circulated to its readers 'news which does not appear elsewhere in this country (England)'[11].

... the reason the [All India Women's] Conference cannot meet is because its effective leadership is under arrest. We understand that the following are amongst the number: The Hon Mrs V L Pandit (India's first woman Cabinet Minister, and President of the AIWC); Shrimati Kamaladevi – the President elect; Mrs Sarojini Naidu; The Raj Kumari Amrit

Kaur; Mrs Brijlal Nehru. A scrutiny of Indian papers shows that women have taken a large part in the nation-wide protests that took place as a result of the arrests in August last... it is clear that a great many of India's outstanding women are either in prison or 'detained', and their work in connection with the All India Women's Conference halted.

The above information should give us pause. The situation calls for intensive effort on the part of British women to end the present tragic impasse between our two countries. We should press too for more detailed news about our Indian colleagues. [December 1942]

The memsahib: an oral archive

While a significant number of women in England supported the cause of Indian Independence, English women in India were not often politically aware. As Margaret MacMillan observed in her recent *Women of the Raj*, 'they were busy worrying about their husbands and children... The greatest of all their incivilities was simply to ignore India'. Yet, as MacMillan also points out in her timely and perceptive book, 'To bundle them up... into the stock figure of the memsahib is to do to them what they did to the Indians... They were merely, most of them, ordinary middle-class women put into an extraordinary situation... they did not come to India for India's sake. They came, the great majority, to be wives; and they found in existence a tightly-knit community which gave them the simple choice of joining or staying outside'.[12] Most of them, of course joined and occupied themselves, as if in a cocoon, with the business of family life; staying outside was simply not an option available and their contacts with Indians were largely confined to the domestic relationship between mistress and servant or child and *ayah*:

Madrassis were a rather high caste, Hindu, group who... had made a kind of corner in ayahing. They were notedly good at looking after children, and to get a Madrassi ayah was almost the ambition of anyone who didn't have a nanny... They had this capacity to completely identify... with the babies and children they looked after... I do think that this had a really profound effect on the development of many English children who were brought up in India... They never took any off duty as such. It wasn't that we were exploiting them... they were so dedicated to their work that it was almost impossible for a good ayah to yield up her charge to anyone else even for a few hours, and this woman was absolutely at the top of her kind. She was wonderful. [Vere Lady Birdwood, IOR; MSS EUR T 7].

Vere Lady Birdwood, born in 1909, brought up in India from the age of three months and married to an Indian Army officer in 1931, remained in India until 1945. Her views and experiences of childhood and marriage are echoed in numerous interviews with women of similar background. The major source of information on the lives of the *memsahibs* is the Oral Archive which has been built up by the IOR since the BBC's 1974 radio series, *Plain tales from the Raj*. In these tapes and transcripts the women speak for themselves about their daily routine, social life and recreation, living conditions and accommodation, the effects of India postings on family life, and the relations between the British, other Europeans, Indians and Anglo-Indians in both social and occasionally working environments:

I don't think we ever consciously thought about the British Raj as such. We simply accepted that this was where fate, destiny, whatever you like, had placed us... We reckoned that we would be there about 30 years or so but we certainly never questioned our right to be there. ... We lived in a sort of apolitical atmosphere... If we thought about Gandhi at all, it was really that he was just a bit of a nuisance and slightly absurd. [Birdwood, *op. cit.*]

It is easy to condemn the *memsahibs* for their ignorance and political apathy but to judge them by standards which are socially anachronistic and male-orientated is to undervalue both their own lives and the detailed evidence of British social life in India which their stories have uniquely provided for historians.

Women's work: the 'caring' professions

A few of the oral archive interviews deal with work outside the home.[13] Between 1939 and 1947 quite a number of middle and upper-class Indian and English women were involved in voluntary war-work, as they had been between 1914 and 1918. Some English women went to India without husbands, specifically to work as teachers, missionaries, nurses or in social welfare. Some Indian women – for example, Cornelia Sorabji, Kamaladevi Chattopadhyaya – went to England to obtain suitable qualifications to enable them to work in India. For the latter the distinction between work, politics and reform was always blurred. On the right to work, as on the right to education and political and social emancipation, the demands of Indian women were firmly set down and established in the first issue of *Stridharma* in January 1918:

Men and women are equal before God, and the blot on the fair fame of India today is the ignorance of her daughters... These must be given, if they wish it, the opportunity to train themselves along any line that attracts them. Some may wish to be teachers, some doctors or nurses of the sick; others may wish to climb intellectual heights or to work in some science or art. The time has come when it should be realised for the sake of India, that India's daughters must be given the opportunity of developing themselves in every branch of education, art or science that they wish to follow. Without doubt there is the desire in their hearts, but most of India's sons have up to now not realised their responsibility in these things, and have held their sisters back... So today demands that all her children shall unite in a new ideal of mutual comradeship and helpfulness, that together they shall go forward to the glory of the New Free India that is coming.

Official material on the employment of women in the late nineteenth and early twentieth centuries is available in the archives of the India Office Public and Judicial Department (IOR:L/P&J) which, until 1924, was responsbile for public service questions affecting India; after this date the Services and General Department (IOR:L/S&G) dealt with establishment and personnel. The India Office Military Department (IOR:L/MIL) is a good source of material on the employment of women in wartime and includes useful information on prostitution and on the operation of the Contagious Diseases Act between 1873 and 1927.[14]

Working women, élite women, suffragettes, social reformers, freedom-fighters, missionaries and *memsahibs*, wives, mothers and daughters are all represented in the printed, manuscript and archival resources. The trick is in finding them, asking the right questions, and setting the answers in a different perspective, in which the men who ruled India and who produced the official record of their rule are set in a more balanced context alongside the women they took with them, or who went of their own accord, and the millions of Indian men and women who participated in the Empire, fought against it, or simply ignored it.

Appendix: English wives and mothers: accounts by women of the events of 1857

The private papers (European Manuscripts) department of the India Office Records includes a large and growing collection of manuscripts and photocopies of contemporary accounts of 1857, some of which were acquired from descendents of the families involved in the events. Many were subsequently published. The following list includes both manuscript accounts in the IOR and printed/published volumes held by the India Office Library.

Bartrum, Katherine
MSS EUR A 67. Contemporary copies of letters, from Katherine Bartrum to her father recounting the deaths in October 1857 of her husband and in February 1858 of her son. MSS EUR A69. MS copy of her diary giving an account of life in Lucknow during the siege and her journey to Calcutta after the death of her husband.
IOL:T 36215 *A widow's reminiscences of the siege of Lucknow*. London, 1858.

Case, Adelaide Teague
IOL: T 35995. *Day by day at Lucknow: a journal of the siege of Lucknow*. London: R. Bentley, 1858.

Chalwyn, Louise
MSS EUR B344/2. Letters dated 1855-57 from Louise Chalwyn, married to Edmund Chalwyn of the Bengal Veterinary Service, describing her life in Calcutta, Hoshiapur and Cawnpore until shortly before her death at Cawnpore in 1857.

Coopland, R M
IOL: T 11217. *A lady's escape from Gwalior and life in the fort of Agra during the mutinies of 1857*. London, 1859.

Duberly, Frances Isabella
IOL: T 35746. *Campaigning experiences in Rajpootana and Central India during the suppression of the Mutiny, 1857-1858*. London: Smith, Elder & Co. 1859.

Ewart, Emma
MSS EUR B267. Three letters, dated May – June 1857 expressing her increasing concern about the safety of the British community at Cawnpore. She and her husband, Lt-Col J Ewart, 1st Bengal Native Infantry, were killed at Cawnpore.

Germon, Maria
MSS EUR B134. Her journal of the siege of Lucknow, 15 May 1857-28 January 1858, describes vividly her experiences during the siege and her journey from there to Calcutta.
IOL: T 17020. *Journal of the siege of Lucknow: an episode of the Indian Mutiny*. Edited by Michael Edwardes. London, 1958.

Gilliland, Mary
Photo Eur 251. Copies of two letters, 28 July and 4 December 1857, written from Sialkot and Lahore describing her experiences and her views of events.

Goldney, Maria Louise
MSS EUR D729 and Photo Eur 187. Correspondence and press-cuttings about disturbances at Faizabad and the death of her husband. Also an account of her own escape with her three children.

Inglis, Julia Selina
IOL: T 4149. *The siege of Lucknow: a diary*. London, 1892.

Jackson, Madeline
Photo Eur 22 and 41. Copies of her memoirs including an account of her escape from Sitapur with her brother to the countryside until taken captive to Lucknow where she remained for five months.

Kirk, Ellen
MSS EUR B268, Letter, June 1857, describing the outbreak of the rebellion at Gwalior, her husband's death and her own escape.

Larkins, Emma
Photo Eur 233. Photograph of a letter, 9 June 1857, written shortly before her death and describing the feelings of those trapped at Cawnpore.

Muter, Elizabeth McMullin
IOL: T 3932. *My recollections of the Sepoy Revolt, 1857-1858*. London, 1911.

Ouvry, M H
IOL: T 36871. *A lady's diary before and during the Indian Mutiny*. (Lymington, 1892).

Paget, Georgiana (Mrs Leopold)
IOL: T 2526. *Camp and cantonment: a journal of life in India in 1857-1859, with some account of the way thither; to which is added a short account of the pursuit of the rebels in Central India by Major Paget*. London, 1865.

Sneyd, Elizabeth
Photo Eur 44. Copy of her account of her family's escape from Fatepur to Alipur and other experiences.

Timbrell, Agnes and Alice
MSS EUR C201. Copy of an account, dated c.1887, by Agnes Timbrell of her family's escape from rebels at Nasirabad; papers of Alice Powell (née Timbrell).

Vansittart, Mary Amelia
MSS EUR B167. Diary, 1857-58, describing her experiences at Agra during the rebellion.

Wagentreiber, Florence
IOR: TR 800. *The story of our escape from Delhi in May 1857*. Delhi, 1894.

Wood, Maria Lydia
MSS EUR B210. Journal and letters, 1855-61, including eye-witness account of the rebellion at Jhelum, July 1857.

References

1. For a comprehensive guide to resources on women of South Asia see Carol Sakala. *Women of South Asia: a guide to resources*, New York: Kraus International, 1980.
2. IOR: MSS Eur A 67/3.
3. IOL: T 17020 *Journal of the siege of Lucknow*, p.82.
4. For example, Florence Wagentreiber *The story of our escape from Delhi in May 1857*, Delhi, 1894; and *Reminiscences of the Sepoy rebellion*, Lahore, 1911.
5. IOL: T 26045 Vol.III, pp.220–21.
6. IOR: MSS EUR F 165 Cornelia Sorabji collection.
7. *See*, for example, Annette Beveridge (IOR: MSS EUR C 176).
8. IOL: SV 189.
9. Mansergh, P N S. *The transfer of power, 1942-47 (Consitutional relations between Britain and India)*. 12 vols, London, 1970-83; Tariq Ali, *The Nehrus and the Gandhis*. London, 1985.
10. *See*, for example *Prison days* by Vijaya Lakshmi Pandit, Calcutta, 1945; *Prison and chocolate cake* by Nayantara [Pandit] Saghal. London, 1954: *Envoy extraordinary: a study of Vijaya Lakshmi Pandit and her contribution to modern India* by Vera Brittain. London, 1965. Kamaladevi Chattopadhyaya is interviewed in the Oral Archive (IOR: MSS EUR T 87).
11. *Bulletin of Indian Women's Movement*, December 1942: All India Women's Conference News (IOR: L/I/1/1920).
12. *Women of the Raj*. London, 1988, p.230 and Introduction.
13. *See*, for example, Irene Edwards (IOR: MSS EUR T 29), an Anglo-Indian nurse working in Bombay during the 1920s. Both Irene Edwards and Vere Lady Birdwood are discussed by Steve Ashton in *Indian Independence*. London, 1985.
14. IOR: L/MIL/7/130809–13902.

Bibliography

A. GUIDES AND CATALOGUES

Ashton, Steve and Tuson, Penelope. *India Office Library and Records: a brief guide for teachers*. London: British Library, 1985.

Moir, Martin. *A general guide to the India Office Records*. London: British Library, 1988.

Sakala, Carol. *Women of South Asia: a guide to resources*. New York: Kraus International, 1980.

Seton, Rosemary. *The Indian 'Mutiny' 1857-58: a guide to source material in the India Office Library and Records*. London: British Library, 1986.

B. SELECTED SECONDARY WORKS

Agnew, Vijay. *Elite women in Indian politics*. New Delhi, 1976.

Allen, Charles. *Plain tales from the Raj*. London, 1975.

Ashton, Steve. *Indian Independence*. London, 1985.

Ballhatchet, Kenneth. *Race, sex and class under the Raj: imperial attitudes and policies and their critics*. London, 1980.

Barr, Pat. *The memsahibs: the women of Victorian India*. London, 1976.

Macmillan, Margaret. *Women of the Raj*. London, 1988.

Lebra-Chapman, Joyce. *The Rani of Jhansi: a study in female heroism in India*. Honolulu, 1976.

Smyth, Sir John. *The rebellious Rani*. London, 1966.

Visram, Rozina. *Ayahs, lascars and princes: Indians in Britain, 1700-1947*. London, 1986.

Albertine Gaur

The life of Asian women as depicted in oriental manuscript illustrations

The department of Oriental Collections (OC) in the British Library, though small in size when compared with other Library departments, is the widest in scope since it is required to cover the literary output of two-thirds of the world's population. Its brief is to act as the national centre for printed books and manuscripts from Asia and North and Northeast Africa and to collect (as far as resources permit) all significant material in the humanities and social sciences from that area. Its staff deals with some 350 languages or language groups, and documents written in about 200 different scripts. A recent census has shown that the total collection now numbers some 42,000 manuscripts (this takes no account of the large number of fragments) written on such diverse materials as paper, vellum, leather, parchment, palm-leaf, papyrus, cloth, silk, metal, wood, bone and ivory; about 650,000 (printed) monographs; some 7,500 serials, and 1,100 newspaper titles. There is in addition a growing number of microforms (*eg* newspapers, official gazettes, manuscripts: text and/or illustration), and a small though not insignificant collection of photographs, prints and rubbings. Historically the books and manuscripts span over four millennia of Asian and North African history, culture and civilisation with documents from 2000 BC being held next to the most up-to-date modern newspapers. Many items are unique and scholars, researchers, students and writers from all over the world come to the Oriental Reading Room to study there, purchase where possible microfilms, slides or photographs, and/or discuss, either in person or by letter, their projects and problems with the specialist staff of the department.

To facilitate better and one hopes a more logical access, and to develop the expertise of the specialist staff, the collections are divided into a number of major geographical and cultural/linguistic areas such as: Arabic (which covers an area from Marocco to Southeast Asia); the Christian Middle East (which includes Coptic, Syriac, Georgian, Armenian, and the languages of Ethiopia); Hebrew and Yiddish; Persian and Turkish as well as material in the languages of Central Asia (written in non-roman scripts); South Asia (which includes India, Pakistan, Bangladesh, Nepal, Sikkim, Bhutan, Tibet and Sri Lanka); Southeast Asia (Burmese, Thai, Javanese, Indonesian, Vietnamese and the many languages used in the islands of this area); Chinese, Korean and Mongolian; and Japanese.

The history of the collection goes back to the year 1753 when, following a bequest made by the well-known physician and collector Sir Hans Sloane, the British Museum was established by an Act of Parliament. As the reputation of the newly founded institution grew many well-known travellers, scholars, government officials, missionaries, and also some servants of the East India Company, either sold, donated or bequeathed the books and manuscripts they had assembled during a lifetime of work and adventure into its safe keeping. In 1867 there were already 7,000 oriental manuscripts in the collection, a number which continued to rise. In addition, during the following years, a period of more generous purchase grants and the various Imperial and Colonial copyright acts, increased the holdings of printed books so rapidly that eventually the Trustees of the British Museum felt only trained specialists would be able to administer the growing collections properly; thus, in 1891, the Department of Oriental Printed Books and Manuscripts (OPBM) came into being.

In 1973 the British Library was established by another Act of Parliament and in consequence the library departments (Printed Books, OPBM and Western Manuscripts) were severed from the British Museum. The department, renamed Oriental Manuscripts and Printed books (OMPB), became part of what was then called the Reference Division (as opposed to the Lending Division in Boston Spa) of the British Library.

In 1982 the India Office Library and Records (IOLR) joined the British Library, bringing its own collections and its own staff. In 1985, in the course of a further reorganisation, the Reference Division became Humanities and Social Sciences (H&SS) and OMPB changed its name once more to Oriental Collections.

Since its foundation in 1801 IOLR had been in an unique position to collect material relating to South Asia and other Asian countries which were either under the direct control or at least under the influence of the East India Company, and later British India. The IOLR is one of the oldest libraries devoted exclusively to oriental studies and holds a wealth of printed, archival and visual materials. Together OC and IOLR form the single largest research library in relation to material from and on Asia and North and Northeast Africa, holding both primary and secondary resources which illustrate all aspects of oriental culture, history and life. Unlike IOLR, OC collects material in non-European languages only and those interested in the study of Asian women might reasonably ask themselves what does the department have to offer to the non-orientalist.

The answer is quite simply: a more or less comprehensive visual documentation of all aspects of women's lives in the east through the large number of illustrations found in many of the 44,000 manuscripts from the Middle East, Turkey, South and Southeast Asia, and the Far East; in the case of the latter, where printing started some 700 years before Gutenberg, also in illustrations accompanying printed material. The problem which confronts the researcher is two-fold: what to look for and how and where to find it.

Let us first address ourselves to the question of what are the key issues which dominate the existence of women living in societies depending on the values of Islam, Hinduism and Buddhism. It must here be remembered that is such traditional societies, the principal bond of cohesion is still based on what Durkheim calls 'mechanical solidarity' and that there is consequently little scope for individual differentiation. Since in addition the economic status of the majority of women is low, there is also little room for rebellious deviation. Thus the use of proto-types and generalisations is apt to paint a picture more akin to facts than would be the case in the more secular, capitalistic, western societies.

Though much common ground exists between Hinduism, Buddhism and Islam as far as the concept of women's place in society is concerned (all three are strictly patriarchal in outlook and place an exaggeraed value on women's 'chastity') there are also clear differences, especially in relation to law and property. Thus, for example, from the purely legal standpoint, the Muslim woman seems to fare better as she can own and dispose of property, conduct business and remarry should her husband die or divorce her. The Hindu woman on the other hand is considered a potential source of power which, if not properly controlled, can bring danger and ritual pollution to her family and society as a whole. Since however the interpretation, and moreover the enforcement of laws, are firmly in the hands of men, those differences are greater in theory than in practice. Most women live their lives in direct relationship with their family (either that of their origin or later that of their husbands) and laws reach them only in an already filtered and pre-selected state. Laws and tradition are moreover open to interpretation: they can be applied in a liberal way with the stress on benefits, or in an exploitive way with the stress on repression. Those who are surprised that the 'modern' Asian woman is still (seemingly voluntarily) bound by the old taboos overlook the fact that not only stand (male) interpreters between her and the state but since 'modern' (and to us 'liberal') laws come mostly from an alien (*ie* western) culture, she is trapped into resistance by her own emotional conditioning. For example: the legalisation of abortion does not automatically enable every Catholic women in the west to make use of it and we should therefore not be surprised when an 'educated' Asian girl still accepts an arranged marriage.

The lives of Asian women revolve thus mainly around their 'otherness', the way they relate to those in power (husbands, fathers, brothers, sons), and the biological aspects of their personality which centre on birth, betrothal, marriage, fertility, children, in-laws, separation, prostitution, widowhood, and death. The social and economic status of the family to which a woman belongs is of course important; it can increase as well as ease restrictions. Muslim queens may be hidden in luxurious women's quarters but they may also play polo and influence the affairs of state; poor Hindu sweeper women may, by virtue of the fact that their men are not able to support them economically, appropriate to themselves sexual liberties their middle class sisters could dare to imagine only at the risk of their lives. In the tenth century Heian period of Japan, Court ladies were instructed in the art of writing, papermaking, and calligraphy, they were poetesses and writers of renown such as for example the Lady Murasaki who wrote *The tales of Genji*, and they were free to initiate and end love affairs. But appearance can be highly deceptive. The level of capricious sophistication that prevailed in Court circles was the prerogative of a very small and already much privileged minority. Moreover the (traditional) education such women enjoyed was in fact no more than a mere accomplishment, designed to make them more attractive to those who ultimately controlled society – namely men.

Among the 44,000 manuscripts in OC and the 37,000 in IOLR at least half will in one or the other way be illustrated and perhaps a quarter of illustrations will contain material relating to women. This, a most conservative and cautious estimate, adds up to some 150,000 individual miniatures.

The main question is of course: how can somebody who does not know any Asian language find a key to those illustrations?

There are several possibilities.

A good starting point are the exhibition cases in the Kings Gallery of the British Museum in Great Russell Street. Entering from the Manuscript Saloon there are at any time about six cases on either side of the room permanently filled with some of the finest examples of Asian book art. Most of the manuscripts on display are illustrated and among those women feature, if not predominantly, then at least in a manner that allows the visitor a glimpse of their cultural background, their tradition-based aspirations and rôle models, and their consequent way of life.

The cases are arranged according to cultural area, beginning, at the entrance, with the Christian Middle East and Hebrew respectively. Manuscripts in the Christian Middle East exhibition case (Ethiopic, Coptic, Syriac, Armenian) exhort the ideological thinking of the orthodox Eastern Churches; manuscript illustrations, when they relate to women, concentrate mainly on the life and the miracles of the Virgin Mary and/or orther prominent female saints. The illustrations themselves have a strong visual impact and provide much detail about appearance, dress, general demeanour and attitude.

The visual representation of women in Hebrew manuscripts revolves mainly around their rôle in the rituals performed in the home (as opposed to those performed in the synagogue). They may relate to the celebration of the Passover festival and can be found in the many *Haggadot* and books of prayers. Here also much detail is available as to women's appearance and deportment not only in relation to Judaism itself but also in accordance to the period and the place where the illustration was painted.

The exhibition case devoted to Arab manuscripts is resplendent with the most magnificent copies of the Koran. By the time of the Abbasid Caliphate in Baghdad, a little over a century after the death of the Prophet (AD 632), the Arabs had already achieved mastery of the art of calligraphy and book ornamentation; illustration however was and remains a point of controversy since nothing capable of throwing a shadow should be pictorially represented. Korans and religious texts are never illustrated and we learn therefore but little about the life of Arab women from these Arab manuscripts.

When, some three hundred years after the Prophet's death, Islam began to establish dominance over an area which was eventually to reach from Spain to Malaysia, taking in Persia, Turkey and India on the way, it ceased to be the religion of just one people and learned to live side by side with a number of highly sophisticated cultures whose own inheritance was not always in tune with the more austere religion of their conquerors. If not in religious matters so at least in literature and in book production compromises were reached. Manuscripts with miniatures showing figurative illustrations had always been an essential part of Court life in India and Persia. Under Islam they became more or less restricted to works of a fictional character, and as a further precaution, the manuscripts themselves were often kept in the women's quarters. In consequence the exhibition cases devoted to Persia, Turkey and India provide rich material in relation to our subject.

Persian tales and legends, centring around the adventures of kings and heroes, such as for example Alexander or Rustam, provided rich subjects for manuscript illustrations. In those stories, part fiction part historical fact, women can be seen in their traditional rôles as wives, mothers, brides, dancers, enertainers or servants. There are the 'Books of Kings', manuscripts bearing such titles as *Akbarnama, Shahnama,* or *Iskandarnama,* and so on. Persian literature has in addition a tradition of fables and romances and it is in the latter that the recurrent motive of the much tested and usually star-crossed lovers provides material for some of the most beautiful and delicately executed miniatures. To this cycle belong the story of Khusraw and the Armenian princess Shirin, the tragedy of Majnun's love to Layla, the story of Humay and Humayun, or that of Bahram Gur's affairs with seven princesses who held him spell bound. (Persian romantic poetry revolves around the motive of the mad heartbroken male lover whereas in Hindu poetry it is always the women who waits, laments and often destroys herself.) The same exhibition case hold Turkish manuscripts, justifiably so since the connection between Persian and Turkish art is close, artists were imported to Turkey from Iran even before AD 1500 and many Persian stories reappear in new guise.

The Indian case is especially rewarding. Manuscripts which will provide a multitude of visual representations of almost all aspects of a Hindu woman's life are those recounting the two great epic stories of the *Mahabharata* and the *Ramayana* (the second being basically a sub-section of the first). There are further the manuscripts of the *Bhagvata-purana* and that of the *Devi-purana* which record the various aspects of the goddess and by doing so demonstrate a deeply-rooted ambivalence towards the female who is conceived as both, nurturing and destructive. Another rich source of information are the various albums of *ragas* and *raginis* depicting musical modes; many of them show courtesans, go-betweens, lovers, or ladies at their toilet. Eroticism (though ostensibly meant to depict the union of the soul with god) can be found in most of the manuscripts relating to the god Krishna, his childhood and his promiscuous relationship with the milk maids in Brindaban, such as for example the *Radhakrishna keli katha.*

In the Southeast Asian case there are usually examples of narrative albums, often with only a minimum of text, showing multitudes of delightful and delicately painted Court ladies; richly dressed, they strike appropriate poses to provide a decorative background for the more serious affairs of state enacted by men.

This leaves the Far Eastern cases: Chinese, Japanese and Korean. Here some of the exhibits, manuscript and block prints (printing started some 700 years before Gutenberg in the Far East) depict women in their religious rôles, as (Chinese) Buddhist nuns, at work, in the home and also as the great (Japanese) courtesans of the 'Floating World'.

In addition to this more or less permanent exhibition in the Kings Gallery the department mounts, periodically, exhibitions on special themes and/or for occasions. The Oriental Reading Room keeps a record of all captions used for exhibits since 1964. There are in addition 30 albums with photographs of departmental material and some 15,000 slides. Though none of those are as yet indexed it is not too difficult to find subject-related material.

Another helpful aid is the *IOLR/OC Newsletter* which appears about twice a year. It gives a list of all research done by readers in Oriental Collections and in the India Office Library and Records. Though addresses are kept confidential, reading room staff are always willing to forward letters. There is also the joint *Annual Report* brought out by the two Asia departments which draws attention to new acquisitions and catalogues (either in progress or completed) by staff.

Finally there are the British Library's own publications. Though only one (*Women in India*) relates directly to the subject, nearly all contain information of pictorial material connected with it. Most offer a wealth of reproductions which in one or the other way guide the reader to relevant manuscript material. All include lists of further reading which provide a key not only to departmental material but also of other manuscript collections, either in Great Britain or abroad.

These publications are (in alphabetical order):

Archer, Mildred. *The India Office collection of paintings and sculpture*. London, 1986.

Brown, Yu-Ying. *Japanese book illustration*. London, 1988. Contains chapters on 'Women's world' and 'The Floating World' which describe and explain material relating to and depicting Japanese women as 'courtesans' and also '... women of all vocations and classes from empress to priestess, to farmer's wife...'

The Christian Orient. London, 1978. An exhibition catalogue.

Gaur, Albertine. *Women in India*. London, 1980. Originally designed to accompany an exhibition of the same title, the book tries to explain the position of Hindu, Muslim, Parsi, Jewish, Christian and Anglo-Indian women in India.

Gaur, Albertine. *A history of writing*. London, 1985, paperback 1987. Has a chapter entitled 'The position of the scribe in society' which contains a sub-chapter on 'Women and writing'.

Goldstein, David. *Hebrew manuscript painting*. London, 1985. The illustrations give examples from Bibles, Prayer books and similar manuscripts in the British Library.

Hooykass, C. *Bagus Umbara, Prince of Koripan*. London, 1968. Relates to a palm-leaf manuscript which tells, and illustrates, the love story between a Balinese prince and Javanese princess.

Losty, Jeremiah P. *Krishna a Hindu vision of god. Scenes from the life of Krishna illustrated in Orissan and other East Indian manuscripts in the British Library*. London, 1980. The booklet explains the mythological background and the ritualistic aspect of the Krishna cult in which eroticism plays a vital part. Some of the illustrations taken from palm-leaf manuscripts in the Library show main events in the daily life of the Hindu women which centres around the service of her husband.

Losty, Jeremiah P. *The art of the book in India*. London, 1982. Originally planned to accompany an exhibition of the same theme, it is a thorough study of Indian miniature painting from the eleventh to the nineteenth century with detailed descriptions of manuscripts in the Library and in other collections.

Losty, Jeremiah P. *Indian book painting*. London, 1986. Indian miniature painting has a history of some 1,000 years and the Library's collection (combining the resources of OC and IOLR) is one of the finest in the world. As far as women are concerned they give a good picture of the lives of Hindu as well as Muslim women.

Meredith-Owens, G M. *Turkish Miniatures*. London, 1969. Explains sources and history of Turkish miniature paintings, its main characteristic, the effect of foreign influences etc.

Merdith-Owen, G M. *Persian illustrated manuscripts*. London, 2nd ed. 1973. There are nearly 300 illustrated Persian manuscripts in the British Library (OC) which include examples from the best period of Persian and Indian painting; the earliest examples, the copy of a poem made in Bagdad, dates back to 1396.

Neressian, V. *Armenian illuminated Gospel books*. London, 1987. Originally designed to coincide with an exhibition of the same title it is a good guide to Armenian manuscript illustration, the main themes used, and the collection of items in the department.

Rohatgi, Pauline.: *Catalogue of portraits in the India Office Library and Records*. London, 1983. The catalogue lists significant portraits in the various collections of the India Office Library and Records; the majority come from collections of oil paintings, sculptures, watercolours, miniatures, prints and photographs in the Prints and Drawings Section. Selections have also been made from the printed books published before c.1920 and photographs from the collection of European Manuscripts.

Titley, Norah M. *Miniatures from Turkish manuscript. A catalogue and subject index of painting in the British Library and the British Museum*. London, 1982.

Titley, Norah M. *Miniatures from Persian manuscripts. A catalogue and subject index of paintings from Persia, India and Turkey in the British Library and the British Museum*. London 1983.

Waley, M I (ed.). *Sultan Abdulhamid II Photograph Collection: early Turkish photographs in 51 albums from the British Library on microfiche*. 1987. The albums (now kept in OC) were originally presented to the British Museum by the Sultan in 1893 and contain over 1,800 photographs (part of Abdulhamid's enormous collection of some 30,000 prints now in the Istanbul University Library) which afford a fascinating view of some aspects of the Ottoman Empire in the 1870s and 1880s.

Wood, Frances. *Chinese illustration*. London, 1985. An easy-to-use guide to the history of Chinese illustration with examples from the collection dating back to the ninth century. There are references to early manuscripts and the beginnings of Chinese printing, traditional themes chosen for illustration, Imperial editions, later printing and export painting, colour printing and illustrations.

Sally Brown

Katherine Mansfield's letters in the Department of Manuscripts

Katherine Mansfield is among the great letter-writers. She reveals herself in every aspect of her character – by turns witty, caustic, playful, passionate, anguished, touching or vitriolic – and displays all the qualities of perception and imaginative evocation found in her short stories. Her life was cut tragically short by tuberculosis and the slowly worsening illness (together with the knowledge of its inevitable outcome) pervades much of her correspondence. She suffered acutely from loneliness, physical pain, debility and occasionally despair, but with rare courage continued the struggle to perfect her art, producing some of her best writing in the last years of her life. Even towards the end, her letters to friends have a brave cheerfulness: writing to her cousin Elizabeth in August 1922 she declares that '. . . it's fun to think of three months in London . . .'.[1] She had in fact only four more months to live.

Sadly, Katherine Mansfield's letter to several important correspondents have not survived. She herself destroyed those to her only lover Florian Sobienowski (for which he demanded £40 from her in 1920) and commanded her devoted companion Ida Baker to burn hundreds of her youthful letters, 'treasured through all vicissitudes',[2] in 1918. Very few of the numerous letters she wrote to her family in New Zealand have so far come to light; there are none to her close friend (and later implacable enemy) D H Lawrence and only one to A R Orage, her sometime literary mentor and editor of the weekly *New Age*. The British Library is, therefore, particularly fortunate in possessing two substantial, and meticulously preserved, collections of her letters to the writer and critic Sydney Schiff and his wife Violet, and the translator S S Koteliansky, as well as letters to Ida Baker and to her cousin Elizabeth Russell, a few to Lytton Strachey and a single letter to the painter Mark Gertler, with whom she had a brief romantic intrigue in 1914.

Working through Katherine Mansfield's papers 25 years after her death, her husband John Middleton Murry commented (in a letter preserved in the British Library's Schiff Papers) on 'the extraordinary alterations of [her] moods and attitudes[3], and reflected that '. . . it's indubitably true that she tended to assume a personality to please her correspondent . . .'.[4] In reading through the British Library letters, one is immediately aware of her different 'voices', and the way in which the character of each of her friends determines the persona which she adopts in writing to them. To some extent, of course, this is true of all of us, but in her case it is particularly striking. Even as a child (she was born Kathleen Mansfield Beauchamp in 1888, in Wellington, New Zealand) she was an accomplished actress and 'performer', moving susceptible visitors to tears with her recitations. She published, or lived, at times under the names Julian Mark, K Bowden (the surname of her first husband, whom she left on the evening of their wedding-day), K Bendall and Matilda Berry; her letters were signed variously as Kass, Katherina, Kissienka, Wig, Tig, and Jones.

In an early letter to her cousin Sylvia Payne, a schoolfriend at Queen's College, Harley Street, which she attended from 1903 to 1906, Katherine writes: 'Would you not like to try *all* sorts of lives – one is so very small – but that is the satisfaction of writing – one can impersonate so many people.'[5] Even where we hear only the merest snatch of a voice, as in the letters to Gertler and Lytton Strachey, it is intriguingly distinct. Writing to Gertler she adopts a wheedlingly intimate tone, apologising for the 'grimy snowball' of rumour and intrigue which 'I'd rather have done anything than start'.[6] With Strachey she is bright, ironic and 'social', wryly describing an unsuccessful Hampstead Party at which 'Poor Murry was rather like a porter who had got at last! his passengers into the railway carriage but somehow wouldn't leave them until the train went – the train *would* not go . . .'[7] In many of the letters there is a sense of nervous restlessness which recalls one of the 50 newly-coined aphorisms brought together in an unpublished piece which she entitled 'Bites from the Apple': 'Life is a tremendous game of "Hide the Thimble", without the delicious, childish certainty that there is any thimble to be found.'[8]

Katherine Mansfield's first real meeting with Sydney and Violet Schiff, wealthy patrons and – as one of her biographers puts it – 'collectors of creative persons',[9] was during a visit to her cousin's Villa Flora, in Menton, in April 1920. She was by then very ill with tuberculosis, and her doctors had advised against another English winter. The Schiffs divided their time between London and the Riviera, combining the life of the mind with the most lavish of material comforts. Although Katherine was occasionally repelled by them and (as a letter from Murray elsewhere in the Schiff Papers reveals) could be cuttingly 'harsh and cruel' behind their backs,[10] her letters to them, both together and separately, are intense, eager, and anxious to praise and please.

In one of the earliest Schiff letters, Katherine is 'delighting in the fact of having met you';[11] 'Life is so much the richer for knowing you both . . . Are you my friends as much as I am your friend?'[12] she asks, a little anxiously, on her return to London in May. Later that month, she announces that she has asked T S Eliot (a friend of Murry's) and his wife to dinner: 'What will they be like, I wonder? The grey door of my room keeps on opening and opening in my mind and Mrs Elliott and Elliott [sic] enter. I can't see her at all . . .'.[13] She eagerly seizes every opportunity to 'talk over Art and Letters',[14] and discuss her own work, with such intelligent and receptive friends. During the course of the correspondence there is much discussion of contemporary writers, especially Lawrence and Joyce. Katherine pronounces 'Prufrock' to be 'the best modern poem. It stays in the memory as a work of art'[15], laments the lack of 'passion', the 'deathly cautiousness' of recent English writing,[16] and advises Sydney that 'Delicate perception is not enough: one must find the exact way in which to convey the delicate perception.'[17] Amidst all there are affectionate references to the quiet, companionable times spent with the Schiffs at Menton, and their villa at Roquebrune, set amidst lemon trees and intensely blue lavender bushes.

Writing from Switzerland to London in December 1921, after a peaceful few months with Murry during which, although extremely ill, she had written a clutch of her most brilliant and successful short stories, Katherine expresses her delight in this friendship with a fierce nostalgia which perhaps reflects the relentless progress of the tuberculosis: 'I want to be with you – to listen, talk, look, observe, absorb, remember, rejoice in ...'.[18] Thereafter the correspondence is, sadly, punctuated with silences and mis-understandings. In March 1922 she writes from Paris that 'I had made up my mind ... that that horrible whispering gallery, London, had decided you both to write no more ...'.[19] Although the Schiffs are addressed as 'Dear, precious friends'[20] in August, the letters draw to a close on a note of awkwardness and strain: 'I am so sorry my letter distressed you ... There is nothing to undo as far as I am concerned ...'.[21] The last farewell of all, in an undated letter sent that autumn, is at once pleasing and rueful: 'Don't, if you can help it, think me *too* horrid'.[22]

In Katherine Mansfield's early letters to her Russian friend Koteliansky, we are presented with another 'voice' entirely, by turns brilliant, coquettish, enigmatic, wistful and all-confiding. Juliette Huxley, in a memoir of the 'Bloomsbury Set', declared that 'K M wrote to [Koteliansky] her truly best letters ... coming from her innermost truth.'[23] Certainly, 'Kot' (as he was known to his circle) was an extremely important figure in her life, the 'secret friend' to whom she wrote at times of greatest happiness and misery. The letters begin in early 1915, four years after his arrival in England from Kiev University. They had met in the preceding year, through D H Lawrence – who was later to turn violently against Katherine and Murry – and their own relationship was not without periods of estrangement, although the rifts were always healed by a renewed gesture of friendship on Katherine's part. At the beginning, Koteliansky is clearly in some sense paying court to her, during a period when she is particularly restless and dissatisfied with Murray; she thanks him gracefully for 'the cigarettes in the charming little box and the chocolates ... and the russian skirt fits well – I like it.'[24] Clandestine meetings are arranged at the Russian Law Bureau, a small office in High Holborn which translated and certified Russian documents. Soon Katherine is signing her letters 'Kissienka' and looking forward to the time 'when we are in Russia'.[25]

The distinct note of flirtation in these early letters to Koteliansky is balanced by a serious wish that he should admire and understand Katherine's overwhelming need to write. In March 1915 she writes from Paris of the nights 'full of stars and little moons and big zeppelins' and her inclination to 'write you a long letter but I am afraid you cannot read my handwriting'[26] (a problem familiar to editors of her correspondence). Later in the same month she sends one of her very happiest letters, in which she describes her dream of 'a little house hidden in a ring of poplar trees ... in some place very far away' and declares 'Yes, Kotiliansky [sic], you are really one of my people ...'.[27] And again from Paris, in May, after a brief and unhappy return to London, comes one of her most lyrical, sustained pieces of description, conveying the delight in the natural world captured in her best short stories: 'It is not only leaves you smell when you stand under the trees today; you smell the black wet boughs and stems – the "forest" smell...'.[28]

When Katherine's beloved brother Leslie was killed in France in October 1915, her shock and grief drove her away from London. Writing to Koteliansky from Marseilles in November, she confides that 'I never see anything that I like, or hear anything, without the longing that he should see and hear, too...'.[29] Later letters recapture her sharper, more malicious self. In May 1916 she sends from Cornwall an account of a spectacular fight between Lawrence and his wife Frieda: 'Suddenly Lawrence appeared and made a kind of horrible blind rush at her and they began to scream and scuffle...'.[30] Her moods veer between frantic hope, resignation and despair as her state of health worsens. The friendship dies for a while and is revived when 'Kot' is summoned to Hampstead in September 1918 with the three words: 'Come tonight, Katherine'.[31] Many of her letters to him express her delight in Russian authors and her pleasure in their work together: from time to time she collaborated with him in Russian translations which needed to be cast in a smoother, less idiosyncratic English than his own quaint (though often inspired) renderings. In April 1919 she writes: 'I dislike IMMENSELY not going over the letters with you... I feel Tchekov would be the first to say we must go over them together... I wish you would come in now, this moment, and let us have tea and talk. There is no one here except my cough...'.[32]

During her years of serious illness, Katherine ('Kissienka' no longer) writes to Koteliansky with increasingly sad, nostalgic affection: 'Does it disturb [your loneliness] to know that you are dear to me. Do not let it. It is such a quiet feeling. It is like the light coming into a room...'.[33] At Christmas 1921 she tells him that he is one of those 'who remain in one's life forever'.[34] (It is surely the 'Russianness' of Koteliansky that draws forth such declarations.) A phrase in a letter of July 1922, which speaks of a 'longing that people shall be rooted in life'[35] looks forward to the poignant journal entry on 14 October, her birthday: 'But warm, eager, living life – To be rooted in life... That is what I want.'[36] During her last months she is still working at Koteliansky's translations. The last letter of all, sent from France on 17 October 1922, shortly after entering the Gurdjieff Institute for the Harmonious Development of Man, at Fontainebleau, attempts rather incoherently to describe the new 'truth' she is trying to embrace in an attempt to heal her 'divided' self: 'The world as I know it is no joy to me and I am useless in it. People are almost non-existent... What is important is to try to learn to live.'[37]

Finally, in Katherine Mansfield's letters to two very different women, her cousin 'Elizabeth' (born Mary Annette Beauchamp) who wrote the world-famous *Elizabeth and her German Garden* (1898), and the doggedly devoted Ida Baker, we hear two more distinct 'voices' in the last years of her life. Those to Elizabeth begin in June 1921, while Katherine is staying with Murry at the Chalet des Sapins, in Montana. Ida remembers Elizabeth 'walking over the snow in her little black gaiters' from her chalet at Randogne.[38] Although there had been occasional rivalry and periods of estrangement between the cousins in the past, they now settled into friendship. Nevertheless, Katherine's letters 'gush' rather too much at times – 'And you know, dear wonderful Elizabeth, I have always longed to be allowed to know you a little . . .' – betraying a slight uneasiness.[39] In writing of her illness she is brusquely dismissive: 'I do think it simply unpardonable to bore one's friends with "I can't get out".[40] About her feelings for Murry, however, and the effect of her tuberculosis upon him, she is disarmingly frank: 'He ought to divorce me, marry a really gay young healthy creature, have children . . . I shall never be a wife . . . Poor John. It's hellish to live with a *femme malade* . . .'.[41]

The occasional brittle, self-conscious note in the letters to Elizabeth derives, perhaps, from the resentment underlying Katherine's fondness for her cousin. Writing to Sydney Schiff in December 1921, she admits that Elizabeth 'fascinates' her but adds: 'And for some reason the mechanism of life hardly seems to touch her. She refuses to be ruffled . . . I find it devilish, devilish, devilish . . .'.[42] She clearly craves Elizabeth's approval of her own writing – 'I should like to write one story good enough to offer you one day'[43] – and is undisguisedly delighted when her cousin heaps praise on *The Garden Party* (published in February 1922): 'Your letter . . . was almost "too good to be true" . . .'[44] A rather uneven tone, however, persists to the end of this small group of letters which seem to mix genuine, if effusive, sentiment – 'I feel I shall never look at a bud or a flower again without thinking of you'[45] with a slightly false self-abasement and awkward attempts to impress Elizabeth with 'fine writing' or *bons mots*.

'Lesley Moore', or 'L M', was the name Katherine chose for Ida Baker (compounded of her own brother's Christian name and Ida's mother's maiden name). She also referred to her at different times as Godmother, Aida, Jones, The Faithful One, The Rhodesian Mountain and the Albatross. Although Ida was excluded from much of Katherine's artistic and intellectual life, she always turned to her in times of crisis. Ida's lifelong devotion to Katherine is simply and touchingly chronicled in the book she published in 1971, *Katherine Mansfield: the Memories of L. M.* Its first description of Katherine is at Queen's College, where they had met in 1903, 'in a full, silk dress, her head tilted a little, her eyes glowing, her lips a little open as she sang to herself . . .'.[46] It ends with a description of Katherine's funeral at Fontainebleau in January 1923: 'I had brought a bunch of marigolds, a flower she loved, and there were not many other flowers there for her. So I stepped forward, looked down, and dropped them in.'[47]

The content of Katherine's early letters to Ida, sent from New Zealand to London in 1906-8 and from London to Rhodesia (where Ida had gone to join her family) in 1914-16, will never be known. While conveying her intense sadness and regret at Katherine's order that such 'dreadful rubbish' should be burned, in 1918, 'L. M.' writes only vaguely of their subject-matter: 'Pages and pages of early girlish enthusiasms, hopes and visions – pictures of her own land and the England of her dreams.'[48] Ida gave all those that followed, dating from April 1918 until Katherine's death, to the Department of Manuscripts in 1956. The earlier ones are mostly addressed to 'Dearest Jones' (the name each used to the other when all was well between them) and signed 'Katie', but after Spring 1921 she becomes simply 'Ida' and the letters are signed 'Katherine' or 'K. M'.

During the last five years of Katherine's life, Ida's steady affection and loyalty were often put severely to the test. Since Murry was engaged in editing *The Athenaeum* in London (and was in any case 'too full of self pity', in Ida's view, to give his wife any help),[49] she served as companion and nurse during the winters in Italy and the South of France, as well as occasional housekeeper in London. Katherine was at times very ill indeed, bitter at what she saw as Murry's defection and unhappily conscious of her new status as an outcast. Although the sequence of letters begins happily, with Katherine expressing her joy and relief at being 'home' again in London after three weeks of 'imprisonment' during the bombing of Paris ('But Jones – one's *own* fire – and lighting the gas and making tea – and oh! the bath water which really was hot...')[50], her mood changes with the dreaded news that she has 'definitely got consumption' six days later.[51] Writing from Cornwall in May 1918, a note of anguish and depression sets in: 'I feel... cold, sealed up, hard... everybody seems to be evil and vile....'.[52] When 'Jones' falls ill (she was working in a hot, cramped munitions factory and living in a YWCA hostel) Katherine berates her for her silence; suffering 'an awful attack of that spinal rheumatism' she forces herself to admit, with an invalid's complete selfishness, that 'I only love you when you're blind to everybody but US.'[53]

The often fractious and caustic tone of these letters is interspersed with (perhaps slightly guilty) outbursts of praise and lavish reassurance. When she rallies a little, Katherine writes with all her old warmth and charm – 'When I went out today the air smelt like moss... The peach leaves are like linnet wings... I hope you had a good journey. Will you please wire me immediately if you want any money...'[54] but as her condition worsens she cries out in angry misery: 'I was not born an invalid and I want to get well... Do you understand?... Help me to escape!'.[55]

In August 1922 Katherine made her will (leaving her carved walking-stick to Koteliansky, her favourite small edition of Shakespeare to Elizabeth, and her gold watch and chain to Ida) before coming to London, where she attended the lectures of P Ouspensky, a Russian who had worked with Gurdjieff for seven years. When, after a series of distressing and unsuccessful x-ray treatments in Paris, she entered Gurdjieff's recently established Institute at Fontainebleau, Ida accompanied her there and stayed two nights, leaving Katherine 'radiant, her eyes shining' but feeling as if she had come from a funeral.[56]

The last letters to 'L. M.' are immensely moving, full of a new, almost childlike simplicity: 'The leaves fall all day and the grass smells good. We are making a Turkish Bath which will be very comforting... I hope you are happy.'[57] The final few describe her immediate surroundings and her 'work': 'My hands are ruined for the present with scraping carrots and peeling onions';[58] 'I shall be glad though when spring comes. Winter is a difficult time...'.[59] One can sympathise with Christopher Isherwood's feelings when he writes to a friend in 1937 about 'the final part of poor Kathy's journal... a book which still makes me cry... that last desperate effort to become "pure in heart" by milking cows at the house of those phoney Russians at Versailles...'.[60] After Katherine's death, from a massive lung haemorrhage, on 9 January 1923, a letter to Ida was found inside her blotter: 'I'm looking for signs of spring already. Under the espalier pear trees there were wonderful Christmas roses... Write and tell me how you are will you? dear Ida?'. It is signed simply 'With love from K. M.'.[61]

References

1. Add.MS 50844, fol.16^v.
2. Ida Baker, *Katherine Mansfield: The Memories of L. M.* London, 1985. p.126
3. Add.MS 52921, fol.20.
4. Ibid., fol.21, 21^v.
5. Vincent O'Sullivan and Margaret Scott (eds.), *The collected letters of Katherine Mansfield*, vol.i, Oxford, 1984. p.19.
6. Add.MS 49597F, fol.13.
7. Add.MS 60679, fol.45.
8. In the *Adam International Review* archive at King's College London.
9. Antony Alpers, *The Life of Katherine Mansfield*, London, 1980. p.313.
10. Add.MS 52921, fol.23^v.
11. Add.MS 52919, fol.115^v.
12. Ibid., fol.117.
13. Ibid., fol.123.
14. Ibid., fol.112.
15. Ibid., fol.179^v.
16. Ibid., fol.180^v.
17. Ibid., fol.117, 117^v.
18. Ibid., fol.160.
19. Ibid., fol.170.
20. Ibid., fol.178^v.
21. Ibid., fol.181.
22. Ibid., fol.182^v.
23. Juliette Huxley 'Ottoline', in *Adam International Reviews*, xxxviii (London, 1972-3), p.93.
24. Add.MS 48970, fol.177.
25. Ibid., fol.293
26. Ibid., fol.166^v.
27. Ibid., fols.168^v, 169.
28. Ibid., fol.171.
29. Ibid., fol.172^v.
30. Ibid., fol.204.
31. Alphers, op. cit., p.286.
32. Add.MS 48970, fol.194, 194^v.
33. Ibid., fol.220.
34. Ibid., fol.238^v.
35. Ibid., fol.264^v.
36. C K Stead (ed.), *The letters and journals of Katherine Mansfield*, London, 1977, p.279.
37. Add.MS 48970, fol.286^v.
38. Baker, op. cit., p.167.
39. Add. MS 50844, fol.1.
40. Ibid., fol.2.
41. Ibid., fol.2^v.
42. Add.MS 52919, fol.168.
43. Add.MS 50844, fol.9^v.
44. Ibid., fol.10.
45. Ibid., fol.10.
46. Baker, op. cit., p.23.
47. Ibid., p.230.
48. Ibid., p.127.
49. Ibid., p.128.

50. Add.MS 49064A, fol.2^v.
51. Ibid., fol.11^v.
52. Ibid., fol.22.
53. Ibid., fols.34–5.
54. Ibid., fols.58,58^v.
55. Ibid., fol.68^v.
56. Baker, op. cit., p.214.
57. Add.MS 49064A, fols.192, 193^v.
58. Ibid., fol.221^v.
59. Ibid., fols.228, 229^v.
60. Sotheby's Sale Catalogue, 15 December 1987, Lot 80.
61. Add.MS 49064A, fols.234^v, 235, 236^v.

Frances Harris

Rich and poor widows: eighteenth-century women in the Althorp Papers

The full range of manuscripts in the Manuscript Collections which could be used as source material for aspects of women's history is too great to be surveyed here. Since the collections touch on most fields of human activity, almost any item is of potential relevance. Literary manuscripts form one important category, and in the archival field certain well-known collections, the papers of Florence Nightingale and Marie Stopes for example, stand out as major primary sources for the study of innovative women in non-traditional rôles. For lesser known and more conventional women in all ranks of society, the wealth of material – household books and accounts, diaries and memoirs (religious and secular), correspondence and papers – is apparent at a glance from the department's published catalogues and indexes.

There are still discoveries to be made even among the oldest and most constantly-used parts of the collections, particularly in so comparatively recent a field as women's history; and additions to the collections are constantly being made. One of the largest and most notable of these recent acquisitions is the papers of the Spencers of Althorp, a family archive of great richness and variety, spanning four centuries of British history. In this short paper I will try to give a small sample of its potential as a source for women's history, by talking about three eighteenth-century women, Sarah, Duchess of Marlborough, Lady Betty Germaine, and Georgiana, Countess Spencer, whose activities are documented in different ways in the collection.

The combined span of life of these three women takes us from the Restoration to the early nineteenth century. All were very different personalities, but they have the common point of interest that for long periods of their lives they belonged to one of the few socio-economic groups which at this period gave women a genuine measure of independence: that of the well-to-do widow. A widow had the social status which marriage conferred, but her property and income, unlike those of a married woman, were usually at her own disposal. Another notable woman of the period, Lady Mary Wortley Montagu (whose experience of marriage was admittedly not happy), found it incredible that any woman who had once been set free by the death of her husband, should voluntarily go into slavery again by remarrying. All three women had opportunities to remarry, but deliberately chose to maintain their independent status.

A large collection of the unpublished memoirs, correspondence, financial and estate papers and wills of Sarah, Duchess of Marlborough (1660-1744) is amongst the Althorp Papers, for the very good reason that it was her wealth, bestowed on her grandson John Spencer, which founded the fortunes of the Spencer family in the eighteenth century. All her life she was a woman with 'a passion for government' – a compulsion to wield power in both private and public life. As a passionate and committed Whig, she was fond of claiming that 'though a woman' she had done all she could to promote the Whig cause and preserve the liberties of England. It was not until she had vainly sacrificed the favour and friendship of Queen Anne to these ends, that she was finally brought to accept the limitations of a woman's influence in politics, acknowledging bitterly that 'the things that are worth naming will ever be done from the influence of men'. She never ceased to chafe against the 'insignificance' of women in this respect, or to wish in moments of national crisis that she was a man and could take an active part in parliamentary and cabinet government. Even so, her frustration had a positive aspect, for the memoirs in which she gives an account of her political involvement, and the related correspondence which she preserved, are an important historical source.

In private life there were fewer obstacles to her exercise of power. It was her boast in old age that no woman had ever been so useful to her family. Her favour with the Queen had been the basis of her husband's career, of her daughters' advantageous marriages, and of the family's whole fortunes. She also claimed with some justice that it was her acumen and vigilance which saved this fortune from such national calamaties as the South Sea Bubble, and as well as from the more insidious embezzlements of stewards and lawyers.

In fact she was very unusual in not having to wait for widowhood to obtain financial independence, since her husband voluntarily placed all her own income from her parental estate and court offices in trust for her sole use, enabling her to manage her own investments quite separately from his. By the time of his death she was therefore a wealthy woman in her own right. As much of a Whig in private as in public affairs, she considered this not as an indulgence on his part, but as an essential human right and liberty. Without it, she commented, she would have been reduced to the level of dispossessed Continental peasantry, 'who neither plough nor sow' because they had nothing they could call their own.

But it was her administration of the family fortunes during her twenty-two years of widowhood which was her most remarkable achievement. As her husband's principal executor and trustee, she devoted much of her time to administering his estate (worth over a million pounds), by investing it in land and government securities. This financial control not only enabled her to influence the interest rates for government borrowing, but also made her virtually head of her own family, a most unusual situation for a dowager in an aristocratic society. These responsibilities, together with the need to retain her independence, made her reject the prospect of remarriage, on the grounds that her situation was 'in many things different from other women's'.

At the same time she invested as much of her own wealth as possible in land. By the time of her death she had acquired thirty estates in twelve counties. These were purchases which she had initiated and managed herself, concerning herself with the minutest details of valuation and administration. Her lists of these properties, with her valuations and comments, are among the Althorp Papers, together with the beautifully executed estate maps which she commissioned.

In widowhood she was able to satisfy her fascination with politics vicariously by controlling the conduct of her grandsons, using the threat of disinheritance to ensure they did her bidding. Her letters to her heir, John Spencer, and the five volumes of her draft and cancelled wills bear witness to the rigorousness of her control. This dominance extended well beyond her own lifetime. Since she was determined that no government would ever be able to control her family's votes in Parliament, she stipulated that both he and his son should forfeit their inheritance if they accepted any public office. The course of her life showed clearly what a woman of energy, force of personality and above all, wealth, could achieve, in freeing herself from the restrictions usually imposed on her sex.

The Duchess of Marlborough's main concern was the establishment of her family. In her widowhood, while in a fit of anger against her heirs, she did spend a considerable sum in endowing almshouses at St Albans, but she afterwards regretted that she had been induced to 'waste' so much of her fortune in this way. The life of her somewhat younger contemporary, Lady Betty Germaine (1680-1769) illustrates the growth of a more systematic charitable activity and social responsibility amongst privileged and independent women. Born into an aristocratic family, the Earls of Berkeley, Lady Betty had married beneath her. Her husband, Sir John Germaine, was a professional soldier of low extraction who had made himself notorious as the correspondent in the divorce case of his first wife, the Duchess of Norfolk. According to the Duchess of Marlborough, who crossed swords with Lady Betty in an electioneering contest, the match came about because she had no portion to attract a better suitor, having in her youth 'had an unlucky accident with one of her father's servants'. Nevertheless the marriage was not only happy, but extremely profitable to her. When Germaine died in 1718 he left her the great wealth in estates and works of art which he had inherited from the first wife.

Lady Betty did not fulfil her husband's recommendation to her to remarry, retaining her freedom, as she put it, to 'follow her own whims'. In her fifty years of widowhood she lived down the indiscretions of her youth and gained a reputation for real though rather idiosyncratic benevolence. An account by Sir William Hamilton who knew her well when he was a young subaltern in the guards is preserved among the Althorp Papers.

Her charities were twofold. In the first place she kept open house at her town house in St James's Square for young men of good family, small fortunes and acceptable moral character, to the point where it became almost a free private club for this social group. Once an invitation had been issued, the recipient could come whenever he pleased. Hamilton, who was one of her favourites, says that 'she made allowances for young men, never reproaching any of us, or asking any questions if we had neglected her for a month or two'. A set portion of her income was devoted to this form of housekeeping. The food was very plentiful but conspicuously unextravagant, often including dishes not normally seen at aristocratic houses, such as 'cockles, cow heel, tripe, [and] ox cheek'.

Lady Betty herself was a firm government Whig, but made it a general rule, in order not to discourage any of her visitors, that there should be no political disputes at her table. Men of opposing parties therefore often found themselves together there, when they met socially nowhere else, and Hamilton remarks that good use was sometimes made of this neutral ground. She kept a regular supply of the latest political pamphlets and newspapers, explaining that 'she took them in to employ those who came to lounge in her house that it might leave her time to follow her own whims'. She loved to treat her company to shows, fairs and public gardens in London, keeping a yellow canvass bag with 'fool money' written on it, to finance these expeditions; and she subscribed to the opera so that she could lend her tickets to any penniless young man who wanted to make use of them.

Although she was happiest in London, as a good landed proprietress she thought it her duty to spend the income of her estate at Drayton in Northamptonshire for the benefit of the local community (something which the Duchess of Marlborough, whose estates were bought entirely as investments, seldom thought necessary). For this purpose she lured a party of friends to stay with her there for some weeks every summer, making the group as large as possible, so that the income from the estate might be the sooner spent. She preserved game on the estate assiduously so that the young men who accompanied her should have good sport.

Lady Betty's activities were not confined to her own circle and tenants. She set aside £2,000 a year of her income to distribute to the London poor. Her street door had a special box for receiving petitions and begging letters, and she spent her mornings reading and dealing with them. Fraudulent claims inevitably mixed with cases of genuine hardship, and Hamilton remarks that 'the sagacity she showed in distinguishing which of them deserved attention was very extraordinary'. Having set aside those which she thought deserving of help, she then engaged some of her young men to escort her to the slums of Wapping or Whitechapel 'or some other extremity of London' to examine into the truth of the petitions for herself and distribute her charity in the form of pensions or gifts.

These recollections of Lady Betty Germaine were written down by Hamilton after her death at the request of her friend, Georgiana, widow of the 1st Earl Spencer (1738-1813). It is clear that Lady Spencer took this example as one of the models for her own conduct in widowhood. She had been widowed in 1783 while still in her forties, and from this time until her death thirty years later she devoted herself to charitable works.

She was a very different personality from Lady Betty Germaine, more conventional, and less spontaneous in her benevolence. There was an element of vanity (for which it is fair to add that she privately castigated herself) in her awareness that she was admired as a doer of good works. It was possible to follow her life almost from day-to-day in her widowhood through the correspondence she conducted with her closest friend, Mrs Caroline Howe, for over fifty years between 1759 and 1814. This survives substantially complete on both sides, amounting in all to about 6,000 letters, and may well be the largest single correspondence the Library has ever acquired.

The most interesting part of her archive, however, is the group of 37 volumes of papers concerning her charities. Like Lady Betty Germaine she set aside a certain portion of her income for charitable purposes and invited petitions from those in need. Unlike Lady Betty she kept these requests for charity, in a neat alphabetical arrangement which has still survived, and with annotations of what action had been taken in response. Many, though by no means all, of her petitioners were women. These papers therefore shed light on the plight of women for whom the death of a husband meant not freedom and affluence, but desitution. The petitioners were from all ranks of society, from working-class women, who supported their families as washerwomen and cleaners by day and as sick nurses by night, to various degrees of distressed gentlewomen who needed assistance in setting up the small schools, shops of needlework businesses which were their only hope of making themselves self-supporting.

These are only a few examples of women's lives as revealed in the Althorp Papers. One might equally well mention the letters of Elizabeth Eyre, recording her determined efforts to set up a sail-cloth manufacture for the Navy in Gainsborough in the 1760s; or the papers of Rachel Lloyd, the housekeeper of Kensington Palace, one of a notable group of eighteenth-century women whose enthusiasm for collecting historical anecdotes and transcribing documents has preserved historical evidence which would otherwise have been lost. In this and other archives much waits to be explored, relating not just to the lives of exceptional or pioneering women, but to those who are equally important because they represent the norm of female experience in a particular social class or period.

Annie Gilbert

Oral history: governesses and teachers 1890–1989

The popular concept of the lives and status of English governesses in modern society has been mainly based on an amalgam of historical evidence, romantic fiction and art, which originated from the nineteenth century.

There was a considerable amount of literature published in the first half of the nineteenth century, both fact and fiction, which referred to governesses. Jane Eyre, portrayed by Charlotte Brontë as a romantic heroine, is probably the most well-known governess in fiction. Brontë, herself a governess, describes one of her profession, as having 'the pale despondent looks' of her class, and one who 'has no existence . . . except as connected with the wearisome duties she has to fulfil.'[1]

Richard Redgrave's painting, *The Governess – she sees no kind domestic visage near*, portrays the governess sitting mournfully in the dark foreground, holding a black edged letter – the morsel of dry toast on the plate beside her underlines the pathos of her position and contrasts sharply with the unbridled happiness of the girls in the sunlight beyond.

Evidence from periodical sources also reinforces the concept that many governesses, though belonging to the oldest, honourable profession open to women, were in the main grave, down-trodden, invisible and without status. 'A governess has no equals and therefore can have no sympathy', *Quarterly Review* (1848). 'What is the position of a governess? She has none', *English Women's Journal* (1860).

The nineteenth century has produced a dichotomous view of the governess; as an individual she is portrayed as a romantic figure, but as a group she belongs to a distinct class of women of invisible and undefined status. This view is perhaps best illustrated in L M Alcott's *Little Women*:

'We have many respectable and worthy young women who are employed by the nobility, because being daughters of gentlemen, they are both well-bred and accomplished you know' said Miss Kate, in a patronising tone, that hurt Meg's pride, and made her work seem not only distasteful but degrading.[2]

Although there are many literary sources referring to nineteenth-century governess, very little evidence exists of their background, motivation, life-style, responsibilities, perceptions of themselves, and the important influences they had on their charges. Yet their influence must have been considerable, since they were responsible for the education and moral upbringing of the children of the upper and middle classes. 'The power of governesses was acknowledged by the middle-aged lady in a turban – she felt the power of the governess' knowledge in the education of her daughters... but nobody thought of the poor, fagged, knowledge herself... being thrown on the world, and going forth among strangers to educate others... '*The Morning Post* (1844) – report on the speech given by Charles Dickens at a dinner for the subscribers to The Governesses Benevolent Institution.

It is against this nineteenth-century background that this oral history first began. The idea was originated by the present Governesses Benevolent Institution – the Board of which has kindly assisted and supported me in this rewarding project.

The main objective is to record on the basis of interviews, the individual and collective experiences of governesses and schoolteachers, who lived and worked in the first half of the twentieth century, and to produce an integrated, archival collection of taped recordings which can then be used for historical research. The collection of recordings will be deposited in the National Sound Archive. The recordings will also be transcribed and made available for research.

The profession of governess is now practically obsolete, but it has left society an important legacy in the education of successive generations of children. All the women, many of whom are now in their eighties and beyond, are members of The Schoolmistresses and Governesses Benevolent Institution. They are able to offer a first hand account of life as a governess.

The Governesses Benevolent Insitution was founded in 1843, its objective was;

To raise the character of Governesses as a class, and thus improve the tone of Female Education; to assist in distress and age those Governesses whose exertions for their parents, or families have prevented such a provision.

In 1847, the GBI founded Queen's College, Harley Street, in order to train young governesses, who were 'demure ladies, rather deprecating in manner and dressed in the rear of fashion.' A retirement home was provided for elderly governesses in Kentish Town and named, in true Victorian manner, Asylum for Aged Governesses.

In 1952, the Institution's scope was enlarged to include assistance to women teachers from the private sector, thus it became The Schoolmistresses and Governesses Benelovent Institution. Present day members of the SGBI either reside in the Society's Queen Mary House in Kent, or in their own homes around the country.

The women who have already taken part in the initial stages of this project have been most willing and active participants, and have, I believe, enjoyed the experience of recollecting and being interviewed.

The structure of the interview is based on a questionnaire, which is designed to cover personal information, professional experiences and subjects of historical interest. The interview, which may be spread over a number of visits, broadly follows the outline set out below:

1. PERSONAL BACKGROUND: Date and place of birth; occupation of parents; size of the family and position therein; the home, size and situation; living conditions.

2. CHILDHOOD: Early memories, traditional games; activities within and without the family; literature; favourite books – reasons for; musical activities; discipline and

parental instruction; family traditions; contact with other governesses; influences; religion; travel.

Recollections of the First World War, effect on the family, reactions, family involvement; rôle of women; suffragettes; aftermath; social changes.

3. EDUCATION: Schooling; conditions and methods; qualifications; leaving age; career aspirations; opportunities, comparison with brothers; reasons for choice of profession.

4. NINETEENTH CENTURY GOVERNESSES: Knowledge of and general comparison of duties; change in status; views on the early women's suffrage movement; the influence of romantic fiction etc; memories and experiences of older governesses.

5. TRAINING: Type and content; methods; standards; conditions; how financed; length of; qualifications; relationships with teachers and peers; holidays; travel; influence of literature, art and music; politics.

6. FIRST PROFESSIONAL POST: How the post was obtained; qualifications required; conditions of employment; occupation of employers; description of household; demarkation of staff responsibilities; salary; duties; teaching methods; hours of work; daily routine (personal and household); responsibilities and status in household; qualities necessary for rôle, qualities aimed for; description of living and working conditions; pension plan; medical expenses etc; relationship with employers, peers and other staff; reasons for leaving post; contact with other governesses, views on.

General recollections of events and position as a governess/teacher in society. In the case of a teacher: omitting household, family etc, but including reactions to and experiences of the 'marriage bar' on women teachers which was introduced in the 1920s.

7. OTHER POSTS: How obtained (*eg*, through an agency or recommendation); description; comparisons; changes, observations as above.

8. SECOND WORLD WAR: Occupation at the outbreak of war; personal reactions and that of the household; education and methods of teaching; effect on children; contingency plans; shortages; duties in the household/armed services/war effort; recollections; experiences of bombing, aftermath, changes and adjustements.

The 1944 Education Act, effect and implementation.

9. THE POST WAR PERIOD: Occupation; lifestyle; general and social changes; events; inventions etc.

10. THE PRESENT: Activities; leisure interests; views and observations; communication and technology; education, the 1988 Education Act; national and international events, etc.

Often answers to structured questions may be interwoven with personal reminiscences, it is from these memories that valuable additional information may emanate; *eg* memories and experiences of famous people, mothers who were suffragettes, involvement in important events etc.

When one is invited to listen to the recollections of a life, it is important to be responsive and open to new avenues of enquiry. In my view, oral history should combine structure and definition with empathy and flexibility. The purpose of the interview is not to invade or interrogate, but to travel back through an individual's life, at her invitation. I have tried to conduct interviews in such a way as to allow the interviewees to play a positive rôle and to give them a sense of the project as a whole. The women are intelligent and articulate and have much to offer.

In the course of this on-going project, two principal features have come into sharp focus: the immense resevoir and multiplicity of information stored in the memories of this distinct group of women, and the importance and value of oral history as an instrument for recording facts and challenging historical assumptions.

It has been a privilege to meet these women, who from their background, education and training, learned to observe and to be aware of changing conditions around them, and who successfully communicated this, and other knowledge, to their pupils. In many cases, life-long friendships have developed between the governesses and their ex-pupils.

The image of the governess as portrayed and documented in the nineteenth century, is of a pale, almost invisible figure of low standing. In marked contrast, the twentieth century governess, through the medium of oral history, emerges as a dedicated, single-minded and independent woman, whose status may now be redefined through the perspective of her own experiences and seen in the light of her influence on and her value to society.

References

1. Gaskell, Elizabeth Cleghorn. *The life of Charlotte Brontë*. London, 1857. p.211.
2. Alcott, Louise May. *Little women*. (2nd edition) London, 1885. p.174–175.

Discussion

In the subsequent discussion the following points were raised:

The likely adverse effect on the social sciences of government retention procedures in respect of files and papers (in any one year, less than one per cent of the papers generated by government departments is transferred to the Public Record Office; case papers from the Departments of Health, Employment and Social Services will probably be destroyed; statistics only will be preserved); the fact that readers must be prepared to do their own research (they should not assume that the level of work on the Althorp papers is the norm); recognition that computerisation and online catalogues will provide easier access to the contents of manuscripts but that automation will be of limited value in the case of archives; the problem of retaining certain types of records (there is no statutory obligation to retain the records of the Equal Opportunities Commission); the need to employ female interviewers when conducting interviews for oral archives (when husband and wife were interviewed in the two India series – *Plain Tales from the Raj* and the *British in India Oral Archives Project* – the questions invariably focused on the rôle of the male – Mary Thatcher of the Centre for South Asian Studies at Cambridge was cited as an illustration of the more balanced results achieved when a woman interviews a woman); the need to recognise that the records of institutions such as the India Office inevitably reflect imperialist and often racist attitudes.

The following participants took part in the discussion: Patricia Barr (writer); Anita Burdett (Institute of Commonwealth Studies); Pat Darter (Equal Opportunities Commission); Sylvia Collicott (Polytechnic of North London); Anna Davin (History Workshop): May Katzen (University of Leicester); Liz Stanley (University of Manchester); and Richard Hayward (SGBI).

B C Bloomfield

Collection development and women's studies

'Collection development' is library jargon and not perhaps immediately intelligible to laypersons so some attempted definition is advisable at the start. Libraries have served as repositories of recorded knowledge since ancient times; usually regarded with some reverence, access to the information contained in them was often restricted to specialists, either religious or secular. Collections in those libraries usually either arose from bequest, gift or a natural process of accretion. The later development of libraries led in the nineteenth century to the rise of a professional class of librarians who saw it as part of their rôle to provide a more open system of access to the collections in their care; librarians then began more actively to manage both the collections and the readership so as to maximise benefits to both. 'Collection development' is a part of collection management and implies a much more active rôle in shaping the book and information collections in libraries; it involves positive buying to strengthen collections, discarding items no longer useful or superseded, tailoring services to the strengths available, and measuring reader demands on the collections to match resources to meet those demands. The concept was developed mainly in the large research libraries of North America and arose from their need to cope with increased reader demand and inadequate historic collections. The techniques of collection development are spreading to Europe because current financial support for libraries here is no longer sufficient to ensure that all librarians can buy all the books their readers want, and because librarians need to try to foresee what future generations of users and researchers will need for their work. Since libraries can no longer afford to buy everything their readers may need, inter-dependence between libraries becomes a necessary fact of life (as it always really was) and co-operation between libraries in collection buying and service provision essential. But the first task for every library is to produce its own definite collection development policy statement with the active co-operation of both staff and users so that it can serve as an agreed agenda for the library's operations. This statement then needs to be implemented by a series of strategies in the areas of acquisitions, preservation and reader services, matching resources, both staff and financial, to the library's defined goals.

Active co-operation between libraries can be in all those activities: acquisitions, preservation and reader services, which are the essential parts of library operations and need to be thoroughly costed and monitored to achieve the most effective results. In the field of acquisitions and resources sharing the 'Conspectus' technique devised by the Research Libraries Group in North America can be of particular assistance.

'Conspectus' is a method of recording in alpha-numeric codes the existing collection strength (ECS) and the current collecting intensity (CCI) of any library's stock. The strength of the existing collection is indicated on a numberical scale extending from 0 (the lowest) to 5 (the highest) and the range of languages covered by an alphabetical code such as 'E' meaning English language only, 'F' principally a mixture of English and other European languages, 'W' material in European and non-European languages, and 'Y' mainly in one or more languages, other than English, from one linguistic or geographic area. The whole range of knowledge is broken up in a series of subject categories loosely based on the Library of Congress Subject Classification and assigned separate class codes. The strength of the library's collections is then analysed under the subject divisions and assigned alpha-numeric codes which can be keyboarded to create a machine readable data-base and then interrogated by subject, library, and other combinations to enable users to discover the best or most suitable library to use in any region or co-operating system. Almost all North American research libraries have entered their data into the RLIN 'Conspectus' system and are using this as the basis for the North American Inventory Project to promote more active and productive co-operation in acquisitions and reader services. In the United Kingdom the British Library and the Scottish national and university libraries have entered their data in a collective file and the National Library of Wales will complete its survey this year. Other major university and research libraries are exploring the costs and benefits of entering the system, which when freely accessible to librarians and users, can direct readers to the best resourced library, or the most convenient, for their research work.

Co-operation in preservation is facilitated by the National Union Catalogue of Microform Masters now in process under the auspices of the National Preservation Office. This records all master microfilm negatives undertaken for preservation purposes so as to avoid needless duplication of scarce time and effort, but it can also be helped by 'Conspectus' indicating existing collecting strength and the assignment of primary collecting responsibility (PCR) in any co-operative system. The British Library has also recently received a grant of US $1.5 million from the Mellon Foundation to promote conservation microfilming, and to this has been added grants of half a million US $ each to the Bodleian Library and the University Library, Cambridge for the same purpose. Other local libraries band together under the 'Newsplan' initiative in co-operative regional projects to assemble and preserve by microfilming complete runs of local newspapers.

Co-operation in reader services involves improving access for readers to information and/or libraries holding that information. The government and the Library and Information Services Councils (LISC) have proposed a system of Local Information Plans (LIPS) which aim to promote agreements between the leading libraries in any region or district under which certain services are provided to readers from other libraries in return for payment or reciprocal services. Trial schemes are already in operation but there has so far been no rush to enter into such agreements. Local agreements for readers from one library to use the services of another have always been commonplace, although it seems in the future they may have to be more formal and regulated. But access also implies access for distant readers and users entailing inter-library loan, facsimile transmission, or remote access to computer-held information. Such arrangements are in operation but the inhibiting factor is cost and unless some system of cost recovery or reimbursement can be found the future development of such schemes will be necessarily slow.

These are the sort of things collection development deals with and some examples of how these techniques may help users in their search for information in libraries. What of women's studies?

History seems to have begun as a simple record of events often compiled under religious auspices. From this developed what is sometimes known as 'political' history: the record of wars, battles, treaties and similar processes which might be called 'men's' history? During the eighteenth and nineteenth centuries in the west 'economic' history developed as a way of studying society and, post-Marx, we have the study of society by class or function. Is the rise of 'women's studies' simply another step along this road organised by the 'splitters' in history, as opposed to the 'lumpers' who believe in weaving all history into a single plain historical narrative? I think there is a case for so regarding them and if so perhaps we can expect to have 'children's studies' and other categorical imperatives arising in the future.

To project this explanation is not to deny the value of looking at history and groups identified by outward and visible characteristics afresh and from a new standpoint. ('Black' studies in the USA is an obvious parallel case.) New truths may become apparent from a different analysis of the evidence and it is the province of librarians with their collection development policies to see that the evidence survives and is accessible for use by scholars. Examples of the sort of thing not easily accessible previously can be seen in Paul Morgan's study of Frances Wolfreson and 'hor bouks'[1] – a study of a seventeenth century women book collector, the work of Emily Faithfull and the Victoria Press (the records of which seem to have disappeared) described by W W Head and William E Fredemann[2], Elizabeth Hageman's bibliography on women writers in Tudor England[3], and the publication in microform of the collection of work by women writers of the nineteenth century advertised by Chadwyck-Healey, Avero Publications and the Nineteenth Century Short Title Catalogue Project (NSTC).[4] Similarly, since the mounting of the Eighteenth Century Short Title Catalogue (ESTC) on BLAISE and RLIN (in the USA) it is now possible to search that published literature in English in ways never previously possible and to extract, for example, all titles relating to women in any one year or decade or other specified parameters. These are a few examples of the ways in which collection development and librarians can organise literature in response to scholarly demands and open new avenues for research.

There may be a case for the contention that previously 'women's studies' have been neglected and that source material for such studies is difficult to find and has not been consciously preserved; but a much greater problem is likely to be finding relevant material in what has been consciously kept in archive and records without discrimination. My colleague Penelope Tuson discovered much material in the India

Office Records once she began to examine those sources; previously no one had bothered to ask the appropriate questions.[5]

And fashions change. A woman reader who had read Aphra Behn in her youth attempted to re-read her in old age only to discover that her sensibility had changed during the Regency period and she was no longer to her taste.[6] Similar changes take place in academic fields of study and what is now fashionable may decline soon to be replaced by other demands. Librarians and collection development policies must be able to adapt to avoid disappointing future scholars; we must continually attempt to second-guess research trends and yet maintain the quality and coverage of our library collections.

Collection development can attempt this in three principal ways: first, by selecting literature with regard to quality and trying to asses its potential importance; second, by co-operating with other libraries and institutions to provide guides to collections in requisite detail making those guides easily and conveniently available; and third, by organising the literature for research in an adequate fashion by the provision of indexes, catalogues, handlists and other finding aids. Let us consider each of these in the context of women's studies.

The first, the selection of appropriate material for women's studies is less straightforward than it may seem. Hitherto national and university and research libraries in the United Kingdom and abroad have in general had sufficient funds to select and acquire material on a broad range of subjects and in a wide range of languages. Now the position is altered and financial stringency rules with a consequent danger that, without co-operation and coordination, gaps in provision and coverage will occur. (An example from the past can be found in the gaps in coverage for American published material that developed in the British [Museum] Library's collections between 1900 and 1950 now being remedied by the efforts of the American Trust for the British Library. The gap-filling exercise has taken account of the needs of women's studies in its work.) Clear statements of acquisition and collection development policies from the major research libraries are urgently needed so that they can be agreed by users and form part of a national plan for coverage seen to be adequate for present and future researchers. At the very least the national libraries benefiting from copyright and legal deposit privileges should work together to ensure this.

The second, co-operation and coordination between libraries in any region, national or international area, is becoming more necessary as institutions and their libraries are forced to specialise in face of the avalanche of publication, the necessity to be selective in acquisition, and the increasing demand from users for more services. Libraries must co-operate in planning acquisition, retention, preservation and provision of services and readers must know – or must be able easily to discover – what to expect from these co-operating libraries otherwise the co-operation is fruitless. What is needed is rapid access to computerised guides to collections based on assessments, like those provided by 'Conspectus' and its ratings, capable of easy and speedy revision. Guides to the literature available in libraries, archives and other repositories are sadly deficient and one of the major tasks for librarians and researchers must be the filling of this gap. Directories of research material simply do not exist in many fields and for many institutions and if this Colloquium does anything it should point up this deficiency and the need to do something about it quickly. Whether the results are published in traditional form or made available through computerised networks is immaterial; unless it is done future research work will be seriously hindered. The sort of thing needed is similar to the work carried out by the British Academy's Oriental Documents Committee and the published surveys of important collections of papers and records compiled by the Royal Commission on Historical Manuscripts. (A similar lack was identified some years ago for sources on Russia and the resulting guide by Janet Hartley funded by the Leverhulme Trust, was published by Mansell last year.[7])

The third and last tactic librarians need to adopt is to organise the literature selected, preserved and retained in forms hospitable to research and this is again more difficult than might be supposed. The traditional alphabetical catalogue of authors' and institutional names and the structured subject catalogues devised and maintained by (and some would say for) librarians over the past century are now anachronistic. The intellectual effort invested in them is not wasted if they are published, but card catalogues in such forms simply demand too much intellectual and clerical effort to be maintained in face of the deluge of published information that falls into libraries and information centres nowadays. Fortunately computers possess both the capacity and the speed to handle the increased input and also the ability to manipulate such information in more innovative ways. Scholars formulate some questions which simply cannot be asked of a card or published library catalogue without searching through the entire file – computers permit the enquirer/searcher to jump across categories like authors, titles, subjects, dates and ask a data base who wrote on a selected subject within a finite period of time or in a particular country or town. What librarians must do is see that in future such catalogues or data bases permit future generations to ask questions not now foreseen. In other words, research must not be constrained by a fixed set of words or concepts in thesauri that can only reflect contemporary modes of thought. Librarians have so far only dealt with keywords as appropriate concepts for such searches – plus the factual information gleaned from the book itself – but whether this will be sufficient for the future needs examination. And whether the storage architecture of computer memories will in future be able to take account of agglutinative principles beyond Boolean logic in searching databases seems likely to become important in the future as files contain more and more information and searches need to be more and more precise to save time and effort. Most people who have used computers to search automated files know the feeling of frustration generated when a search results in perhaps 2,000 or more relevant entries found. It can only be likened to the feelings of a former library user using the card catalogue which refers from one added entry to another without ever disclosing the main entry and information sought! Associated with these abstruse questions are simple questions of access as mentioned before. If libraries pursue policies of co-operation and coordination, publish the most detailed guide to sources, and catalogue and index their material in great detail with absolute precision, if all these things are accomplished readers/users/scholars must still be able to get at the books or information, whether in their own libraries or in distant repositories. Questions of access and document delivery will be increasingly and acutely important; but that is nothing to do with 'collection development' and will need to be discussed in other places.

References

1. Morgan Paul, 'Frances Wolfreson and "Hor Bouks"'. *Shakespeare: text, language, criticism. Essays in honour of Marvin Spevack,* edited by B Fabian and K Tezeli von Rosador. Hildesheim, Olms, 1987, pp.193–211. (A revised version will be published in *The Library* during 1989.)
2. Head, W W. *The Victoria Press...* London, Victoria Press, 1869; William E Fredemann. 'Emily Faithfull and the Victoria Press: an experiment in sociological bibliography'. *The Library,* 5th series, XXIX (1974), pp.139–64, plus the note by J S Stone in *The Library,* 5th series, XXXIII (1978), pp.63–7.
3. Hageman, Elizabeth. 'Recent studies in women writers of Tudor England, 1485-1603.' *English literary renaissance,* XIV (1984), 409–425. (I owe this reference to Mr Paul Morgan and Dr M Jannetta.)
4. *Nineteenth century short title catalogue newsletter,* 5 (May 1988), [7] and publisher's announcement.
5. Tuson, Penelope, *and* Jasbir Singh, Amar Kaur. 'Archival collections in the India Office Records' *Women of Sourth Asia: a guide to resources,* edited by Carol Sakala. New York, Kraus International Publications, 1980, pp.456–7.
6. From Lockhart's *Life of Scott* quoted in *Before Victoria,* by Muriel Jaeger, London, Chatto, 1956, p.136.
7. The Royal Commission on Historical Manuscripts has a series of 'Guides to sources for British history' among which are: 1. *Papers of British Cabinet Ministers, 1782-1900* (1982); 2. *Manuscript papers of British scientists, 1642-1940* (1982); 4. *Private papers of British diplomats, 1782-1900* (1986), etc. The sort of thing needed is exemplified by Helena Wedborn (*ed.*) *Women in the first and second World Wars: a checklist of the holdings of the Hoover Institution...* Stanford, Hoover Institution Press, 1989.

Note:
The British Library adoption of 'Conspectus' is best described in Stephen Hanger's article, 'Collection development in the British Library: the role of the RLG Conspectus'. *Journal of librarianship,* XIX (1987), pp.89–107. Also the book by Brian C F Holt *and* Stephen Hanger *Conspectus in the British Library,* London, 1986.

Pat Darter

Small is beautiful – but is it feasible? Small special women's collections in the UK

In June 1987 I gave a paper on women's studies libraries at a seminar on Information for Women's Studies held at Sheffield City Polytechnic[1]. The libraries chosen were 'independent' in the sense that they were each an autonomous collection – that is not just a subject collection within a larger general library. As such they had a valuable, although frequently unpublicised, rôle in the provision of information on a national level. The first part of this present paper is an update on the current situation of those libraries. My title may already have given a clue that all is not well and so I have tried to gather together a number of common themes and problems – something which I hope may not be too depressing but which will at least alert the library/information community to a potentially serious situation so that we may start to consider what remedies are available. Finally and fairly briefly I want to mention a number of international initiatives intended to improve access to information on women's studies on both a European and international scale, and the part which the UK can play in these.

Let me first of all describe a number of specialist libraries in the field of women's studies. Factual information such as hours of opening, stock, equipment etc about these independent collections can be found in Appendix A. The libraries in question are: the Equal Opportunities Commission; the Fawcett Library; Feminist Archive; Feminist Audio Books; Feminist Library; Lesbian Archive; Nottingham Women's Information Library; Women Artists Slide Library; Women's Health and Reproductive Rights Information Centre; and Women's International Resources Centre.

1. EQUAL OPPORTUNITIES COMMISSION: The Commission has recently launched a new strategy document[2] which implies that its work is not to be as wide-ranging as was previously the case. This, together with the financial crisis facing the EOC, may well have implications for the selection policy of the Information Centre. Another problem is the dichotomy of providing an internal information service to the Commission and at the same time being a major national source of information on the current status of women.

2. FAWCETT LIBRARY: Since one of the other papers deals exclusively with this library I will only make one brief, and I hope not too unkind, comment. Having taken over this library the City of London Polytechnic seems to have done little to capitalise on this marvellous resource. There is no women's studies degree there and

so the library is not seen as an integral part of the information resources, consequently funding has become an increasing problem. A good account of their efforts at fund-raising can be found in a recent issue of the journal *Charity*[3].

3. FEMINIST ARCHIVE: Now re-sited in the centre of Bristol and with some funding from Avon County Council the future looks more hopeful for the archive. However more staffing resources are needed if the materials housed there are to be made more accessible.

4. FEMINIST AUDIO BOOKS: Since loosing their funding from the London Boroughs Grant Scheme, the library has struggled to keep going. It provides a valuable service but it may be just a question of time before it is forced to close.

5. FEMINIST LIBRARY: The withdrawal last year of funding by the London Boroughs Grant Scheme was a drastic blow to this collection. Although a number of organisations expressed interest in acquiring the library, the collective decided to carry on an independent existence. There is now a question mark over how long they will be able to remain in their present accommodation. The future does indeed look bleak and a major rescue operation will be needed if this fine resource is not to be lost.

6. LESBIAN ARCHIVE: Surprisingly this collection did manage to retain LBGS funding and although there have been internal staff problems during the past year, its future is reasonably assured. A recent issue of their newsletter[4] gives a good account of the resources in the archive.

7. NOTTINGHAM WOMEN'S INFORMATION LIBRARY: As yet a very small collection with the emphasis on local information. However, unless an assured source of funding becomes available this library too could be in difficulties.

8. WOMEN ARTISTS SLIDE LIBRARY: A valuable resource within a very specialised area which, since the move to Fulham Palace, enjoys a good deal of success.

9. WOMEN'S HEALTH AND REPRODUCTIVE RIGHTS INFORMATION CENTRE: Another very specialised collection again existing on a shoe-string.

10. WOMEN'S INTERNATIONAL RESOURCE CENTRE: A valuable resource since the other libraries in this list have only a limited amount of information on women in other countries. The centre has also co-operated with ISIS International in providing training for women working in documentation centres in the third world.

The recurring theme which emerges from the first part of this paper, is unfortunately that of financial difficulties. Even the EOC, which on paper appears the most financially secure, is not safe from some worries. For 1989/90 the purchasing budget of the library has been reduced to £20,000 – the same as 1980-81; allowing for the rise in book/periodical prices during these years this must represent something in the order of a 50% cut in funding. Problems over what can or cannot be purchased are not the only result of poor financing; at least the EOC and the the Fawcett Library can afford to employ professionally qualified library staff, most of the other libraries rely on volunteers and with the best will in the world this inevitably affects the organisation and the exploitation of their materials. Given the current crisis in funding faced by all voluntary organisations the future for these collections is beginning to look bleak.

Who then is going to collect and document women's studies material in the future? The obvious answer is: the colleges where women's studies are taught as an academic discipline – but would this be a satisfactory solution? Is their book selection geared to pick up the small press publications and ephemera that are the strength of specialist libraries? How will women's studies fare in the cold wind of realism sweeping through our campuses? – it hardly carries the same commercial 'clout' as business studies and economics. Even then there is the long-standing problem of how to find books on women's studies in a large general collection. The numbers of students using the EOC, the Fawcett Library, and previously the Feminist Library, could not all have been doing so because the resources of their college libraries were inadequate but because the materials they required were in one compact collection instead of being spread throughout a much larger collection. Above all what about the problem of access? Few college libraries admit anyone other than their own students and a number are even loathe to participate in inter-library lending schemes. Women's studies could thus become a sterile academic discipline, while for anyone not attached to an academic institution the pursuit of knowledge in this area would be a very limited and frustrating exercise.

The situation we now have is one where more women's studies courses (from GCSE upwards) are coming on-stream, the demand for resources is therefore increasing, and yet the specialist collections are at their lowest ebb for many years. Can we look to the British Library for a life-line? What about the following suggestions:

1. The British Library to take over funding of the Feminist Library which could then be housed in an ex-BL building once the move to St Pancras is complete. If the building were also large enough to accommodate the Fawcett Library then the combination of these two collections would become an outstanding resource of national and international repute.

2. The British Library to co-fund the Feminist Archive together with the Avon County Council (and possibly other library authorities in the South West) so that it becomes a regional centre for contemporary resources. Nottingham Women's Information Library, and the Pankhurst Centre in Manchester, could be further bases for expanding such a network. Provided the scope and purpose of these collections is thought through, the amount of funding need not be large, and by making them part of a national network rather than a local centre they would hopefully be removed from the political arena and thus not suffer the same fate as the resources centre in Bradford following the change of power there last year.

3. Data bases. As has already been stated the strength of these specialist collections lies in what can best be described as 'grey literature'. As such their resources largely fall

outside the scope of BND and so are 'lost' in bibliographic terms. Most of these libraries have produced catalogues or periodical lists and by doing so provided a basis for further developments. Three areas provide potential for data bases: books, periodicals and periodical articles.

a. BOOKS: BiblioFem[5] ceased publication a few years ago. It would be inappropriate here to discuss the reasons but I would nonetheless have thought it could be used as a basis for a joint catalogue of these collections.

b. PERIODICALS: Following the Sheffield seminar referred to at the beginning of this paper, the EOC coordinated responses from a number of libraries to produce a draft union list of periodicals. Staff time is no longer available to update this and yet how else will you find out where for instance copies of *Feminist Arts News*, *Ms London* and *Writing Women* are to be found.

c. PERIODICAL ARTICLES: This would probably be the easiest and most useful development of all. 'Studies on Women Abstracts'[6] and 'Assia'[7] are both well established. This year has seen the production of 'Women in BHI'[8], and in addition the EOC maintains a card-index of some 15,000 periodical references which it hopes to computerise in the near future.

Yes – I am sure I have glossed over a number of technical problems, no – it is not going to be easy, but the need is there, this is a valid area for research, the basic materials are available and what is now required is the will to bring these ideas to fruition.

Finally, and following on from that plea for data bases, just a brief word about developments outside the UK in bringing together resources on women's studies. Moves are being made within the United Nations to organise not only the material produced by this organisation but also to help less developed countries organise their own resources. For a brief description of this system, *see* Appendix B.

Nearer to home, and perhaps more important to us, are current developments within the EEC. In January of this year I attended a meeting of a 'Documentation Working Party' in Brussels. This consisted of librarians/documentalists from the national equality agencies (or their nominees) of each of the member states of the EEC. The proposal discussed was the establishment of an EEC data base on equal opportunities for women. This is of course a tremendous undertaking and as an initial step each representative will submit bibliographies within a number of chosen subject areas. The sheer volume of material, let alone deciding what is British as opposed to American, means that I have decided in the first instance to limit my response to books in the EOC Information Centre. However, I am very well aware of how incomplete a response this will be; if the data base of which I spoke earlier had existed, then my task would not only be a lot easier but British resources would be properly represented within the project.

The EEC has a plan of action for libraries and funds are available for new projects. I can only repeat – the raw materials are there, the need for information is there – it is up to us to get organised!

References

1. Pankhurst, R *and* Graves, S (*eds.*). *Information for Women's Studies: seminar proceedings*. Sheffield City Polytechnic, 1988.
2. 'From policy to practice: an equal opportunities strategy for the 1990s.' Equal Opportunities Commission, 1989.
3. Cerasale, G. "Unique" record of women that "top" women ignore'. In: *Charity*, January 1989, pp.16–17.
4. *Lesbian Archive and Information Centre Newsletter*. No.2 1988.
5. *BiblioFem: a joint catalogue of the EOC and Fawcett Libraries 1950–1986*.
6. 'Studies on Women Abstracts' In: *Carfax Publishing Company*.
7. 'ASSIA (Applied Social Sciences Index and Abstracts) In: *The Library Association*.
8. 'Women in BHI (British Humanities Index)'. In: *The Library Association*.

Appendix A

1. EQUAL OPPORTUNITIES COMMISSION INFORMATION CENTRE
Address: Overseas House, Quay Street, Manchester M3 3HN.
Telephone number: 061–833 9244.
Opening hours: Monday–Friday 9.00 am–5.00 pm.
Funding: Grant-in-aid from the government.
Founded: 1977.
Collecting policy: to acquire material related to the implementation of the Sex Discrimination Act and Equal Pay Act.
Stock: *c*.20,000 books and pamphlets; *c*.330 current serials; *also* newspaper cuttings, posters, records, videos, badges.
Staff: 7 full-time paid posts (including two professional librarians).
Equipment: photocopier, microfiche reader/printer.
Additional resources: Index of periodical articles; Research Index; Statistical Databank; List of periodical holdings.

2. FAWCETT LIBRARY
Address: City of London Polytechnic, Calcutta House, Old Castle Street, London E1 7NT.
Telephone number: 01–283 1030 ext.750.
Opening hours:
Monday (term time): 11.00 am–8.30 pm
Monday (vacation): 10.00 am–5.00 pm
Wednesday, Thursday, Friday (all year round): 10.00 am–5.00 pm
Closed Tuesdays and week-ends
Funding: partial funding from CLP, subscriptions, donations.
Founded: 1926 (but 're-founded' by CLP 1977).
Collecting policy: to cover most aspects of women's place in society.
Stock: 40,000 books and pamphlets; 700 periodical titles; 500 boxes of archives; *also* newspaper cuttings, photographs, posters.
Staff: 1 full-time paid post, (professional librarian), 4 paid part-timers *plus* volunteers.
Equipment: photocopier, microfiche reader-printer.
Additional resources: BiblioFem; Newsletter; occasional talks/lectures organised by 'The Friends'.

3. FEMINIST ARCHIVE
Address: Trinity Road Library, St Philips, Bristol.
Telephone number: 0272 350025.

Opening hours: Wednesday 2.00 am–5.00 pm, Saturday 10.00 am–5.00 pm.
Funding: Partial funding from Avon County Council, donations.
Founded: 1978.
Collecting policy: to document the women's liberation movement (with particular emphasis on ephemera).
Stock: Books and pamphlets; periodicals (mainly sample copies, few complete runs); *also* posters, badges, photographs, postcards.
Staff: part-time volunteers.
Resources: Bulletin (infrequent).

4. FEMINIST AUDIO BOOKS
Address: 52–54 Featherstone Street, London EC1Y 8RT.
Telephone number: 01–251 2908.
Opening hours: Tuesday *and* Thursday 11.00 am–6.00 pm.
Funding: donations (accommodation provided by LBGS).
Founded: 1986.
Collecting policy: titles are chosen by disabled women to reflect all aspects of feminism.
Stock: 100 titles on tape (copy of all tapes sent to Feminist Archive).
Staff: part-time volunteers.
Equipment: photocopier, tape-recorders, microphones.
Additional resources: printed catalogue, acquisitions list and bibliographies, '*Women Tape Over*' (monthly selections from feminist magazines); advice pack on how to tape, support groups and public readings.

5. FEMINIST LIBRARY
Address: Hungerford House, Victoria, Embankment, London WCN 6PA.
Telephone number: 01–930 0715.
Opening hours: Saturday and Sunday 2.00 am–5.00 pm, Tuesday 11.00 am–8.00 pm.
Funding: Subscriptions, donations.
Founded: 1975.
Collecting policy: to reflect all aspects of contemporary feminism.
Stock: *c.*4,500 books and pamphlets; *c.*700 periodical titles (150 current); *also* unpublished papers, leaflets.
Staff: volunteers.
Equipment: photocopier, microfiche reader.
Additional resources: Index of women's studies courses; Research Index; Newsletter.

6. LESBIAN ARCHIVE
Address: BCM Box No.7005, London WC1N 3XX.
Telephone number: 01–405 6475
Opening hours: Monday 11.00 am–5.30 pm, Thursday 11.00 am–8.30 pm, *also* second Saturday of each month 11.00 am–5.00 pm.
Funding: London Boroughs Grant Scheme.
Founded: 1984.
Collecting policy: to reclaim lesbian history and celebrate lesbian lives.
Stock: *c.*700 books and pamphlets, *c.*250 periodicals (not all current); *also* newspaper cuttings, music, badges.
Staff: 2 full-time paid posts *plus* volunteers.
Equipment: photocopiers, cassette players.
Additional resources: Newsletter; social events and benefits.

7. NOTTINGHAM WOMEN'S INFORMATION LIBRARY
Address: 30 Chaucer Street, Nottingham.
Telephone number: 0602 411475.
Opening hours: Tuesday, Thursday and Saturday 11.00 am–4.00 pm.
Funding: Part-funding from local authority, grants, donations.
Founded: 1988.
Collecting policy: to provide information on all issues of interest to women.
Stock: books and pamphlets, periodicals.
Staff: voluneers.

8. WOMEN ARTISTS SLIDE LIBRARY
Address: Fulham Palace, Bishop's Avenue, London sw6.
Telephone number: 01–731 7618.
Opening hours: Tuesday–Friday 10.00 am–5.00 pm (preferably by appointment).
Funding: London Boroughs Grant Scheme, GLAA, Arts Council, Hammersmith and Fulham, donations, subscriptions.
Founded: 1982.
Collecting policy: to document the work of contemporary and historical women artists.
Stock: 12,000 slides; *also* theses, books, journals, posters, cuttings, exhibition catalogues.
Staff: 1 full-time, 4 part-time (all paid posts).
Equipment: photocopier, slide projector and viewers, slide copier, video-recorder.
Additional resources: Journal; conferences, workshops and exhibitions; bibliographical index of women artists; *also* index of black women artists; Catalogue of books and exhibition catalogues; Bibliography (unpublished) of women artists.

9. WOMEN'S HEALTH AND REPRODUCTIVE RIGHTS INFORMATION CENTRE
Address: 52 Featherstone Street, London EC1Y 8RT.
Telephone number: 01–251 6332.
Opening hours: Monday, Wednesday, Thursday, Friday 1.00 pm–5.00 pm.
Funding: London Boroughs Grant Scheme (accommodation only), subscriptions, book sales.
Founded: 1982.
Collecting policy: to be an information centre for women's health issues.
Stock: 2,000 books and pamphlets; 60 periodicals.
Staff: 3 full-time equivalents (paid).
Equipment: photocopier.
Additional resources: Register of women's health groups; Newsletter; occasional fact sheets.

10. WOMEN'S INTERNATIONAL RESOURCES CENTRE
Address: 173 Archway Road, London N6.
Telephone number: 01–341 4403.
Opening hours: Monday–Friday 11.00 am–6.00 pm.
Funding: London Boroughs Grant Scheme, Oxfam, Christian Aid, EEC.
Founded: 1985.
Collecting policy: to document women's issues internationally particularly as they affect women in their own countries.
Stock: 2,000 books and pamphlets, 50 journals.
Staff: 4 full-time paid *plus* volunteers.
Equipment: photocopier.

Appendix B

A COMPUTERIZED BIBLIOGRAPHIC INFORMATION SYSTEM ON WOMEN

The Branch for the Advancement of Women has developed a computer-based bibliographic information system on women, which has the acronym WIS, and is operated on a personal computer. The system runs on IBM PCs and IBM PC compatibles with a hard disk and a floppy diskette drive. It is controlled by a data base management system called Micro CDS/ISIS, which has been developed by the United Nations Educational, Scientific and Cultural Organization (UNESCO) and is widely used throughout the world for small-scale bibliographic data base systems.

The descriptions are in principle taken from the United Nations Bibliographic Information system (UNBIS) Thesaurus, although a list of supplementary descriptors relating to women's issues is also being developed by the branch.

At present, the branch has used the system to list more than 700 documents on women produced throughout the United Nations system since 1 January 1986. The primary objective of the system is to provide bibliographic information on the implementation of the Forward-looking Strategies for the Advancement of Women. Searches can be made on request for government offices, non-governmental organizations, research institutions and the United Nations system. The system also aims to improve national capabilities to maintain documentation information and to facilitate systematic international exchange of bibliographic information on women by encouraging national machinery to set up their own computerized bibliographic information systems. The user's manual has been prepared in a format that enables interested persons, even those with limited knowledge and experience in computer operation, to operate the system.

It is hoped that permission will be obtained from UNESCO shortly so that the system can be distributed. Discussions to this end are continuing.

See: *Women 2000*. No.1, 1988. United Nations (Branch for the Advancement of Women), Vienna.

David Doughan

The Fawcett Library

The Fawcett Library is Britain's main historical resource on women and feminism, and is also a major library of contemporary women's studies. As well as conventional monograph material (books and pamphlets published from 1592 to date), the Library holds considerable quantities of ephemeral material in various forms (mainly in support of feminist campaigns from the 1850s to the present); more than 700 periodical titles, with runs of up to 100 years; nearly 600 boxes of archives (papers of individuals and organisations) and a major autograph letter collection; press cuttings, posters, flyers etc; a small photographic collection; and banners and other objects from the women's suffrage movement. The main academic emphasis of the Library is historical and political; however, current material is actively collected, and the political range includes revolutionary radical feminism, the Women's Institute, and the Campaign for the Feminine Woman.

History

Originally the library of the London and National Society for Women's Service (formerly Suffrage), the Women's Service Library (as it was then known) gained its first full-time librarian in January 1926. This was Vera Douie (1894-1979), who remained in post for over 41 years, retiring in 1967 with a well-deserved OBE. It was Vera Douie who turned the Women's Service Library from an interesting small society library into a major research resource with an international reputation among historians, social scientists and feminists.

In the 1930s, the library acquired purpose-built accommodation in the Women's Service House, in Marsham Street, Westminster, which became a meeting place for many prominent women of the time. Particular interest in the Library was shown by Vera Brittain and Virginia Woolf, both of whom contributed substantially to the book-stock. However, the building suffered severe bomb damage in 1940-41 (fortunately, not before the Library was evacuated to what is now St Anne's College, Oxford), and in consequence the Library found itself without a permanent home. In 1949 it was offered the hospitality of the City of Westminster's Great Smith Street Library, where it remained until the opening of Fawcett House (27 Wilfred Street, Westminster) in 1957, which became its home for the next 20 years.

In the early 1970s, the rate of inflation, together with the growth of the Library, made it increasingly obvious that the Fawcett Society (as it was now called) was unable to cope with running the Library on its own, and various moves were made to find it a home in an academic institution. Finally the City of London Polytechnic came to the rescue, and housed it, in March 1977, in a basement in Old Castle Street, London E1, where it has been ever since.

Over the years, the Fawcett Library has attracted various other smaller collections which were in danger of dispersal. The most notable are the Cavendish Bentinck Collection (founded 1909; acquired 1931); the Josephine Butler Society Collection (formerly the library of the Association for Moral and Social Hygiene, founded in the late nineteenth century and acquired in 1956); and the Sadd Brown Library (acquired 1939). For fuller details, see below under 'Stock'.

Stock

The core of the Library's stock is its books and pamphlets – more than 40,000 of them – dating from 1592 to the present, and dealing with all manner of material relating to the position of women in society: the political status of women; the women's suffrage movement; the women's liberation movement; women and the law, education; the labour market; housework; marriage; sexuality; prostitution; health; psychology; religion; dress; fashion; cooking; visual arts; theatre; cinema; literature; language; music; etc. A particularly interesting feature is the wide range of biographies (including autobiographies) of individual women, ranging in time from Nefertiti to Maya Angelou, and of a diversity which includes Edith Summerskill, Margaret Thatcher, Mandy Rice-Davies, Tina Turner, St Catherine of Siena, Sarojini Naidu, and Han Suyin. Most of the stock concerns women in Britain, the Commonwealth (including such ex-Commonwealth countries as South Africa and Pakistan), Ireland and the USA, but there are significant holdings on other countries, most notably the Soviet Union, China, and Japan. Although the overwhelming majority of the material is in English, various other languages are represented, *eg* French, German, Italian, Spanish, Greek, Hungarian, Russian, Swedish, Dutch, Bulgarian, Hindi, Arabic, Japanese, etc.

Periodicals represent an extremely important part of the Library. General 'commercial' women's magazines are held from 1713 to date (though twentieth-century magazines are for reasons of space, usually held in sample copies, rather than in complete runs); feminist periodicals begin in 1858 with the *English Woman's Journal*, and continue through to such contemporary titles as *Spare Rib, Everywoman, Feminist Review,* and *Trouble and Strife*. Many older periodicals are available to readers on microform only.

Other types of print material include ephemera – leaflets of all ages, from such campaigns as the Repeal of the Congatious Diseases Acts; the Women's Suffrage movement in all its phases and factions; the Equal Pay Campaign; campaigns opposing anti-abortion legislation; the campaign in support of Wendy Savage, etc and newspaper cuttings which are organised by subject from the 1920s on, though many scrapbooks contain much earlier material. Recent cuttings, alas, are much more limited in their coverage than earlier ones, taking in only the 'quality' dailies – a testimony to the vastly increased amount of space in the press devoted to what could be described as feminist issues.

The three special collections each have their own emphasis – the Cavendish Bentinck concentrates on the old, the rare and the valuable, and is the Library's only locked book collection. It thus acts as a convenient shelving facility for material deemed too vulnerable to be left on open shelves, such as issues of the *Englishwoman's Domestic Magazine* and the *Ladies' Treasury*, with their hand-coloured fashion plates, and first editions of such authors as Mary Wollstonecraft, the Brontës and George Eliot.

The Josephine Butler Collection starts in the 1860s with the passing of the Contagious Diseases Acts, and not only contains much material concerned with the Acts and their repeal, but also considerable quantities of material dealing with prostitution and sexuality and related issues, such as criminology and psychology, present legislation on child abuse, kerb-crawling, and proposed 'red light' districts.

The Sadd Brown Library is maintained by a trust in honour of Myra Sadd Brown, suffragette and founder of the British Commonwealth League (now the Commonwealth Countries League). It covers women in Commonwealth and ex-Commonwealth countries, and has recently attracted donations of books from the New Zealand High Commission.

The archives consist in roughly equal quantity of papers of organisations and individuals. The latter include such prominent feminists as Josephine Butler, Emily Wilding Davison, Maude Royden, Teresa Billington-Greig, and Millicent Garrett Fawcett. There is also an Autograph Letter Collection which contains numerous letters by a wide variety of women (and men) – for example, Queen Victoria, Florence Nightingale, Elizabeth Garrett Anderson, various Pankhursts, Harriet Martineau, W E Gladstone, J S Mill, Thomas Hardy, Bernard Shaw, T S Eliot, etc, as well as many other less well-known, but no less interesting, women. Organisations whose papers are held include most of the major suffrage societies, various white-collar unions such as the National Association of Women Civil Servants, such feminist bodies as the Six Point Group and the Open Door International, female emigration societies, and organisations formed to combat the traffic in persons and/or campaign for social purity, such as the National Vigilance Association. Archival material is still being acquired, on a small scale.

The photographic collection is relatively small and restricted in scope. Its main strengths are in portraits of prominent feminists, and early twentieth-century material (mainly the suffrage movement and working women, particularly in World War I), though later photographs can often be found. The Library co-operates closely with the Mary Evans Picture Library, which acts as its agent for photographs, and can supply high quality copy prints (at a price).

Use and organisation

Both patterns of use, and users themselves, are very varied, and not always predictable. Annually, the Library receives about 4,000 visits from readers, who make about 3,000 loans. In addition, about 500 postal enquiries are received, as well as very many (uncounted) telephone enquiries. Users may come singly or in groups; about a quarter of them come from within the Polytechnic; most of them have an academic purpose in mind (ranging from GCSE History to post-doctoral research), but some are independent writers and researchers, some are professional authors, some are feminist activists and some are just women after a good read. In addition, regular use is made of the Library by the press and broadcasting organisations. Similarly, enquiries range from the extremely simple (*eg* on what date did women first get the parliamentary vote?) to the very complex (*eg* about the relationship of Labour women to the Labour Party from 1905 to 1930) (*see* Blagden 1985).

Access to most materials (except the Cavendish Bentinck collection and the archives) is open, and there are few restrictions (apart from copyright) on photocopying. Members may borrow 2 books published after 1960 for 3 weeks (renewable); borrowers on inter-library loan (via Boston Spa and London Wing only!) are treated a little more generously.

Much of the printed material is catalogued to UKMARC standards, using the *Libertas* system, and from April 1989 it will be available via JANET. BNB cataloguing is accepted as the norm, which involves subject arrangement by Dewey – not an ideal situation for a feminist library, but part of the price the Library pays for centralised cataloguing as a constituent of the Polytechnic library system. Some of the older material, including pre-1970 cuttings, is catalogued by UDC (which does something to reconcile the staff to Dewey).

Staffing and finance

Overall responsibility for the Fawcett Library is taken by Maureen Castens, Head of the Library Service at the City of London Polytechnic. The paid staff of the Library consists of one full-time professional librarian, one part-time library assistant, and one-day a week each of an archivist, a photographic specialist and a cataloguer. In addition, some tasks (book processing, newspaper cuttings, organisation of ephemera, etc) are dealt with by unpaid volunteer helpers.

The Fawcett Library is part of the City Poly Library Service, which means that its premises, heating, lighting, catalogue hardware and other similar 'below the line' costs are met by the Polytechnic. In addition, the Polytechnic pays the wages of the full-time librarian. As part of the library system, the Fawcett Library can also call on relief staff from other sites in case of need – and in theory, the Fawcett staff can be called on to reciprocate, though in practice this hardly ever happens. Finally, the Polytechnic pays for the Fawcett Library periodical subscriptions, and makes other occasional subsidies to the stock on the increasingly rare occasions when funds become available.

Other Fawcett Library expenditure is paid for by funds generated by the Fawcett Library itself. The Library has over the years amassed a fairly large capital sum interest from which it pays salaries, book purchases, etc. Money is raised partly through membership fees, charges for services, and publication sales; however, there are many donations from various sources, mainly through the Friends of the Fawcett Library, who have recently been organising a major fundraising appeal. From time to time the Library has also been successful in obtaining grants for specific programmes from other bodies, such as the British Library, the Leverhulme Trust, the EOC, ILEA etc. In addition, a number of publishers contribute considerably to the Library by free donations of new books and current periodicals.

External (and public) relations

The Library has friendly links with a number of other institutions whose concerns are similar, or which overlap. Prominent among these are the Feminist Library; the Women's Artists' Slide Library; the Equal Opportunities Commission Library; the Museum of London; Pankhurst House (Manchester); the Internationaal Informatiecentrum en Archief voor de Vrouwenbeweging (Amsterdam), and the Schlesinger Library of Radcliffe College in Cambridge, Mass, with which the Fawcett Library had a successful Fulbright-sponsored exchange of staff in 1986.

The Library regularly lends material (for a fee) to galleries and museums mounting exhibitions; the most recent exhibition has been the one accompanying the BBC's *Out of the Doll's House* series. Its facilities are also used from time to time by broadcasting organisations (with on-screen credits wherever possible), most recently again by the BBC for a programme on Josephine Butler in a series on *Eminent Victorians* by A N Wilson.

In the past, the Library has tried raising its profile by in-house publishing of women's studies papers, by publishing a newsletter (until staff time ran out), and by producing, from 1978 to 1986, the microfiche bibliography *BiblioFem* (until money ran out). However, the area where the Library's name is most visible is on the acknowledgements pages of a wide range of books concerned with women and feminism. The Library staff have no false modesty about these, and will proudly display them in large quantities to anyone rash enough to ask. The Library has also been involved in moves to increase co-operation between institutions in this field, most prominently through a project for a women's studies network initiated by Rita Pankhurst, Head of Library Services up to 1987.

Accommodation

The Library is very conveniently situated for researchers in London, especially those who are already using such centrally located libraries as the British Library at Bloomsbury; the London University Libraries (including and especially the British Library of Political and Economic Science and the libraries of the Institute of Education and the School of Oriental and African Studies); the Wellcome Institute for the History of Medicine; the London Library; etc. However, it is not particularly easy to find, and once found, it is not notable for easy physical access (though wheelchair access can be provided, given notice). It can be said that anyone who actually gets to the door of the Fawcett Library has passed a number of motivation tests.

Once they have reached the Library, readers discover themselves in a basement (formerly a book store) with no natural daylight and limited seating (about 14 readers can be accommodated at a time, but it is something of a squeeze). Storage space is maximised by the use of compact shelving, which can lead to difficulties when two or more people want to consult books at different points in the same stack. Fortunately, what might be thought of as a risky situation for reader safety has not proved so in practice; in twelve years, not even a minor injury has been suffered. However, despite the use of such space-saving measures, the Library risks becoming cramped in the fairly near future even for the storage of books. Certainly there is no adequate display space for the remarkable visual material held in the Library. Reader convenience is also not all that it might be: toilets are one floor up (two floors for men) and a walk along a corridor; food, drink and student lounge are four floors up, across a bridge, up and down a few steps, and along a corridor. Opening times are also more restricted than would be ideal, with only one evening open in term (and none in vacation), and no weekend opening; largely the result of staff shortage.

Conservation

This is a major cause of concern. Many documents, particularly from the period 1920-60, are printed or written on wood pulp paper, and are now rapidly deteriorating. In addition, normal wear and tear, especially in the case of circulating books, and stresses induced by photocopying, mean that older material, or material which is less well bound, may be literally coming to pieces. This leads to a number of difficult decisions. For a library like the Fawcett, the cost of major deacidification projects is prohibitive. Similarly, the library cannot afford to do its own microfilming, and arrangements with commercial publishers of microfilm have their own drawbacks – the publisher's idea of what is most marketable may not coincide with the staff's perception of what most needs conserving, and moreover careless filming can do more damage to the original than ordinary wear and tear. The Fawcett Library has in the past co-operated in major microfilming programmes with IDC of Leiden, and in an advisory capacity with Harvester Microform, but this has only covered a few score periodical titles, the Autograph Letter Collection, and the Josephine Butler letters.

The unwelcome conclusion to the problem of conservation without really extensive funding is that staff must either watch material disintegrate before their eyes, or be increasingly restrictive in allowing access to material – a dilemma for those librarians committed to increasing the availability of the material in their charge.

Prospects

Over the past twelve years, the Fawcett Library has become very closely linked with the City of London Polytechnic, and its fate is bound up with that of the Polytechnic.

This means that the Library benefits from being under the protection of the institution; however, this safeguard is limited when the institution itself is under pressure, as is the case with most higher education in Britain at present. In particular, the City of London Polytechnic has a problem with its locations; several major leases are approaching their end, and as they are on prime development sites, there are problems in renewing them at a cost which the Polytechnic can afford. So the Library, alongside teaching departments, faces the prospect of relocating to new accommodation within the next four years.

Staffing is also a source of concern. Last October, Catherine Ireland, the Fawcett Librarian, took voluntary severance, and the Polytechnic is unable to afford a replacement. Present staffing levels mean that an adequate day-to-day service can (just) be provided to readers, but they make it very difficult to find the time to do anything beyond this – forward planning, publicity, fundraising, conservation work etc.

The answer to most of these problems is money. Libraries in general, and research libraries in particular, are increasingly being urged to generate their own income. How the Fawcett Library could do significantly more in this area is a subject to which we have been giving some thought, but most suggestions to date have raised at least as many problems as they solve – such as the vexed question of charging for services. Even leaving to one side the more bizarre possibilities of the 'information-as-commodity' approach ('I can tell you where to find that book but it will cost you 20p'), market forces in the narrow sense currently used are not at all friendly to research on feminism or women's history. Generating significant income from services presupposes affluent consumers who are able and willing to pay considerable sums; but few women have above-average disposable income, those doing serious research are usually well below average in this respect. Thus, charging for services beyond the present membership/day fees would almost certainly be counterproductive; and even if staff were available as paid researchers, it is most unlikely that any income generated would be in hundreds of pounds, let alone the hundreds of thousands of pounds the Library would need to secure a future largely independent of national or local government funding. Certainly, in the short term, the Library will be concentrating on more conventional means of fundraising through its appeal, specific grants, and the service charges it already exacts from broadcasting organisations, the press, publishers, etc.

Still, not all prospects are gloomy. At the worst, the Fawcett Library is in a better condition than the Feminist Library, which is currently struggling for existence. Projected ideas for the future of the Polytechnic could mean the Library being moved to a smart modern site in Docklands. Finally, use of the Library shows no sign of slacking off; readers are by and large keen, industrious and appreciative, and staff morale remains good. Certainly, comparing the state of the Library now with what it was in 1976 shows just how much has been achieved in the past thirteen years, both in women's studies and in the Fawcett Library, which has now survived and flourished for 63 years. We expect it to continue for at least as long again.

Some suggested additional reading:

Blagden, Pauline, 'Women's studies: an examination of library use by researchers in the field with special reference to the Fawcett Library' *Library Research Digest*; 14 City Poly LLRS Publications, 1985.

Fawcett Library Annual Report 1987-1988

Line, Maurice B. 'The research library in the enterprise society' *LSE Quarterly*; vol.2 no.4, winter 1988.

Women's Studies International Forum; vol.10 no.3, 1987. (Special issue of the Fawcett Library. This is far and away the fullest account available of the Fawcett Library's holdings and history, and is essential reading for any serious study of the Library).

Rosemary Seton

Women missionaries as represented in the Missionary Collections in the School of Oriental and African Studies Library

After a season of darkness and struggling, light broke and relief fell: my cramped existence all at once spread out to a plain without bounds; my powers heard a call from Heaven to rise, gather their full strength, spread their wings, and mount beyond ken. God had an errand for me; to bear which afar, to deliver it well, skill and strength, courage and eloquence, the best qualifications of soldier, statesman, and orator, were all needed: for these all centre in the good missionary.

Jane you are docile, diligent, disinterested, faithful, constant, and courageous; very gentle, and very heroic... As a conductress of Indian schools, and a helper amongst Indian women, your assistance will be to me invaluable.
St John Rivers in *Jane Eyre* by Charlotte Brontë, published in 1847.

The rôle of women missionaries in the evangelical missionary enterprise of the nineteenth and first half of the twentieth century is a significant, broad, and fruitful subject of study. It is a topic to which until recently all too little attention has been paid. Documentation in the archives of three Protestant British Missionary Societies in SOAS Library, namely the London Missionary Society, the Methodist Misionary Society and the Presbyterian Church of England provides ample evidence on such topics as the social background, motivation, recruitment, and training of women missionaries, the contemporary perception of their rôles, the organisation of their work and lives, and their attitudes to the cultures in which they found themselves. Although their sphere was more circumscribed than that of their male counterparts, women were able to achieve a greater degree of freedom and opportunity in mission work than would have been allowed them in contemporary British life. As a group they form an interesting early example of professional women working alongside men. It is not possible, within the scope of one paper, to do more than provide a brief illustrated sketch of some of these themes but I hope I will do enough to convey more than a hint of the possibilities of the resources at our disposal.

Women had for long been generous contributors to missionary work. Findlay and Holdsworth, historians of the Wesleyan Methodist Missionary Society, estimate that 'quite half of the amount yearly raised for the missionary funds was due, directly or indirectly, to the labours and influence of the women of our Home Churches.'[1] The first female missionaries went out to the east as unpaid assistants to their missionary husbands. In addition to their domestic responsibilities they were called upon to run schools, orphanages and cottage industries, visit homes and help with medical work. There is little record in the archives of these early female endeavours but published memoirs and funeral sermons testify to feminine virtues which seemed so admirably fitted to the missionary rôle. One bereaved husband wrote of his wife that she was 'always gathering up the smallest fragments of time and turning them to some account'.[2] The Reverend E Storrow declared in a funeral sermon for Hannah Mullens preached in Calcutta in 1861 that 'she uniformly acted on the principle of taking as little as possible from others, and giving them as much as she could. So great indeed was her self-abnegation that it degenerated into a fault.'[3] But despite an awesome workload which must have contributed to her early death (at 35) *viz*, 'four *zenana* morning schools; ... [an] other eleven *zenanas* which she visited in the afternoons; ... a class almost every day in her own boarding school; ... a Bible class in the Cooly Bazar Sunday School, and [the] writing [of] a book for the instruction of native females'[4], there was felt to be a need for single female workers who could commit their entire lives to missionary work.

It was early perceived that women had a special contribution to make in the work of evangelising the heathen. The pioneer Protestant Missionary in China, Robert Morrison asked the Directors of the London Missionary Society to consider in 1824 'The expediency of sending ... some unmarried ladies of experience and education ... with the design of teaching English and the principles of our religion to pagan girls[5] and *The Missionary Register* published in 1820 an emotional appeal on behalf of the Native Females of British India 'who are totally destitute of Education, and to whom every vestige of mental cultivation has been denied. Their fingers have never touched a needle, a pair of scissors, a book, or a pen; and they are entirely excluded from all intellecutal intercourse with the other sex.' The article further noted that 'every improvement of the Female Mind and Character will re-act on the Fathers, the Brothers and the Sons within its circle; and will greatly quicken the emancipation of the whole body of the natives of India, from the ignorance and superstition under which they are enslaved.' To answer this need a female 'of superior qualifications, agreeable manners, benevolent temper, and unfeigned piety', additionally, 'well qualified to superintend a School for training Native Female Teachers' was called for.[6] A Miss Mary Anne Cooke duly arrived in Bengal to teach under the auspices of the Calcutta School Society and by 1823 fifteen schools with some 300 pupils had been opened. But single women missionaries before the second half of the nineteenth century were exceptional. Many shared the view of Daniel Wilson, Bishop of Calcutta who objected 'in principle to single ladies coming out unprotected to so distant a place with a climate so unfriendly, and with the almost certainty of their marrying within a month of their arrival.'[7] The most active Society in this respect was the Society for Promoting Female Education in the East, founded in 1834, which by 1860 had sent out some 90 teachers. But up to 1870 the London Missionary Society had sent out only eight fully accredited female missionaries.

By the middle of the nineteenth century the view was gaining ground that until the women of India and China were conquered for Christ the whole missionary enterprise was in jeopardy. Not only would their own narrow, unenlightened and oppressive lives be transformed and uplifted by the Christian message but, upon conversion, they would lead, inspire and influence the menfolk of their families to follow their example. In particular the secluded lives of higher class Indian women was seen as a barrier to the growth of Christianity in Indian homes. Dr Thomas Smith, who is credited by some as the originator of *zenana* work, declared in the *Calcutta Christian Observer* for 1840 that: 'if the men of India will not permit their female relations to come to us for instruction, we must send out teachers to them.'[8] In the 1860s and 1870s *zenana* work acquired momentum and the women of England organised themselves into a positive frenzy of sewing circles, busy bees, sales of work, bazaars, prayer leagues and collecting auxiliaries to support this extension of missionary work. But now they were asked to do more than support. They were asked, besought and even hectored to sacrifice the comforts of civilised life and the attractions of marriage, motherhood and homemaking for, in the words of a contemporary pamphlet, how could they 'be content to sit at ease in Zion whilst millions of your sisters suffer untold shame and anguish.'[9]

The first of the major British Missionary Societies to undertake *zenana* work, was the Baptist Missionary Society in 1869. In 1875 a document calling for the establishment of a Ladies' Committee to supervise the training, selection and advising of female missionaries was circulated by the officers of the London Missionary Society. Having found that its constitution did not allow for the participation of ladies in the management of its affairs the Society passed a special resolution and the first meeting of the Ladies' Committee was held on 6 October 1875. The Ladies' Committee acted as an examination committee for female candidates until 1907 although, in other ways, the work of women missionaries was not organised separately as it was in most other missionary societies. In 1891 the London Missionary Society allowed women to become Directors of its Board, the first of the great missionary societies to do so. The Women's Missionary Association of the Presbyterian Church of England was established in 1878. The first Annual Meeting took place in 1880 when 42 branches and an income of £671 17s 3d were reported. The Association had to 'depend on the men of the Church to conduct these public meetings ... It was not until the spring meetings were started in 1893 that we held a public meeting for women only and conducted it ourselves'[10] Among Methodists the Ladies' Committee for the amelioration of the condition of women in heathen countries had been established in 1858 but it did not take on *zenna* work until the 1880s.

High standards of education, behaviour and appearance were expected from aspiring female missionaries. It was, for example, required of the successful applicant to the post of head of what was described as a Hindu Ladies' High Caste School at Mysore in 1882 that she be 'a good Christian and Methodist ... a good musician, and one who possesses a facility for languages ... she should ... be a lady and possessed of great force of character. Whoever comes will need all the commonsense, ability, grace and Christian faith and patience which she possesses'.[11] Some applicants not surprisingly did not live up to these high expectations. The Ladies' Committee of the Wesleyan Methodist Missionary Society was very critical of the first batch of 25 applicants for missionary service. 'It would save some trouble if friends and advisers would bear in mind that a year's training at Westminster cannot make up the deficiencies of an entirely neglected early education'.[12] Only eight of the 25 were thought worthy of being taken seriously. Of an applicant to the London Missionary Society it was commented that 'if she can be sent to a place where appearance or manner are not of importance, I think she will prove an efficient missionary'.[13] The series of Candidate's Papers in the archives of this Society are a useful source of information on the education and background of applicants who were asked to complete a detailed application form and supply moral and educational references. Candidates were asked about their educational attainments, and to provide proof of their Christian character, beliefs and experience and their expectations of missionary service. The minutes of the Ladies' Committee provide additional evidence on the desired qualities. The candidature of a Miss Amory in 1894 seemed to meet all the Committee's requirements – 'Her age was 22, her health was good... she spoke well at meetings and in open air services.'[14] Very sensibly, great stress was placed on the health of candidates and each had to undergo a medical examination. From 1896 those applying to the London Missionary Society could choose to be examined by a female doctor. Female missionaries had to be young (candidates of 29 years or more being turned down out of hand) single and without family responsibilities. Most societies gave their intending female missionaries some training though usually of an improvised nature and only for a year or two. It was not until 1912 that a permanent college to train women missionaries was established by the London Missionary Society, the Baptist Missionary Society and the Women's Missionary Association at Carey Hall, Selly Oak, Birmingham. A period of practical experience was often arranged. Emma Foggit who went out to China with the LMS in 1907 was based during her training at the Settlement for Women Workers in Canning Town. 'I find the work most interesting and it is very varied in character. It largely consists in visiting, addressing gatherings, working in the girls clubs, holding children's services and doing dispensary work.'[15] Such practical work did not always prove sufficient preparation. One female missionary wrote home that she had 'witnessed things that would never have cropped up at Kentish Town Mission.'[16] A proportion of early missionaries were honorary missionaries, *ie* women of independent means who could support themselves or, where the claims of family took priority, a substitute, though the proportion of self-financed missionaries was lower in nonconformist missionary societies than in anglican ones. In most cases a salary of about £100 per annum or approximately what an elementary school teacher could earn at home was paid.

Female missionaries continued to be involved in teaching work in both schools and orphanages. One new entrant wrote enthusiastically of her schoolroom with its gallery, 'since then, desks, reading stand and blackboard have been added,' and of her sense of fulfilment. 'I am very happy in my work, for I feel it to be an unspeakable and utterly undeserved honour to be thus engaged'. This despite her reservations about her abilities to control her 'dusky pupils' who were 'full of sprightliness and mischief'.[17] In addition to a basic curriculum, 'extra' subjects like French and music were often taught, as well as the Bible, hymns and prayers. Later on, school trips and camps were arranged such as one near Bangalore, where 'we had some glorious walks – nearly nine miles one morning. And we had all sorts of games and sing songs, and everybody was as happy as could be.'[18] Other work carried out by women included famine relief work and social service work of various kinds. But evangelising work amongst women took a high priority. There could be problems as one of the earliest practitioners of *zenana* work, Hannah Mullens, amusingly relates. 'We were seated in their verandah, as usual, surrounded by at least twenty eager learners... when suddenly a harsh voice [of an 'old uncle]' was heard below stairs, vehement and loud in the extreme, and so choked with anger that the only words I could distinguish were 'What, again! Again! After all I have said, these missionary ladies are here again!'... Our frightened scholars slid away and hid themselves in all parts of the house.'[19] The work was often done through the agency of Biblewomen. One missionary wrote '– we have a splendid worker in our Biblewoman Mrs Kwang... [who] has worked in that position for 27 years... Mrs Kwang is a great believer in home visits, she visited one home at intervals for seven years before she was admitted, but she won them at last, and is now a welcome visitor.' But evangelical work needed many Mrs Kwangs as well as the educationists and female evangelists to instruct her. There were frequent appeals for more helpers. 'Are there not any of our girls... who are fitted for this kind of work, and who are willing to make the necessary sacrifice... I can assure them that in a very short time all sense of sacrifice will have disappeared.'[20]

Soon, another dimension of work opened up. Calls for women doctors and nurses appear in missionary literature from about 1800 onwards. From Secunderabad the Revered W Burgess in 1880 urged the Ladies' Committee of the Wesleyan Missionary Society to urgently consider the need of *purdah* women and send out a 'lady doctor not skilled simply in prescribing and compunding, but thoroughly adept in surgery'[21]. Reverend Josiah Cox of Wu-Chang urged in a letter written during a furlough in 1880 the need of similar work in China, 'You must endeavour to take some share in the blessed work of alleviating the suffering and mortality of your sisterhood in India and China.'[22] The *LMS Quarterly News* of 1894 offered to 'young medical women of England, looking for a practice, perhaps yearning for a sphere' the opportunities of work in China 'where you may have patients from morning to night' and become 'centres of hope to thousands of poor women'.[23] The first woman doctors to be sent out by the London Missionary Society were Dr. Elizabeth Harris appointed to Hankow in 1892 (she married Dr Thomas Gillison in 1893 but continued medical work), Dr Ethel Tribe appointed to Amoy in 1895, and Dr Lillie Saville who went out to Peking in the same year. Increasingly too, nurses were appointed by all the main missionary societies not only to work in general wards in the mission hospitals, or in the dispensaries attached to them, but in women's wards and hospitals. Nor was the greater goal forgotten in hospital work. Elizabeth Gillison wrote of her disappointment that many who were urged to come in for operations failed to do so. 'During hospital stays we have a wonderful opportunity of getting to know them and of teaching them of our Heavenly Father and His great love.'[24] Another, describing work in the Wesleyan mission hospital at Hankow wrote that she wished 'you could look in and see your three agents at work some of these mornings, one in the waiting room of the dispensary, instructing the women in Gospel truths; one in the consulting room, diagnosing; and another... dispensing medicines, and every now and then having a look into the large ward close by to see that all is going on right there.'[25] Helen Stevens, Superintendent of the Nethersole Memorial Hospital in Hong Kong told of how she and Miss Davies '... have a plan to train those who come from the country to be Bible-women, and in mid-wifery also, that they may go back among the villages, and in the country, helping the women for our dear Lord's sake, and also finding *special* opportunities to tell of all His wondrous love.'[26]

Reference to the sacrifice which women made on answering the call of missionary work is frequently made. The life of a female missionary was conceived of as a single one. Among some American missionary societies married women missionaries were allowed to hold independent appointments but in most British societies it was usual for women to give up their posts on marriage; although, as we have seen, they continued to work, unpaid, alongside their husbands or, as one Society's historian put it, 'without any contractual obligation'.[27] If marriage took place within five years of their initial appointment they were expected to reimburse the cost of their training, outfit and passage. Many female missionaries did not marry and their lives could be rather solitary. 'From the early part of the year 1893... until October... I was alone here [in Peking]... and in consequence the daily pressure of work was too great to admit of my replying to the many kind letters received from you from time to time, and for which I have been deeply grateful. These kind, loving letters have cheered many a lonely hour.'[28] Others, on occasion, rather neglected their own needs: 'I occupy the unique position of being the only woman in South China living alone in the heart of the Country a hundred miles away from the nearest English-speaking friend... After I had been here alone for eight weeks Miss Davies and Mrs Stevens made me a visit, and took me back with them to Hong Kong for a few weeks. I had been rather run down, food here being rather poor and badly cooked, but soon recovered there, being kindly cared for by the friends.'[29] In addition to the letters sent from home female missionaries were often supported by the efforts of women's auxiliaries, who collected and worked on their behalf, sending out goods for sale or supplies such as 'needles, pins, hairpins, hooks and eyes, small court-plaister cases, scissors, thimbles, tapes, white cotton, cord, buttons, thread, black sewing silk, and pocket pin-cushions'[30] for the needs of the missionaries themselves. Sewing groups and working parties provided opportunities too for listening to news of missionary needs and achievements although, evidently, some pains had to be taken in organising these effectively. A pamphlet published by the London Missionary Society in 1907 warned organisers to 'be careful that the reading is not in a voice hardly audible at one end of the room, and is of a more lively nature than statistics of a school of which no one present ever heard the name before.'[31]

As we have seen women had been prominent supporters of missionary work throughout the period surveyed. By the middle of the twentieth century there were substantial numbers of women workers in the field. Up to 1895 the LMS had appointed 65 women missionaries. By 1945 there were 122 out of a total workforce of 276. Between 1847 and 1947 the Presbyterian Church of England had appointed 162 men and 140 women though the first woman was not appointed until 1878. The presence in such numbers of female missionaries was not universally welcomed by their male colleagues. Norman Goodall, in his history of the London Missionary Society comments that 'some of the men have shown up at their worst in the failure to adjust their service to the colleagueship of women.' He quotes the view of Wardlaw Thompson who was Foreign Secretary of the London Missionary Society from 1881 to 1914 that 'the policy of sending out large number of women missionaries is one which requires to be very carefully watched. We have some splendid workers among them, able and capable and devoted. We have some others whose personal crotchets and angularities greatly detract from the value of their help to their fellow missionaries, and we have some who, I fear, have neither ability nor angularity, and who receive £100 a year for very little service'[32] Sometimes, the arrangements made for the organising of women's work seemed designed to cause friction and difficult relations in the mission field. This was particularly so among Methodists and English Presbyterians where women agents appointed by women's committees at home found themselves subject to the authority of the parent organisations through local missionary councils. The historian of the English Presbyterian mission comments 'WMA agents were to cause the Council frequent headaches by their independent action and reluctance to admit to male jurisdiction. Many years were to pass before United Councils were instituted on the Mission field, and harmonious co-operation became the order of the day.'[33] However, there are examples from minutes, reports and correspondence of women co-operating with men in committee work, in attending and participating in conferences and speaking at and leading devotions at missionary gatherings. Such participation it is true was not in proportion to their numbers. Perhaps many women missionaries shared the feelings of one who confessed that, 'it is so much easier to do the work than to talk about it.'[34]

References

1. Findlay, G G and Holdsworth W W. *The history of the Wesleyan Methodist Missionary Society*. London, 1922, vol.IV, p.18.
2. *Memoir of Mrs Louisa Mundy of the London Missionary Society's Mission at Chinsurah, Bengal. By her husband*. London, 1845, p.154.
3. *A funeral sermon for Mrs Mullens, preached at Union Chapel, Calcutta by the Rev. E. Storrow, 1st Dec. 1861*. Calcutta, 1861, pp.7–8.
4. Ibid p.9.
5. Letter, dated 7 September 1824, from Robert Morrison to the Directors of the London Missionary Society. SOAS: CWM Archive, South China Incoming Correspondence Box 2/2/D.

6. *The Missionary Register*, Oct. 1820, British and Foreign School Society, 'Appeal in behalf of the Native Females of British India'. pp.433–435.
7. Quoted in S C Potter, *The social origins and recruitment of English Protestant Missionaries in the nineteenth century*. University of London, PhD. Thesis, 1974, p.221.
8. Quoted in Richard Lovett. *The History of the London Missionary Society 1795-1795*. London, 1899, vol.II, p.247.
9. Ibid, p.237.
10. Band, Edward. *Working His purpose out; the history of the English Presbyterian Mission 1847-1947*, London, 1948, p.577.
11. Letter, dated Mysore 12 November 1881, from Reverend H Haigh to the Committee of the Ladies' Auxillary for Female Education, Wesleyan Missionary Society. *Occasional Paper*, January 1882, p.456.
12. Report of the Ladies' Committee for ameliorating the condition of women in heathen countries, female education etc. Wesleyan Missionary Society. *Occasional Papers*, March 1861. pp.149–150.
13. Quoted in S C Potter, op cit., p.230.
14. SOAS; CWM Archive, Minutes of Ladies' Examination Committee, Tuesday, 11 June 1895.
15. SOAS: CWM Archive, Candidates' Papers 1900–40, Emma Foggitt.
16. Goodall, Norman. *A history of the London Missionary Society 1895–1945*. London, 1954, p.12.
17. Letter, dated Natal 6 June 1861, from Miss Lamb to the Reverend M C Taylor, Ladies' Committee for ameliorating the condition of women in heathen countries, *Occasional papers*, January 1862, p.215.
18. *Woman's Work on the Mission Field*. vol.iv no.14, April 1922, p.322.
19. R Lovett, *op cit.*, p.249.
20. SOAS: CWM Archive, North China, Reports, Report from Frances Stuckey, Peking, 1921.
21. Letter, dated Secunderabad 1880, from Reverend W Burgess, to the Committe of the Ladies Auxillary for Female education, Wesleyan Missionary Society. *Occasional Paper*, January 1881, p.263.
22. Letter, dated 10 December 1880, from Reverend J Cox, ibid, p.263.
23. London Missionary Society, *Quarterly News of Woman's Work*, April 1894, p.38.
24. Ibid. p.50.
25. Letter, dated Hankow 1881, from Mrs Bell, Wesleyan Missionary Society, Woman's Work conducted by the Ladies' Auxillary. *Quarterly Paper*. October 1891, p.736.
26. London Missionary Society. *Quarterly News of Women's Work*. January 1894, pp.69–70.
27. N Goodall, op.cit., p.13.
28. Letter, dated Peking, January 1894 from Georgina Smith, LMS, *Quarterly News of Women's Work*, April 1894, pp.69–74.
29. Letter from Sara Rowe [Poklo], ibid., p.103.
30. *London Missionary Society, Women's Auxiliaries, How to help the Work*, 3rd Edition, revised. London, 1901. p.8.
31. London Missionary Society, Women's Auxiliaries, op.cit. p.9.
32. N Goodall, op.cit., p.12.
33. Edward Band, op. cit., p.110.
34. *LMS, Quarterly New of Women's Work*, January 1894, p.15.

List of Sources

1. COUNCIL FOR WORLD MISSION (London Missionary Society)
Ladies' Committee founded 1875.

Ladies' Committee Minutes 1875–1907.
Candidates' Papers 1875–1950.
Correspondence 1875–1950.
Personal Papers.
Photographs.
Reports.
LMS Quarterly News of Women's Work, 1887-1895.

2. METHODIST CHURCH OVERSEAS DIVISION (Methodist Missionary Society)
Ladies' Committee for the amelioration of the condition of women in heathen countries founded 1858.

Minutes 1858-1939.
Correspondence 1911-50.
Reports 1923-50.
Financial Papers.
Ladies' Committee for amelioration of the condition of women in heathern countries, Occasional Papers 1861-
Ladies' Auxillary for Female education, papers 1874-
Woman's Work as conducted by the Ladies' Auxiliary 1885-
Report of Women's Auxiliary 1923-
Report of Women's Work 1935-

3. PRESBYTERIAN CHURCH OF ENGLAND
Women's Missionary Association founded 1878.

Records 1878-1961 comprising Committee minutes, correspondence including circularised monthly letters, Foreign Missions Committee and Women's Missionary Association Joint Conference Minutes 1920-24, reports and miscellaneous publications.

The three archives are available on microfiche. Copies can be ordered from IDC AG, Poststrasse 14, 6300 Zug, Switzerland.

Ursula Owen

Feminist publishing

The name was a problem at first: hardly anyone saw the joke or knew the original meaning – Virago, a heroic woman. One forgets how disturbing and unmarketable feminism was in the early 1970s. But in 1978 Fay Weldon wrote in *The Times Literary Supplement* that 'the solid substance of their list and the very feel of their books has all but changed the connotation of the word. Say Virago to me now and I visualise an industrious and intelligent lady in her middle years.' The enterprise seemed to be going to work.

The women's movement of the 1960s and 1970s was, to a remarkable degree, a writer's movement. Many of the early movers and shapers, starting with Simone de Beauvoir, had begun as writers and reached public attention first through books. The movement's grassroots were bound up in writing as well. Feminists of the 1970s found art and politics inextricably connected, for this 'second wave' grounded itself in personal change, believing that daring to expose and discuss hidden, often forbidden, topics was a vital basis for attacking social and political issues. By a new feminist definition, the personal was political – and this became the central slogan of the movement.

For a new generation it is not easy to imagine just how invisible most women's issues were before this second wave movement – or how isolated most women felt, whatever their lives. Although women were writing, the opportunity to be published was a matter of what they wrote *about*. Two stories from the early 1970s illustrate some of the problems women writers faced. Mary Gordon, an American novelist, whose first novel *Final Payments* became a best-seller, tells this one:

Once I was told a story by a famous writer. ' I will tell you what women writers are like,' he said. The year was 1971. The women's movement had made men nervous; it had made a lot of women write. 'Women writers are like a female bear who goes into a cave to hibernate. The male bear shoves a pine cone up her ass, because he knows if she shits all winter, she'll stink up the cave. In the spring, the pressure of all the built up shit makes her expel the pine cone, and she shits a winter's worth all over the walls of the cave.

That's what women writers are like,' said the famous writer.

He told the story with such geniality; he looked as if he were giving me a wonderful gift. I felt I ought to smile; everyone knows there's no bore like a feminist with no sense of humour. I did not write for two months after that. It was the only time in my life I have suffered from a writer's block. I should not have smiled. But he was a famous writer and spoke with geniality. And in truth, I did not have the courage for clear rage. There is no seduction like that of being thought a good girl.

And, in a different vein, here is Joyce Carol Oates:

The question was asked of me by an earnest young man, who like most of the Poles we met, spoke excellent English: Why was my writing so violent? Might it be 'perhaps my childhood', had my 'unique temperament' distorted my vision of mankind and of history?

That this familiar question was asked of me in Warsaw, where in September 1944 the insurrection against the Germans by the Polish underground had begun, with the eventual consequence that 200,000 Poles were slaughtered, that it was asked with a hint of reproach that clearly resonated through the crowded gathering struck me as painful and ironic and dispiriting and, in a sad way, amusing.

'Why do you focus on the violent?' The question was asked in Oslo, in Helsinki, in Brussels, in Budapest, and in that city in Eastern Europe known for its encircling wall. In West Berlin the question was asked with great courtesy and tact not many miles from where Adolf Hitler proclaimed the Second World War and Dr. Goebbels advanced the notion of 'total war'... When I point out that, in fact, my writing isn't usually explicitly violent, but deals, most of the time, with the phenomenon of violence and its aftermath, the interviewer will nod and take notes and inquire about childhood 'Was it tragic? Have you been frightened by life?'

'Would you ask the question of a male writer?' I responded the last time it was put to me. After some hesitation, the answer came 'No'.

'Why no?' I asked.

Herewith a long pause ensued. My interrogator knew the answer to the question but declined to answer it. Or perhaps he was thinking. I hope he still is.

Virago came out of the early years of a women's movement which concerned itself with silences, invisibility, the denial or marginalising of women's experiences in a male-dominated culture. Writing became one weapon to break that silence, to reveal and celebrate women's lives, bringing urgent dispatches from the female heart. And the movement also brought a new audience of readers who realised that the received view of cultural history had marginalised women's experiences. It has been a complicated, far from finished process; as Jane Miller says, in *Women writing about men* (1986):

Women writers have seen themselves as rewriting, as telling familiar stories differently, as forging new forms of language out of the old... Women have had to return to their personal knowledge in order to explain what it is they recognise in other women's lives and why that recognition is important.

Virago was set up as a publishing house where women could take risks, trust their instincts, dare to be vulnerable – and be understood.

Virago has many birthdays: 1972, when Carmen Callil had the idea; 1973 when she registered the company; 1975 when we (now a company of three) published our first book in association with Quartet Books. Then, in the summer of 1976 the American *Publisher's Weekly* ran an article – 'Mr Hopeful Starts a Publishing Company' – and, savouring the irony, we read it eagerly. Armed with a cash flow sheet and a publishing proposal for the first three years, we set off to find independent backing, and with a bank overdraft of £25,000, a loan of £10,000 (from supportive friends and relatives, some inside, some outside publishing) and £1,500 capital we embarked on what is now the Virago list. In our year with Quartet we had learned two things: how vital it is to have *total* financial control over your business (something hardly any women in publishing had at that time); and how any requirement to refer to others on editorial decisions, however benevolent those others might be, is a constraint. Even so, we were surprised how quickly our new situation gave us the psychological freedom to spread our wings.

The question was, and is, not just what to publish but *how* to publish, because Virago had marketing as well as literary and political aims – attempting to reach not just feminists but people who were not necessarily feminist sympathisers, who might fear or dislike feminist ideas. We knew there was an audience which would love the books we loved, but we were determined to get into the high street as well as the radical bookshops. The books had to look good, they had to be as cheap as possible but we had to stay solvent. We aimed for the maximum amount of publicity on each book and in our early years were lucky to receive strong support from women's page editors on daily papers; it took longer to break through the suspicions of the traditional reviews pages, and longer still to reach the popular women's magazines and television.

We knew we could print between 5,000 and 10,000 copies of the titles, but not the 25,000 to 100,000 or more a mass market paperback requires to keep its price down. So the 'trade paperback' pioneered by Paladin and then Picador, with its larger format, elegant cover and slightly higher price, was a vital part of our operation. Virago's success has helped establish the trade paperback in the market-place, and it in turn has served us well. We learned too that series publishing is often an appropriate vehicle for our titles, and effective in marketing terms.

Our first years were spent working in Carmen's dining-rooms (she moved) with three cats for company, after which we graduated to the fourth floor (no lift, many complaints) of a building in Wardour Street, sharing it with a palmist, a barber, a drinking club and a pinball arcade. In this single room we grew from a company of three to one of seven, from publishing eleven books a year to forty, from a turnover of £50,000 to one of nearly half a million. I don't remember any conversations about whether we'd succeed or fail: we just worked like dogs – commissioning authors, ordering paper, learning to do budgets, choosing cover designs, packing review copies and dragging them in sackloads to the post office. There was a lot we didn't know. Years later we could look back and, out of interest, draw up a list. It makes terrifying reading. Like many small enterprises, we started on low salaries, optimism and ignorance. We knew little about contracts, export and home sales, production, royalties, distribution, finance. But we controlled our own company, and had the power to publish. Through telephone conversations half overheard, through decisions made in minutes by shouting across the room, we all learned a lot about each other's jobs – for from the first there was division of labour in Virago. In addition we set up an advisory group of about thirty women – journalists, teachers, publishers, writers among them, who made an enormous contribution to our early years, suggesting titles and authors, reading for us, talking about us to their friends, giving us huge moral support.

We have achieved visibility beyond our wildest dreams. Even now, when competition for media space has grown, when there are other feminist publishing houses and mainstream feminist books competing for bookshop space, when we are no longer new and therefore 'news', when the political climate is much less sympathetic to feminism, the selling of our books flourishes, our presence in the high street, and the independent bookshops grows each years. With the help of the women's movement, we have won our place in the bookshop through customer demand. We have a brand image our readers have come to trust; people buy our books because they liked the last Virago book they read. We get letters daily suggesting, criticising, expressing pleasure. We are as much married to our readers as to our authors.

The size and display of women's writing in bookshops today is in sharp contrast to how things were in the 1960s and early 1970s. Many women tell us how they are encouraged by *seeing* so much women's writing available. And other feminist publishing houses have similar experiences. There are now eleven such publishers in Britain and Eire – Virago, the Women's Press, Pandora, Stramullion, Sheba, Onlywomen, Jezebel, Attiz Press, Womanwrite, Black Woman Talks and Arlen House.

There are many more women with power in general publishing now; they may not all be feminists, but many of them have been influenced by the women's movement, and their influence means more books by feminists appear on general lists. And, of course, in the 1970s, the publishing world discovered that some feminist books sell in vast numbers – *The Women's Room*, the novel of the women's movement by Marilyn French, *The Female Eunuch*, Germaine Greer's famous tract, *Sexual Politics*, Kate Millett's early critical analysis of D H Lawrence and other male writers; while others have remained steady backlist titles for many years. Feminism has, in some of its manifestations at least, been good business. With our backlist presenting half our turnover, the signs are that our authors and titles will remain visible for future generations as well as our own.

In choosing books we have always had three things in mind. First the discovery of the hidden voices of 'ordinary' women has been a guiding theme. *Fenwomen*, an oral history of women in an English village by Mary Chamberlain, was our first commissioned book, and *Life As We Have Known It*, edited by Margaret Llewelyn Davies our first reprint. Virginia Woolf said in her introduction to those writings by working-class women: 'These pages are only fragments. These voices are beginning only now to emerge from silence into half articulate speech. These lives are still half hidden in profound obscurity.' Such a book was part of the feminist enterprise to recover women who had been 'hidden from history', and to break away from the idea that books can only be about what the critic Lorna Sage has called 'personages'.

Books like these have also gone some way, though not far enough, to put domestic and personal matters firmly at centre stage; they, and others like them, were an impressive counter to what had been, and still remains, a dominant notion in our culture – that women's experiences are limited and limiting. Anthony Burgess, in his reviews, expresses this view repeatedly; he could say of Olivia Manning, 'She was never, like so many women novelists, limited to experiences of her own sex.' Or again his 'virile objections to Jane Austen' (as the critic Mary Ellmann put it): 'I recognise that I can gain no pleasure from serious reading that lacks a strong male thrust, an almost pedantic allusiveness, and a brutal intellectual content.' This ghettoising of women's writing, as of their experience, is something we have always been determined to challenge. If love, friendship, birth, death, work, travel, affection comprise a limited world, it is a ghetto many of us would choose to live in.

This 'female tradition', if we may call it that, is present also in many of the books in the most famous part of our list, the series which has been particularly responsible for our visibility in the bookshops, the Virago Modern Classics. For the second vital part of our enterprise was bridging the gap with the past. 'Women,' as Beatrix Campbell and Anna Coote said in *Sweet Freedom*, their account of the women's movement of the 1970s, 'continually have to reinvent their rebellion.' The history of women's movements (for there have been others) has been one of starting again, of 'searching through libraries and coming, with astonishment, upon the accounts of women who had had the same hopes, problems and experiences' (Carmen Callil, 1986). We were determined to reclaim a history, a feminism and a literature which had been lost or neglected. In this we were not only in tune with feminist historians like Sheila Rowbotham, but were influenced by new writing in social and cultural history which was among the most important work being done in the 1960s and 1970s, most significantly E P Thompson's *The Making of the English Working Class* and Raymond William's *Culture and Society*.

The Virago Modern Classics were launched in 1978 with Antonia White's famous convent school story, *Frost in May*. It was followed closely by two novels by Christina Stead. The books in this series have been chosen to show the imaginative range of women's writing and to celebrate the scale of female achievement in fiction. Many of the works of even the best known authors – Rosamond Lehmann, Stevie Smith, Edith Wharton, Elizabeth Taylor – were, suprisingly, out of print when the list began (though in the past ten years the competition among publishers' lists for this kind of book has hugely increased, which has meant that many out-of-print novels have seen the light of day again). Other names on the list are not so identifiable. For another aim of the list was to try to counter the narrowing notion that only 'great' novels are worth reading. We have those too, and modernist as well as naturalist novels. But the Virago Modern Classics are, above all, intended to give pleasure and do what all good novels do – in Marx's words: 'issuing to the World more political and social truths than have been uttered by all the professional politicians, publicists and moralists put together'.

A critic's comments on Eudora Welty suggest some characteristics of this part of the list: 'What interests her is the moral and physical landscape of her characters, their domestic lives, clothes, conversations, their kitchens and pantries, their gardens, the food they eat, the cars they drive. She does not cultivate the high pitch or beat the big drum.' Or here is Christina Stead:

My purpose in making characters somewhat eloquent is the expression of two psychological truths: first, that everyone has a wit superior to everyday wit, when discussing his personal problems, and the most depressed housewife, for example, can talk like Medea about her troubles; second, that everyone, to a greater or lesser extent, is a fountain of passion, which is turned by circumstances of birth or upbringing into conventional channels – as ambition, love, money-grubbing, politics, but which would be as well applied to other objects and with less waste of energy.

Lorna Sage summarises this neatly: 'When you come down to it, what Christina Stead is implying is there's plenty for everyone, a most subversive suggestion, then as now.'

To discover new fiction and first novelists, we had to go out to find writers in more unorthodox ways than other publishers. Manuscripts from the grander agents did not pour through our letter box. But even at the start we were sent hundreds of unsolicited manuscripts every month, and some of our authors have emerged from those parcels. Others came from writers' groups, or were recommended. The question of whether there is such a category as feminist fiction has been debated for many years. As with most publishers of fiction, the quality of writing comes first but, in the early years, there were recurring themes in some of the novels we were sent connected to what was happening then to women's lives. This is much less true now – fiction from feminist publishers has broadened in scope and imagination.

Much of our new fiction takes traditional forms and pushes out the boundaries: it is often a question of realism with an altered viewpoint, another perspective, or giving a voice to those who have had short shrift both in literature and in life (Pat Barker's novels of working-class life in the north of England are a good example of this). In recent years we have published fiction by black British and American women, conscious of how, early on, we concentrated too heavily on the experience of white women, how black women have felt excluded from the account, and conscious too of the difficulties for a largely white women's press in getting such publishing right. And from the beginning we have published fiction in translation, aware of the parochialism of much British publishing, and of the importance of such writing for our enterprise.

Like all publishers with a political base, we have wanted to change the world. Publishing new thinking by women on urgent contemporary issues has been a third concern. Early books such as Adrienne Rich's book on motherhood, *Of Woman Born*; Angela Carter's brilliantly original view of sexual innocence and experience, *The Sadeian Woman; Alice Through the Microscope*, which broke fresh ground in looking at science as a man-made discipline; and Beatrix Campbell's *Wigan Pier Revisited*, provoking disturbing questions about women, poverty and the labour movement, are still in print. Politically and socially the mid-1980s are light years away from the previous decade; there have been vast changes on the world political scene. And the preoccupations of feminism have changed too. Race has become a central theme in the feminism of the 1980s and *The Heart of the Race* tells of black women's lives in Britain today. Maya Angelou's five-volume autobiography of a black woman's childhood and adulthood in America has struck an extraordinary chord in this country. Irish women in Britain, incest and child abuse, the rôle of socialism in feminist ideology, the lives of Egyptian women, Chinese women, Aboriginal women, told in their own words, are some of our books for the 1980s. We continue to publish a wide range of non-fiction – poetry, literary critcism, health books, autobiography and biography, history, popular culture, art, psychology, books for teenagers.

Times change, and any alert political publishing house has to keep in touch with the changes, keep abreast, indeed be ahead of the game, because we now compete with larger houses with considerable funding who want some of these books on their own lists. Feminism has, though still only in its more 'palatable' forms, become good business, and sometimes big business. Yet if feminism was an unpopular word in the market-place in the early 1970s, it has become so again, for new reasons.

It is not a word used much in the media any more – indeed, some sections of the media have been saying for years that feminism is 'over'. Young women often associate the word with separatism; black women often feel the word applies only to white, middle-class feminists. And yet women who are reluctant to call themselves feminists often share in feminist enterprises and ideals. In the early 1970s, socialist feminism was the dominant voice in the movement, with its belief that the structures and ideologies of male dominance and the requirements of the profit motive are linked, so that the divisions between women and men are firmly supported by the economic system, and women and men can work together to alter the position of women. In the late 1970s radical feminism became the most powerful voice of the movement, believing that women have separate and special knowledge, emotions, thoughts and moralities which exist in fundamental and unchanging opposition to 'male culture' and 'male authority', and which is in fundamental opposition to the world of men.

Virago came out of socialist feminism, but we were not simply socialist feminists, nor were we separatists. What we tried to represent is best described in the words of Dora Russell's daughter about that pioneer of socialism and women's rights:

> She really believed in the value of women as women. She didn't want them to be mere companions of men, she wanted them to be in every way equal, in every way influential. She thought that women ought to be deeply involved in politics because there were so many things they understood that men did not. What she said was that she wanted women not only to have equality and rights but also for the very essence or what they represent to count in politics and in society.

But we have also wanted people to define their own feminism, not to have a view of what is 'properly' feminist or not: we have wanted to celebrate women's achievements; and we have wanted to have fun. We concluded early that to alter the culture we had to occupy the middle ground as well as the margins, and, where necessary, to draw blood. The idea that our books are not 'mainstream' has always seemed curious. The subject matter of our books, we believe, concerns everyone. It is often the titles on the list of so-called general publishing houses which seems superfluous and peripheral.

It is easier to start a publishing house than to keep it going, especially when it starts as a small company and grows to medium size. One soon learns that being undercapitalised at the start tends to mean one continues undercapitalised. The money you make is ploughed back immediately into new books. Virago grew enormously fast. By 1980 we were feeling some concern at the amount of time spent by the staff (still only nine) on administrative matters and money raising. When in 1982 Carmen Callil was approached by Chatto, Bodley Head and Cape to be managing director of Chatto and for Virago to join the group, we decided, after much heart-searching and negotiating, to take this step. As Carmen Callil said:

We basically had three choices: we could borrow money from the bank to finance us, but that would have been crippling and would not have given us the investment or services we needed; we could sell parts of the company to interested outsiders for money which would have given them control; or we could do what we did, which was to sell the whole company to a group which had an established organisation of independent publishers in a deal which had written into it safeguards orchestrated by ourselves.

The Chatto, Bodley Head and Cape Group was made up of three companies, offering services such as sales, accounts, warehousing, royalties, but remaining independent from each other in editorial and other crucial respects. The three were owned by a holding company, whose board consisted of the people who ran the three companies. Virago joined as an equal fourth member. Costs on the joint overheads were shared between the companies. That turned out to be a problem for Virago. When we joined the group in 1982, it consisted of three companies with great publishing prestige and financial success: it was, for a while, an ideal arrangement. Our sales rose considerably, we became more visible in the high streets, even on station bookstalls; we were relieved of the administrative duties of the company, and could concentrate on developing other aspects, such as editorial and marketing strategies. But though the group turnover increased substantially, as did ours, so disproportionately did the group overheads and management costs, most of them out of Virago's control. As *The Times Literary Supplement* put it, 'The group umbrella was full of holes. As in Magritte, it was raining pinstripe men.' By the end of 1986 the group situation was grave and was affecting Virago's financial situation; the end-of-year accounts registered our first loss. The history of women's enterprises has too often been one of breaks, or interruptions. We were determined that our list, bridging as it did generations of women, must survive. Something had to be done.

There were other, larger changes, going on in publishing at the time. In 1986 and 1987 conglomerates seemed to form almost daily. There was much talk of the 'bland, internatioinal best-seller', of loss of author contact, advances paid that could never be earned, and a high turnover of editorial staff so that authors were never sure they would stay with their editor. Meanwhile, the retail trade was developing EPOS (electronic point of sale), making stock control a much more streamlined business. In this atmosphere it became clear to us that, as a 'niche' publisher, with a well-established audience and a remarkably strong backlist we should once again become an independent company. In a world of ever larger conglomerates we could use our smallness to our advantage – keeping close contact with authors, cultivating our niche in the market, staying quick on our feet out there with promotion and publicity and, once again, having total financial control of our own company. The rest is history to people in the book trade: five directors embarked on a management buy-out, which took a year to complete (partly because in the middle of negotiations Random House bought the entire group and some renegotiation had to take place). By the end of the year we had written an eighty-page business plan, and learned a good deal about Cityspeak ('washing your own face' and 'who are you in bed with' will never seem the same again). With the investment of Rothschilds Ventures Limited, Bob Gavron and a 10% slice to Random House, Virago became an independent company again.

But since it is not possible to separate the economic and creative sides of a publishing house, no publishing house can be truly independent. Mary Wollstonecraft said, 'Independence I will ever secure by contracting my wants, though I were to live on a barren heath.' In one sense we do not want to contract our wants. We want to reach an even wider audience, which we are convinced is there. Yet we want to stay radical in the widest sense of the word. Our early decision to reach the high street audience and people who do not regard themselves as feminists meant that in a sense we became part of the Establishment, but not *of* it.

I believe that the audience the feminist presses have established for women writers will grow. Already the children of the 1970s' generation of feminists are buying our books, reading them, writing to us about them. Writing *for* us, too. The women's movement, however fragile it might have become (that will change again – there are political cycles as well as trade cycles), has altered the lives and expectations of generations of people, women and men. The younger generation, girls *and* boys, takes for granted that these changes are here to stay and that the books that reflect them will stay on the shelves.

Some ideas which were startingly new in the 1970s are now common currency. Even the language has incorporated them: patriarchy and sexism are discussed on television and in the newspapers; married women with children now expect to work if they want to, and can find a job (though motherhood as a job still has a very low status). More women refuse the idea of powerlessness and economic dependency – though this is still a huge problem for many working-class and black women. And there are other changes. But it would be unwise to feel too much complacency and certainty. The success of feminist publishing in Britain is a cause for rejoicing. But 'success' is not without its problems, and fashion can be a treacherous partner. Some things are remarkably unchanged – women's economic position in relation to men's, for instance. Britain remains a very patriarchal, classbound country which pays only lip service to serious equality for women. We have certainly influenced more women than men, and the male-dominated English literature cannon in schools and universities remains almost untouched. Virago has, from its beginning, been concerned to make some impact here, but we have not made the progress we hoped for (although we are now working with an educational publisher to produce school editions for our titles). The 'greats' – Jane Austen, Charlotte Brontë, Virginia Woolf, George Eliot – are on the syllabus: but many impressive women writers are nowhere to be seen. And in other disciplines – history, anthropology – the problem is the same.

In British academe in the 1980s, it is *gender* that is studied – more respectable as a subject than feminism – but there is not as much connection with women *writers*. Women writers have flourished as a result of the women's movement, and many have been influenced by it. But, although feminism now has a strong cultural presence, it is less anchored to change, and the books that are published reflect this. In the 1970s one was aware of women as an *absence* in the market-place; in the 1980s feminism, by other names, is a growth industry. But still the more radical and exploratory texts are ignored by the media – a powerful form of censorship. And still the ethnic minorities are hugely under-represented in publishing. There is a burgeoning fiction market, including a new concern with genre writing (all the feminist presses have developed an interest in this). But though women are so much more visible in the number of books and their range of subject matter, there is no deepening of political engagement as a result.

Yet there are many reasons for optimism and tenacity. No other country compares with Britain for a feminist presence in bookshops, and women of all generations seem to be writing with an ever-increasing range and confidence. For all the political and cultural frustrations of Thatcher's Britain, the rewriting of the 'human adventure' by women continues, and feminist publishing shows all the signs of being here to stay.

Note

Dr P Mann (*A survey of women's reading habits with special reference to romantic fiction*) withdrew from the Colloquium at a time when the programme was already published.

Fortunately Ursula Owen from Virago Press allowed us to table her paper *Feminist Publishing* and also to reprint it in the Colloquium Proceedings with the permission of P Owen (*Publishing the future*, 1985). Though Ms Owen could not attend in person a representative of Virago was present at the Colloquium and able to take part in the discussions. Ms Owen's paper adds a new and much needed dimension to the Colloqium Proceedings and we are grateful for her contribution.

Discussion

In the subsequent discussion the following points were raised:

The need for co-operation between libraries in matters of acquisition and preservation; the possibility of the British Library sharing its resources: the extent to which 'Conspectus' will offer sufficiently detailed analysis for women's studies; the need to make women's studies a priority area for British Library acquisitions; recognition of the important contribution made by smaller but specialist libraries (they are usually under-funded and dependent on voluntary help); the need for adequate library provision in teaching institutions which establish courses in women's studies: the rôle of computers in facilitating subject analysis; the problems posed by the Library's discard policy and the difficulty of predicting future research needs and interests; the rôle of public libraries in providing information for non-academic researchers; the status of the Fawcett Library (ownership of the special collections cannot be transferred to the Polytechnic library); the problem of access to the British Library for teachers and school children (the Education Service of the India Office Library and Records and Oriental Collections has been extended to all departments within the BL Humanities and Social Sciences Division).

The following participants took part in the discussion: Steve Ashton (BL, Education Service); Jean Boyd (writer); Anita Burdett (Institute of Commonwealth Studies); Anna Davin (History Workshop); Rosalind Delmar (writer and lecturer); Tom Geddes (BL, Collection Development, West European – Scandinavian Branch); Elizabeth James (BL, Collection Development, English Language Branch); Lyndal Roper (Royal Holloway and New Bedford College); Dorothy Sheridan (University of Sussex Library); Ken Watson (Sheffield City Polytechnic Library); Annabel Wigner (Plumstead Manor School).

Rosalind Delmar

How can the British Library help feminist research?

Introduction

Feminist research is a relatively new area, having developed over the past two decades. Its first appearance was as an outcrop of a political movement, the women's liberation movement. A desire to understand more about the place of women in Britain and the rest of the world, a need to know how women had organised and thought about their lives in the past, and a wish to experiment with different ways of thinking about sexual difference and sexual division, generated both informal study groups within the movement and individual research.

The work produced by these groups and individuals helped to stimulate a demand for adult education courses around the subject of women, which were organised by a diversity of providers, and as women's studies began to make an appearance in more formal educational settings. By now women's studies courses exist (in fact if not always in name) in many polytechnics and universities, for both undergraduates and post-graduates. Many of those who teach and participate in such courses are engaged in independent feminist research.

Although the impetus for feminist research came from the women's movement and needed an active politics as a condition of its birth, there is no reason to assume that it will remain entirely dependent on this politics in order to stay alive. In the universities, women's studies courses are proving attractive to students from abroad, particularly from the United States, and in this way are becoming a source of external income. In the polytechnics women's studies is likely to be offered as an incentive to attract mature women students to one college rather than another, given the decline in the school-leaving population and the need to increase adult participation in higher education.

A parallel can be drawn with the expansion of the 'women's market' in publishing. From having once been seen as a narrow specialist interest, women's publishing has grown so that few publishers are without their 'women's list'. In the long term resources will have to be generated and maintained to meet the needs of those engaged in women's studies.

What is meant by feminist research?

For the purposes of this paper, I am defining feminist research very loosely, as that work which takes as its starting point the proposition that there has been a different social, economic, political or psychological development between the sexes. Feminist research is concerned to investigate the origins, means of articulation and effects of this differentiation, its variation over time, women's response to the situations in which they have found themselves, and the meanings which have been generally ascribed to sexual division and sexual difference. Women, as well as the institutions and relationships which help define their circumstances, like the family, the educational system and so on, tend to be a predominant focus for investigation.

The work and preoccupations of feminist researchers tend to be wedded to particular fields of study: sociology and the applied social sciences, history and English literature. This is a result of three main factors:

1. The stress on social and cultural conditions in the criticisms of women's place offered by feminism.

2. The sort of material which feminists use to demonstrate their case (drawing as they do and have done on history, literature, philosophy, psychology, anthropology, sociology, art history and aesthetics).

3. The traditional organisation of knowledge in the polytechnics and universities in which women's studies now exist, and where much feminist research is now based: women's studies courses tend to be offered within specific departments and in the context of specialist courses.

Thus feminist research takes place within the Humanities and Social Sciences, and spreads over a wide range of material within this general field: it is often genuinely inter-disciplinary. What unity exists comes from a general focus of interest.

I would single out two broad aims of feminist research which are relevant to this paper. The first is the sometimes undervalued aim of recovery: finding out and publishing or advertising what women have done or are doing, highlighting those aspects of the wider social, economic or political order which have been or are of particular relevance to women, and so on. Recovery has been the theme of many of the papers presented today. Secondly, there is the aim of reinterpretation: finding out what happens when you put the material on women together with other material, and develop the means to think through the problems which then emerge.

Examples of such work can be drawn from the area in which I have been most recently working, that of late seventeenth century feminist writing. Under the rubric of recovery one can place a group of books produced out of the current interest in and commitment to the discovery of women's presence in history. For example, *Kissing the rod*, edited by Germaine Greer, Jeslyn Medoff, Melinda Sansone, and Susan Hastings, a collection of women's poetry from the seventeenth century; *The female wits*, by Fidelis Morgan, which collects some of the plays written by women; then, more analytic, Elaine Hobby's *Virtue of necessity*, a review of the written material published by women throughout the century, Janet Todd's *The sign of Angellica*, which covers mainly fictional writing in the seventeenth and eighteenth century and Antonia Fraser's survey of women's lives, *The weaker vessel*. And there have been new biographies of individual women like Mary Astell, sometimes called the first English feminist. On the side of reinterpretation there has been Carole Pateman's book, the *Sexual contract*, a rereading of social contract theory from the perspective of the marriage contract, a work not in itself mainly concerned with what women at that time wrote. These are just a few examples; it is not a comprehensive list.

These broad aims of feminist research depend on each other, and on the existence and maintenance of good archives. My own research on the use made by and criticisms extended by feminists to Lockean thought at the end of the seventeenth century depends as much on the maintenance of collections to do with Locke as that to do with women's writing. In this way the needs of feminist researchers and those of others coincide, a point to which I will return. The exploration of archives from a different perspective does however result in the turning over of different material – for example, the discovery of a collection of poetry written by Mary Astell in the Rawlinson MSS at the Bodleian Library by her biographer Ruth Perry. At the same time it brings a confrontation with old and difficult bibliographical issues, like those of attribution.

Specific needs

Like many users I have every reason to be grateful to the Library staff for their help, information, and courtesy. It is somewhat embarrassing to seem to be criticising such a valuable institution and such dedicated people. I hope that my comments will be taken in the constructive spirit in which I have tried to think them through.

In the British Library Strategic Plan the point is made that the Library cannot afford to collect the whole publishing output from this country or abroad, and that therefore priorities have to be set for collection development. One of the key strategies of the plan is 'a developing programme of wider services both through increased access to the collections and the development of revenue-generating services. Increasingly, services will be focussed more sharply on meeting the needs of particular groups of users.'

It is in the interest of feminist researchers that women's studies should be seen as a priority area for collection development. The specific needs which feminist researchers have in relation to the Library could be best addressed through the appointment of someone with a specific responsibility for women's studies within the Library. Such an appointment would facilitate the wider advertisement of the Library's holdings and the production of publications relevant to womens studies.

There is a strong need for even a preliminary resource book on women's studies, based on an assessment of what is held in the Library's collections, including its visual and cartoon collections. Mr Bloomfield's paper on *Collection development and women's studies* makes this point in a valuable way. 'Guides to the literature available in libraries, archives and other repositories are sadly deficient and one of the major tasks for librarians and researchers must be the filling of this gap', he writes. 'Directories of research material simply do not exist in many fields and for many institutions and if this Colloquium does anything it should point up this deficiency and the need to do something about it quickly.'

I wholeheartedly agree with his point that it is immaterial whether the results 'are published in traditional form or made available through computerised networks', and share his concern that 'unless it is done future research work will be seriously hindered.' Such publications would have every chance of commercial success, here and abroad. An analytical catalogue of periodicals/articles, perhaps available on CD-ROM would also be a valuable guide for research.

If women's studies were to be made a priority area for collection development, with specific appointments to both explore the archives and develop future collections, this would be a great asset for future scholars. It would be important to ensure the acquisition of American and European books and journals in this field, in order to maintain a stock of knowledge for British researchers. Given the cuts being made in library acquisitions elsewhere, the establishment of a women's studies collection at a recognised centre would be invaluable. Attached to this might be the creation of a collection of PhD theses on microfilm.

Consideration should be given to the development of the archives of the future. How can the British Library accrue the documentation relevant to the growth of, for example, the contemporary women's liberation movement, its pamphlets, leaflets, cyclostyled sheets, journals and letters?

The value of participation in informal groups as a means of disseminating information about library resources should not be underestimated. The participation of interested library staff in those informal groups which work on and in women's studies, like the Womens History Seminar and the Womens Studies Information Network enriches the work of those groups enormously, and should be encouraged by the Library. Feminist contributions to cataloguing could be incorporated into the Cataloguing In Publications Programme as well as within the general subject index.

General needs

It is a paradox of research that the more that is done, the more is needed. Even those areas which once appeared known about, like the nineteenth century women's movement, need extensive reappraisal, and existing archives have yet to be fully explored. This underlines the importance of good maintenance of existing collections.

There is another reason for feminist researchers to be concerned about the maintenance of existing archives: the relative absence of standard editions of feminist works. As long as there are no standard editions of early works, scholars will need to turn to the original material held in collections like that at the British Library, and they will require the support services which anyone else researching this area would need: on the basis of my own experience I would stress the importance of the conservation services. It is amazing how long books can remain at the binders. If one thinks about feminist research from this point of view it can be seen that the needs of Library users who are engaged in feminist research coincide with those of other users.

The patterns of use of feminist researchers are as variable as those of other users. They may use the Library as their main research centre, or (as I do myself) as library of last resort. They may be engaged in private research, embarking on a PhD thesis, or gathering material for lectures or a new book. What they are most likely to have in common will be their sex, so that a subsidiary question attached to the provision of facilities for women's studies and feminist research is that of facilities for women at the Library. It would be good to know that some provision will be made at St Pancras.

The British Library Strategic Plan links its 'programme of wider services' both to 'increased access to the collections' and to 'the development of revenue-generating services.' This linkage is to be expected in the current atmosphere of pressures to reduce dependence on grant-in-aid. Both access and finance, have a special inflection for feminist research.

'Increased access to the collections' can mean either access by more people, or more open access to the collections, or both. The precise combination which feminist research presents, that of a relatively new and under-researched area, whose practitioners are as likely to be new to research as not, raises quite sharply the general question of access to a wider range of researcher. Feminist researchers may not always be attached to an academic institution, and feminist research often takes place in an non-academic context, so the accessibility of the Library to non-academic users is an issue for feminist researchers and women's studies in general.

Is it the intention of the Library to remain as open as it has historically been to the independent researcher? The impression is sometimes given by some library staff that new users are expected to be graduates engaged in some form of post-graduate research. This can only be off-putting to the non-academic user, and goes against the Library's rôle as a national library, open to all who cannot find the material they need elsewhere.

Even in the case of academic researchers I have been surprised by the negative feelings about the Library I encountered in informal discussions. It was often seen as a rarified place for London-based researchers. There seemed to be a general and primary ignorance about the Library. Experienced researchers, who on the face of it might be expected to face no difficulties, seemed ill-at-ease with the Library and unclear about the potential resources the Library had to offer.

Most of the users I talked to use the Library as many people use a new piece of software for their computers. They don't have a sense of the Library and its resources as a whole, but rather find out what is available as and when they have specific needs. There is no over-view of the possibilities offered by access to such a wonderful resource. There's nothing wrong with this, but it did seem to point to absence of information on the Library's part.

I wondered if there might be guided tours of the Library for readers, regularly scheduled, not necessarily with a particular area in mind, although this might turn out in the long run to be a good idea. A further possibility would be short courses, organised around specific collections, with might sometimes be coordinated with the work of particular groups of students engaged in specific courses. Another need which the Library publications services might fulfil is for a general bibliographical guide for researchers. And there also seemed to be a premium on good, well-briefed staff at the information desks. This seemed as important as the development of a user-friendly on-line catalogue, and it is to be hoped that the human touch will not be phased out in favour of leaflets, videos and computer systems.

Perhaps one reason for the uncertainty of the Library users I talked to was the projected move to St Pancras. What will it mean in terms of access, facilities, catalogue provision, etc? Is the old catalogue to be abolished? Will there be more open access? It seems important to start to give researchers a sense of what the move to St Pancras will mean for them.

Finally, I would stress once more the need to protect the interests of the independent researcher. The spread of women's studies does mean that nowadays many feminist researchers will have financial support through their institutions for their use of facilities which must be paid for: computer searchers, photocopies, etc. But others will be self-financing, and it is important that they should be charged at a realistic rate. Every care should be taken to ensure that a two-tier scale of users based on the length of their purse does not emerge. As David Doughan pointed out in his paper: 'generating significant income from services presupposes affluent consumers who are able and willing to pay considerable sums for them; whereas few women have above-average disposable income, and those who are doing serious research usually are well below average in this respect'.

Its sensitivity to the needs of independent researchers has helped make the British Library not just a national but an international asset, a symbol throughout the world of the intellectual freedom of enquiry, an institution to which, as a user, I and many others feel privileged to have access. Whilst I was thinking about this paper and visiting the Library there was a tank parked in the forecourt of the British Museum, an unlikely symbol of the cultural heritage cared for within the Museum. It occurred to me how important to the Library is the preservation and the care of the independent researcher, whose continuing existence is a part of that 'heritage' the Library is concerned to preserve. And reciprocally, how important it is that users should have the chance to support the Library in its development and growth.

Discussion

This session provoked the most animated discussion. The British Library was criticised as an elitist organisation, which caters almost exculsively for the needs of post-graduates. Basic information, about the Library's holdings, even its opening hours, is lacking. If such information exists, it has a restricted audience.

Concern was also expressed that the Library should not adopt a narrow view of women's studies and that it should consider the needs of those not involved in higher education. The danger of a Eurocentric approach was emphasised. Priority should be given to the development of black women's studies. It was also suggested that the Library could do more to share its holdings with other institutions and that it should educate its users by organising tours and seminars. Considerable importance was attached to the appointment of a Women's Studies Officer and to the publication of a preliminary guide, leading ultimately to a series of bibliographic guides, outlining the Library's resources for women's studies.

In reply, the advantages of the move to St Pancras were explained. The collections will be located on a single site, the automated catalogue will drive the book handling system, improved conservation conditions will be introduced and five new reading rooms will be opened. The aim is to make the services more reader-orientated and to improve links between curatorial staff and reader services. The Library's current admission regulations were explained. The Library is not a post-graduate institution: it is open to all who cannot easily find the material they want elsewhere. There is room for improvement in the Admissions Office, but with seating for only 800 readers the Library cannot adopt an 'open-door' policy. It was also argued that women's studies is already a priority area. The Library acts in response to what is published and, although there are loopholes, it takes all material published in the UK by copyright deposit. Scepticism was also expressed, largely on financial grounds, about the appointment of a Women's Studies Officer.

While welcoming the improvements envisaged at St Pancras, several participants challenged the negative tone of some of these responses. In particular, it was pointed out that other institutions provide special facilities for groups with particular needs. The use of the Romilly Room at the Public Record Office was cited as an example. It was also suggested that financing the post of a Women's Studies Officer should not present an insuperable problem. An application for a grant could be submitted to Leverhulme or to the British Academy. Women's studies could also be promoted through the Friends of the British Library and through the establishment of a separate Library Group.

The following proposals were agreed at the end of the session. They will be submitted in a letter to senior British Library management:

1. Women's studies should be a priority area for British Library collection development.

2. A Women's Studies Officer (possibly as head of a separate department) should be appointed.
3. The British Library should publish a guide, based partly on the Colloquium papers, to its holdings on women's studies.
4. British Library acquisitions should include all American and European books, copies of these, and women's movement ephemera.
5. The maintenance and preservation of women's sources should be given high priority.
6. Facilities for women should be provided at St Pancras.
7. Access should be given to a wider range of readers and the cost of on-line services to non-academic users should not be prohibitive.
8. There should be access to the British Library for women's groups.
9. The approach to women's studies should not be Eurocentric.
10. The Library should share its resources with other libraries.
11. Women's studies should be interpreted in its broadest sense.
12. A Library Group for women's studies should be established.
13. Short courses for women should be arranged.
14. The participants at the Colloquium should join and thus be represented on the Friends of the British Library.

The following people took part in the discussion: Sally Alexander (History Workshop Journal); Alison Bailey (BL, Reading Room Enquiry Desk); Anita Burdett (Institute of Commonwealth Studies): Sylvia Collicott (Polytechnic of North London); Ruth Coman (Project Services Director, St Pancras Planning): Anna Davin (History Workshop): Eamon Dyas (BL, Newspaper Library); Albertine Gaur (BL, Oriental Collections); Tom Geddes (BL, Collection Development – West European – Scandinavian Section); Brigid Haines (BL, St Pancras Planning); Eddie Higgs (Public Record Office): Margaret Makepeace (BL, India Office Library and Records); Mary Kennedy (Birkbeck College); Jane Rendall (University of York); Maureen Ritchie (University of Kent); Liz Stanley (University of Manchester); Ilse Sternberg (BL, Collection Development, English Language Branch); Rosina Visram (Writer).

Albertine Gaur

Summing Up

The idea of this Colloquium was born on 24 June 1987 during a one-day Seminar on *Information for Women's Studies in Universities and Polytechnics* at the University of Sheffield which Penelope Tuson and I attended. There was a good mixture of participants, the papers were stimulating, the discussions lively. But as the day wore on we began to realise that there was a group of users – in many cases potential users – who did not feel that their needs were, or could be, satisfied by the British Library. Talking it over on the way back we were dismayed; we felt we had done our best to be user-friendly: the India Office Library and Records had published a special *Guide for teachers* to open up the use of its archival material; Oriental Collections was in the process of doing the same. We had all produced a substantial number of small booklets, each arranged around a particular subject or collection, some of them richly illustrated, designed to appeal to the specialist as well as to those engaged in more generalistic areas of research. The Library had continued to stage, despite ever-decreasing resources, a varied programme of exhibitions – yet somehow the message had not come through, as far as women's studies were concerned our best had so far obviously not been good enough.

We began to analyse the complaints and agreed that they centred around three main areas: (1) despite valiant efforts by the Library's Press and Public Relations Office there was still not enough information about the structure, intention and aims of the Library easily available; (2) this lack of information had apparently led to a number of misunderstandings which had directed researchers to wrong parts of the Library (*eg* to Boston Spa for women's newspapers and journals instead of Colindale); and (3) those who had ventured into Bloomsbury had found access to special subjects areas difficult and frustrating. We felt something had to be done, the most obvious solution was one which had been successfully applied to several language/area studies, namely a colloquium, where staff and users could meet, exchange ideas, put forward suggestions and explore possibilities for future co-operation.

When we broached the matter with senior management we received a sympathetic reply. Yes, we could make arrangements for a Colloquium of Women's Studies but it was suggested that we should make it one day only (instead of three); with the rider that should the response be encouraging a second (if necessary longer) colloquium could be held at a later date. This meant that participation would have to be at national instead of international level, and though we were at first somewhat disappointed, the restriction was to prove a blessing in disguise. Almost as soon as we had started our preparations, the Library, like many other similar institutions, suffered further cuts in funding and found it necessary to withdraw financial support from all subsequent colloquia. This posed a number of problems. We had to secure the use of a large enough room free of charge; we had to find funds for meals since we could not very well stage a one-day colloquium designed to demonstrate our user-friendliness and then ask participants (many of whom travelled at their own expense from various parts of the UK) either to pay for their food, or send them out to fend for themselves in the middle of Soho and thus limit even further the time available for the all important discussions which usually take place over coffee and tea and lunch, where ideas are discussed and new partnerships forged; and we somehow had to find money within our slender departmental budgets to send out letters, with at least abstracts of paper, and thus prepare the ground for discussions. In the event we secured the Novello Room free of charge (the normal fee was then £600 per function); Penelope (and the India Office Library and Records) allowed us to use for food some of the money she had earned for the Library from consultancy fees in the Gulf States; and at the very last moment Ruth Coman, who is in charge of St Pancras planning, offered to have all papers copied on her budget.

We also had luck. The Marketing and Publishing Office of the British Library agreed to publish the proceedings providing there were sufficient papers to make publication worthwhile. This meant that we had to have more papers than could comfortably be read out, even in short form. We solved this last problem by cutting the time for all papers contributed by Library staff so as to be able to offer our guests the courtesy of more time (on the principle of 'family hold back').

What then did we hope to achieve with the Colloquium?

- We wanted to provide (subject orientated) information about the collections in Bloomsbury and Colindale and thus open them to the needs of users engaged in women's studies.
- We wanted to draw attention to the rich holdings of source materials, manuscripts and archives, which are in the keeping of the Library.
- We wanted to give Library staff, especially our younger colleagues a chance to research the collections on a subject basis (the time honoured approach has so far always been by language), to meet some of our users and learn directly about their needs.
- We wanted to hear about other collections in the UK, learn about the problems those in charge of them experienced and compare them with our own.
- We wanted to tell each other about projects relating to women's studies and the bibliographical control of primary and secondary material connected with it.
- We also wanted to place the papers dealing with collections and projects within a framework which, on the one hand elucidated the state of women's studies in British universities, and on the other hand drew attention to the needs, experiences and problems of users in the British Library.
- Most of all however we wanted to provide a forum for frank discussion, creative

criticism, and an exchange of opinions which we hoped would provoke suggestions and recommendations able to point a way towards the future. We did not want to pay each other polite compliments – we wanted to be constructive.

Did we achieve our objectives?

I think we can safely say that we have made a good start. If the beginning of wisdom is truly an initial shock, this shock has been administered to some of the Library's staff. Our outside participants have given us a vote of confidence by offering to join the Friends of the British Library and thus assist us in our work towards becoming more useful to them. We have met each other, we have been frank with each other. The recommendations put forward in the course of the last discussion will go to the management of the Library and even if not all of them can be implemented (there looms as always the question of funding) some certainly will and one has reason to hope that things will never be quite the same again. The dialogue has started, it is really now up to all of us to make sure that it continues.

Penelope and I would like to express our gratitude to all who have helped to bring about this meeting.

Appendix

Changing views of women: a British Library exhibition

A small exhibition of books and manuscripts entitled *Changing views of women* was on display in the King's Library, Great Russell Street, between 17 March–4 June 1989. The exhibition tried to look beyond the images of women as mothers and wives, child-rearers and home makers. It reflected the achievements of individuals who spurned the rôle models of their day and also highlighted societies with very different views of women. In addition the exhibition aimed to give an account of the wide range of material available in Humanities and Social Sciences (H&SS) of the British Library in supporting research in the field of women's studies in the United Kingdom and abroad.

List of exhibits

1. *In verloren minuten: dagboeken en herinneringen van vrouwen 1896-1979*. Edited by Annete Mevis, Weesp: Fibula-Van Dieshoeck, 1979. (YA 1986.a.7631) THE NETHERLANDS.

2. *Emancipatiebeleid. Verslag over de periode januari 1978-april 1980*. Rijswijk: Ministerie van Cultuur, Recreatie en Maatschappelijk Werk, 1980. (SJ 350/683) THE NETHERLANDS.

3. *Sor Juana Inés de la Cruz, Carta athenagórica*. Puebla de los Angeles: Diego Fernández de Leon, 1690. (4226.aaa.42) MEXICO.

4. Portrait of Sor Juana Inés de la Cruz (1648-1695) by Miguel Cabrera, in *Ensayo de psicologia de Sor Juana Inés de la Cruz*. Ezequiel A Chávez, Barcelona, 1931. (4868.g.8) MEXICO.

5. *Mulheres moçambicanas*. Organizoção da Mulher Moçambicana, 1983. (The opening shows a photograph of the International Women's Day celebrations in Maputo). (Ya.1988.a.9395) MOZAMBIQUE.

6. Joaquín Ezquerra del Bayo *and* Luis Pérez Bueno. *Retratos de mujeres españolas del siglo XIX*. Madrid: Julio Cosano, 1924. (10635/1.9) SPAIN.

7. *Les trobairitz: poetes occitanes del segle xii*. Edited by Meg Bogin, (Collecció clàssiques catalanes; 3–4), Barcelona: La Sal, 1983. (YA 1987.a.14869) SPAIN.

8. *Frauengeschichte: Dokumentation des 3 Historikerinnentreffens in Bielefeld, April 81.* (Beiträge zur feministischen Theorie und Praxis; 5), München: Verlag Frauenoffensive, 1981. (X 520/32138) GERMANY.

9. Käthe Kern. *Frauen, entscheidet euch!*, Berlin: Dietz Nachf. [1931]. (YA 1987.a.9265) GERMANY.

10. Maria Sibilla Merian. *Der Raupen wunderbare Verwandelung und Blumen-Nahrung...* Nürnberg, 1679-83. (445.c.15) GERMANY.

11. *Handbuch der Frauenbewegung.* Editors Helene Lange and Gertrud Bäumer. Part 5, *Die deutsche Frau im Berufs: praktische Ratschläge.* Berlin: Moesser, 1906. (845.i.25) GERMANY.

12. Albert Thura. *Gynaeceum Daniae Litteratum...*, Altona: Apud Jonam Korte, 1732 (276.g.15) SCANDINAVIA.

13. Grethe Jacobsen. *Kvindeskikkelser og kvindeliv i Danmarks middelalder.* Copenhagen: Gad, 1986. (YA 1989.b.641) SCANDINAVIA

14. Merete Stistrup Jensen, *Kvindesprog*, (Kvindeforskning; 24). Aalborg: Aalborg Universitetsforlag, 1987. (X.0519/828(24)). SCANDINAVIA.

15. *Hertha.* Stockholm: Fredrika-Bremer-Förbundet, [1859–]. (PP 4833.0) SCANDINAVIA.

16. Madame H J M de Coicy de Montigny. *Demande des femmes aux États Généraux, 1789.* (R. 409 (9)) FRANCE.

17. Madeleine de Scudéry. *Almahide...*, Paris: Augustin Courbe, 1660-3. (243.g.3) FRANCE.

18. Marguerite de Navarre. *L'Heptameron des novvelles...*, Paris: B Prevost pour G Robinet, 1559. (C.7.a.14) FRANCE.

19. Krest'ianka, kollektivizurui' derevniu, idi v riady krasnykh traktoristok. Moskva: Gosudartsvennoe isdatel'stvo, 1930.' In: *Seht her, Genossen!: Plakate aus der Sowjetunion.* Dortmund: Harenberg, 1982. (X.429/15087) SOVIET UNION.

20. *Soviet Women*, Moscow: State Art Publishers, 1939. (8147.dd.2) SOVIET UNION.

21. Gwendolyn Books. *Riot*, Detroit: Boadside Press, 1969; a copy signed by the author. (X.909/37816) UNITED STATES.

22. Virginia Penny. *How women can make money, married or single, in all branches of the arts and sciences, professions, trades, agricultural and mechanical pursuits.* Springfield, Mass, [1870]. (8415.dd.24) UNITED STATES.

23. Tenessee Celeste Claflin. *Constitutional equality, a right of women...*, New York: Woodhull, Claflin, 1871. (8416.f.33) UNITED STATES.

24. Susannah Strickland. *Roughing it in the bush, or, Life in Canada.* London: Richard Bentley, 1857. (10470.b.28) CANADA.

25. Bhagvanta Hari Khare. *How is Woman treated by Man and Religion?* Bombay: Javaji Dadaji, 1896. (08416.de.9) INDIA.

26. *The Woman as good as the Man, or The equality of both sexes.* Translated from the French by A L. London, 1677. (8415.b.17) ENGLAND.

27. *The Wonder of Wonders: or a True and Perfect Narrative of a Woman near Guildford in Surrey, who was Delivered lately of Seventeen Rabbets, and the Legs of a Tabby Cat... In a letter from a gentleman at Guildford to his friend, a Physician at Ipswich, Suffolk...*, Ipswich: J Bognall, 1726. (1178.h4. 1–16) ENGLAND.

28. Raden Adjeng Kartini. *Letters of a Javanese Princess.* Translated from the original Dutch by Agnes Louise Symmers, London: Duckworth, 1921. (10906.bb.6) INDONESIA.

29. Cao Dagu Nü jie (Cao Dagu's *Admonitions for women*), ink and colour on silk, eighteenth century or later. (Add.MS 17344) CHINA.

30. *Gu Hu tou hua Lie nü zhuan* (Biographies of exemplary women illustrated by Gu Hutou), text attributed to Liu Xiang (c.79 – c.6 BC), Yangzhou: Linghai Jielou, 1825 (based on the Yu shi Song dynasty edition). (15303.c.2) CHINA.

31. *Hun yin fa tu jie tong su ben* (The marriage law in pictures: popular edition), Shanghai: Huadon People's Publishing House, 1951. (15625.f.11) CHINA.

32. *Hyakunin jorô shinasadame* (One hundred women classified according to rank), the work of the artist Nishikawa Sukenobu, Osaka, 1723. (16074.e.44) JAPAN.

33. *Genji monogatari kotoba* (Extracts from the Tale of Genji), a folding album of paintings and poems. Attributed to Sumiyoshi Jokei, mid-seventeenth century. (Or. 1287) JAPAN.

34. *Nihon sankai meibutsu zue* (Pictures of products of the land and seas of Japan) by Hirase Tessai, illustrated by Hasegawa Mitsunobu, published in Edo c.1800. (16035.c.2) JAPAN.

35. *Perbendaharaan yang kaamasan* (The Golden Treasury), an anthology of poetry by Osman Hashimi, collected and published by his wife Che' Pok Badariah Ahmad, Kuala Lumpur, 1932. (14654.c.1) MALAYSIA.

36. Virginia Woolf. *A sketch of the past.* 1940. (Add.MS 61973) ENGLAND.

37. Sylvia Plath. *Insomniac.* 1961. (Add.MS52617) ENGLAND.

38. Charlotte Brontë. *The search after happiness*, 1829. (Ashley MS 156) ENGLAND.